All Judges Are Political—
Except When They Are Not

THE CULTURAL LIVES OF LAW

Edited by Austin Sarat

All Judges Are Political—
Except When They Are Not

Acceptable Hypocrisies and the Rule of Law

Keith J. Bybee

Stanford Law Books

An Imprint of Stanford University Press

Stanford, California

Stanford University Press
Stanford, California

©2010 by the Board of Trustees of the Leland Stanford Junior University.
All rights reserved.

Printed in the United States of America on acid-free, archival-quality paper

Library of Congress Cataloging-in-Publication Data

Bybee, Keith J., 1965–
  All judges are political—except when they are not : acceptable hypocrisies and the rule of law / Keith J. Bybee.
      p. cm.
  Includes bibliographical references and index.
  ISBN 978-0-8047-5311-1 (cloth : alk. paper)—ISBN 978-0-8047-5312-8 (pbk. : alk. paper)
  1. Judicial process—United States. 2. Political questions and judicial power—United States. 3. Rule of law—United States. I. Title.
  KF8775.B93 2010
  347.73'12—dc22   2010011546

Typeset by Classic Typography in 11/13.5 Adobe Garamond

For Jennifer, Evan, and Ava

Contents

I   Legal Realism: Dead and Alive   1

II   Elements of Common Courtesy   35

III   The Rule of Law as the Rules of Etiquette   75

Notes   107

Bibliography   149

Table of Cases   167

Acknowledgments   169

Index   173

All Judges Are Political—
Except When They Are Not

Part I
Legal Realism: Dead and Alive

IN THE WINTER OF 2003, THE *NEW YORK TIMES* announced the triumph of "legal realism," the theory that suggests judicial decisionmaking is essentially a matter of politics.[1] The announcement occurred in the course of reporting on Justice Thomas Spargo's energetic participation in the political process. When campaigning for a New York town judgeship in 1999, Spargo handed out free cider and doughnuts, distributed coupons for free gas at a convenience store, sent free pizzas to school teachers and government workers, and bought a round of drinks for everyone at a local watering hole.[2] Once elected town justice, Spargo kept up his political activities by speaking at partisan fundraisers and, more famously, by participating in obstreperous protests at the Miami-Dade County Board of Elections, with "the aim of disrupting the recount process" after the 2000 presidential election.[3] Spargo's political enthusiasm earned him a judicial promotion. In 2001, he was elected to the State Supreme Court in Albany County.

Spargo's politicking was less popular in other quarters. The New York State Commission on Judicial Conduct charged Spargo with violating the state rules governing judicial behavior. In response, Spargo filed suit claiming that the state code of judicial conduct was unconstitutional. The federal district court agreed. Applying the United States Supreme Court decision *Republican Party of Minnesota v. White*, the court ruled that Spargo was free to be as politically active as he had been.[4] Thus the *New York Times* was prompted to declare a conquest for legal realism, a victory for "the jurisprudential philosophy that calls for a frank acknowledgement of the role politics and other real-world factors play in judicial decisionmaking."[5]

Interestingly enough, Spargo himself was among the first to call legal realism's victory into question. Although he thought that the ruling was "absolutely good" because it freed judges to be more involved in the political life of their communities, he otherwise believed that the decision pushed a political understanding of the courts too far. "When people think of Tom Spargo," Spargo said, "many would consider my reputation as a kind of partisan hack lawyer or Republican law expert. But when you get on the bench, then all that is behind you. . . . [F]rankly, I have not had a political thought in any of the work that I've done as a judge." It was one thing to acknowledge that politics played a part in judicial life, but it was altogether something else to argue that judicial decisionmaking was all politics. When it came to legal realism, Spargo seemed to suggest, it was best to accept a little bit, but not too much.[6]

Spargo's ambivalent reaction to his own exoneration seemed hard to believe. How could he consistently lay claim to the roles of both politician and judge? He had assiduously courted voters through frankly political electioneering. On the basis of his behavior, one could easily infer that Spargo was a judge who could be counted on to represent the interests of his political supporters. Yet, if this were true, then Spargo had misled litigants and the general public by claiming to be unbiased. By trying to have it both ways, simultaneously playing partisan politics and claiming judicial impartiality, Spargo risked looking like a hypocrite: his courtroom behavior appeared to be an act, an effort to affect a degree of neutrality and open-mindedness which he did not possess. He claimed to give litigants a serious hearing, but his behavior suggested that he was just giving them the pretense of being heard.[7]

In principle, Spargo easily could have avoided landing in such a bind. He could have stuck to a single role and thus eliminated the appearance of hypocrisy. For example, he could have responded to his courtroom victory by insisting that judicial decisionmaking is a thoroughly political enterprise. The goal, Spargo might have claimed, is not to pretend that judges operate on the basis of neutral legal principles but to recognize that judges are political actors with power over controversial policy questions. As a result, Spargo could have argued that open judicial politicking is a welcome sight. Vigorous judicial elections contested by aggressively political candidates allow voters to select and control the officials responsible for making legal policy. Reasoning along such lines, Spargo might have sincerely defended his actions as a critical contribution to democratic politics.[8]

Alternatively, Spargo could have denounced the claims of legal realism from the outset. He could have argued that although elected politicians are necessarily obligated to represent the voters who placed them in office, judges are only required to "represent the Law."[9] The job of the judge, Spargo might have claimed, is to reason strictly on the basis of legal principle, to assimilate each dispute before the court into a coherent legal order, and to articulate a framework of rules capable of regulating subsequent judicial decisions. Spargo could have run a low-key, nonpartisan campaign and muted his political participation once on the bench. Indeed, he could have argued against the whole idea of judicial elections and insisted that a judge's loyalty to the law rightly renders him indifferent to popularity. Had Spargo sincerely cultivated a reputation for independence and impartiality, he would have eliminated the risk of being seen as a "partisan hack lawyer." He would have had no reason to contest charges leveled by the Commission on Judicial Conduct, since he would have never engaged in any judicially untoward actions in the first place.

And yet Spargo did not adopt either of these alternative strategies. Instead of choosing between the roles of active politician and impartial judge, he clung to both and defended his behavior by arguing that judges are political actors—except when they are not.

The legal realism that Spargo at once embraced and renounced has a venerable lineage. In 1897, Oliver Wendell Holmes, then a member of the Supreme Judicial Court of Massachusetts, warned his Boston University School of Law audience against supposing that "the only force at work in the development of the law is logic." "This mode of thinking is entirely natural," Holmes admitted. "The training of lawyers is the training in logic. The processes of analogy, discrimination, and deduction are those in which they are most at home. The language of judicial decision is mainly the language of logic. And logical method and form flatter that longing for certainty and repose which is in every mind." The natural mode of thinking about the law clearly feels right, but Holmes argued that it is in fact wrong. Certainty, Holmes famously said, "is illusion and repose is not the destiny of man. Behind the logical form lies a judgment as to the relative worth of and importance of competing legislative grounds, often an inarticulate and unconscious judgment, it is true, and yet the very root and nerve of the whole proceeding."[10] Lawyers and judges may talk of sound logic, impersonal principle, and impartial judgment, but the law is actually driven by politics.

In the decades following Holmes's address, a loose group of scholars that came to be known as legal realists took up Holmes's remarks and fashioned them into a way of thinking about the judicial process. The realists devoted themselves to exposing the role played by politics in judicial decisionmaking and, in doing so, they called into question conventional efforts to anchor judicial power on a fixed legal foundation. The realist rejection of objective judicial reasoning proved to be quite popular and has been widely adopted. Less than one hundred years after Holmes spoke, a prominent legal historian noted that the claim "we are all realists now" had been made so often in legal scholarship that it was a kind of truism.[11]

The remarkable fact about legal realism, however, is that in spite of its impressive provenance and current popularity, it occupies an uncertain position. When one considers the context in which American courts operate, the picture of legal realism that emerges is decidedly mixed. On one hand, many Americans acknowledge that the judicial process is infused with politics; on the other hand, almost everyone seems to believe that judicial decisions are determined on nonpolitical, purely legal grounds. Spargo is far from being alone. In the public discourse about the courts, the claims of legal realism are simultaneously proclaimed from the rooftops and disavowed in the streets. The American judiciary is said to be squarely situated *in* politics, yet it is not, somehow, thought to be entirely *of* politics.

In Part I of this book, I examine the shape and significance of legal realism's ambivalent status. I find that the courts—at both the state and federal levels—are generally viewed as hybrid institutions, caught between general expectations of impartial judicial decisionmaking and widespread beliefs about politically motivated judicial rulings. Moreover, I find that the uncertain standing of legal realism provides fertile ground for public suspicion. The political nature attributed to the judicial process often appears to be at odds with claims of judicial impartiality, naturally leading many to wonder whether judicial appeals to law are anything more than ad hoc rationalizations deployed to obscure political purposes.

One might argue that this state of affairs is not particularly significant. Conflicting public views and their attendant suspicions are, after all, matters of appearance and perception. Americans are reacting to the surface of the judicial process, and superficial assessments of how courts look may have little to do with how judges actually behave. Perhaps the public's opinion of the courts is less an inherently interesting phenomenon than a simple perceptual error in need of correction.

Although I agree that Americans are making judgments about appearances, I disagree that such judgments are either unimportant or simply mistaken. In part, my disagreement is motivated by the fact that the public's views are supported by scholarship: research suggests good reasons to believe that the modern judicial process really is an uneasy mix of legal and political factors. Beyond the validation provided by scholars, the public's views merit attention in their own right. Judicial legitimacy has long been understood to derive from what judges do *and* from how they look doing it. Public confidence in the judiciary ultimately depends not only on the substance of court rulings but also on the ability of judges to convey the impression that their decisions are driven by the impersonal requirements of legal principle. Public suspicion of the courts is therefore worth paying attention to because it threatens judicial capacities. Litigants may not respect court orders when they suspect that a judge is advancing a political agenda. Indeed, citizens may be led to doubt the authority of government as a whole when they suspect a powerful institution is misrepresenting its manner of operation.[12]

But this is only part of the picture. As I will argue over the course of this book, the public's half-politics-half-law understanding of the courts not only chips away at judicial legitimacy but also forms an essential part of the current legal order. Public skepticism about whether judges actually mean what they say is potentially corrosive, but it also points to an enabling dynamic that makes possible the exercise of legal power. My overall goal is to illustrate and critique the means by which suspicions of judicial hypocrisy feed into the legal process, producing a rule of law that facilitates mutually beneficial accommodations among individual citizens and at the same time sustains hierarchies across different groups.[13] I take the first step toward my overall goal by describing how legal realism today is simultaneously accepted as conventional wisdom and decried as an inaccurate distortion.

Law and Politics in the State Courts

The fact that Justice Spargo staked his claim to conflicting political and judicial roles in a highly public fashion is unusual. But the circumstances that gave rise to Spargo's behavior are hardly unique to him. The overwhelming majority of state appellate judges in the United States (an estimated 87 percent of appellate judges in thirty-nine states) must, like Spargo, stand for election. Many of these judicial elections, like the elections in which Spargo ran, are not only openly partisan but increasingly indistinguishable from ordinary political contests.[14] Judicial campaigns around the country have become more expensive and now set new records in almost every election cycle. In 2004, the race for the Illinois Supreme Court cost more than did eighteen of the thirty-four contests for the United States Senate held that year.[15] In 2006, the race for chief justice of the Alabama state supreme court was at once "the most expensive in state history" and "the most expensive campaign anywhere in the nation."[16] These increasingly expensive judicial elections regularly feature extensive television advertising and the active participation of single-issue interest groups and political parties. As a result, many candidates seeking judicial positions must think about how to woo campaign donors, court constituencies, and craft a winning message. The Supreme Court's decision in *White*, the ruling that struck down limits on judicial campaigning and served as the basis of Spargo's legal victory, only promises to accelerate the prevailing trend.[17]

At the same time, judicial candidates who have successfully managed their political campaigns are widely expected to act in an unbiased, distinctly non-partisan way once they are in office. Polls show that substantial majorities of Americans believe state courts should be shielded from politics and allowed to make decisions based on an independent reading of the law.[18] Consistent with popular belief, an overwhelming majority of state judges report that the "making of impartial decisions" is one of the most important responsibilities they have.[19] A majority of the Supreme Court justices appear to concur: although the high bench cleared the way for more openly political judicial campaigns in *White*, the Court has also ruled that the risk of bias in a judicial election may be so great as to violate the Constitution's Due Process Clause.[20] Whatever claims state judicial candidates may make, and whatever constituent support these judicial candidates may win, the Court ultimately requires judges to guard against partiality. This does not mean, of course, that a state judge must approach controversies without any pre-existing beliefs about what the law requires. As a practical matter, judges inevitably come to the bench with some preconceived legal views. The expectation of judicial impartiality does not ask judicial candidates and sitting judges to abandon their legal preconceptions, so much as it calls upon them to not let preconceptions "harden into prejudgments," preventing them from giving fair weight to the facts, law, and arguments that will be presented in the cases before them.[21] The American Bar Association considers this ideal of judicial impartiality to be so broadly shared that it is an "enduring principle." "Judges occupy the role of umpires in an adversarial system of justice; their credibility turns on their neutrality. To preserve their neutrality, they must neither prejudge matters that come before them, nor harbor bias for or against parties in those matters. They must, in short, be impartial, if we are to be governed by the rule of law rather than by judicial whim."[22]

Many state judges thus appear to be suspended between conventional expectations of impartial judicial conduct and the growing electoral necessity of shrewd political calculation and frankly partisan behavior. Whether or not they publicly agree with Justice Spargo, these state judges find themselves compelled to play the roles of savvy politician and neutral jurist, forced to act as if they believe in a bit of legal realism, but not too much.[23] Like Spargo, state judges attempting to straddle the divide between politics and law strain credulity: their political behavior calls into question their legal commitments, suggesting that the discussion of law in state judicial decisions is merely a pose designed to disguise the pursuit of partisan interests.

The notion that state judges are political is indeed commonly held. The very same polls that highlight the public's faith in the impartiality and fairness of state judges also reveal clear public awareness of the influence of political considerations.[24] Consider, for example, thirteen separate surveys of public opinion about state courts that were conducted in the twenty-year period from 1989 to 2009.[25] All of these surveys contained similar questions about judicial fairness and similar questions about the impact of politics on judicial decisionmaking. Averaging across all thirteen polls, 67 percent of those surveyed agreed that their state judges were generally impartial, while 70 percent thought that politics was at work in the judicial process.[26] In all different parts of the country and across significant periods of time, Americans consistently value the fairness of state judges and yet doubt the degree to which state judicial decisions can be explained simply by pointing to the law.[27]

Judicial Elections

Given all of the preceding, one might conclude that partisan elections are at the root of the problem in the states. Election is the most common method of state judicial selection, and when conventional expectations of impartial judging are mixed with partisan electoral contests, judicial candidates must concede (at some level) that judging is political even as they insist that their own judging will be conducted without regard for politics. Perhaps state judges might be spared the task of treading such an "elusive and perhaps illusory line" if they were selected for office in a different way.[28]

The most prominent alternative means of judicial selection in the states—an alternative specifically designed to insulate judges from partisan politics—was first introduced by Missouri in 1940. Under the "Missouri Plan," nonpartisan commissions recruit and evaluate judicial candidates and then recommend rosters of possible appointees to the governor. Those appointees selected by the governor may remain on the bench for subsequent terms subject to noncompetitive retention elections in which voters are asked only if they approve of the incumbent. Thirty-four states currently use some variant of the Missouri Plan to select certain judges and require at least a portion of their judges to face retention elections.[29]

Judicial retention elections usually have a low public profile and are often far less expensive than other forms of judicial election.[30] A large percentage of the judges subject to retention believe that such elections effectively reduce partisan politicking in the selection process.[31] In fact, judges who have faced retention elections not only agree that such elections mute partisan politics but also overwhelmingly favor keeping retention elections in place—a level of support that undoubtedly is propped up by the fact that sitting judges survive retention elections at very high rates (one study found that over a thirty-four year period judges were retained in all but 52 of 4,588 elections).[32]

The sleepy, low-risk environment of a noncompetitive retention election arguably bolsters the appearance of judicial impartiality. After all, if the lesson of partisan judicial elections is that judges "who campaign like politicians become, in effect, politicians," then the largely campaign-free retention elections should prevent judicial candidates from looking political.[33] By sharply limiting the pressure to pander to a popular audience, retention elections would appear to promote the highest standards of judicial integrity and professionalism.[34]

Yet judges subject to noncompetitive retention elections actually find that they are not entirely removed from either political influence or public suspicion.[35] The merit-based appointment process itself may involve substantial politicking and lobbying behind the scenes.[36] Conventional partisan electioneering is generally at a low ebb in retention elections, but a high percentage of judges nonetheless report that these contests still affect their behavior, leading them to be more sensitive to public opinion, to avoid controversial rulings, and to curry favor with the local bar.[37] Large-scale statistical studies confirm that judicial behavior is powerfully shaped by retention elections.[38] Public opinion appears to have taken note: polls show that individuals living in states with noncompetitive retention elections are just as likely to believe "judges' decisions are influenced by political considerations" as individuals living in states with partisan judicial elections.[39] The Missouri Plan combination of merit appointment and retention elections does often convert judicial selection into a low-key affair. But this highly constrained process does not quell the public suspicion that state judges are basing their rulings on something other than the evidence and legal arguments presented in any given dispute.

The persistence of public suspicion even where the judicial selection process has been reformed suggests that the bind in which state judges find themselves cannot be pinned on partisan elections alone. According to Alan Tarr, the deeper problem is a lack of public agreement about how to "assess judicial fidelity to the law."[40] If there were a stable, widely shared consensus on how judges should interpret the law, then judicial elections would not in themselves pose a problem; whether a judge was elected in a party contest or retained in a noncompetitive referendum, it would be easy to tell whether or not she was behaving impartially by measuring her decisions on the bench against accepted standards of legal interpretation. Unfortunately, there appears to be little such consensus on legal interpretation today, at least with regard to the politically charged constitutional disputes that make up an important component of the state docket.[41] Rather than a clear notion of what the law requires in such hard cases, there is a proliferation of diverse legal arguments covering the entire spectrum of policy alternatives. And where the law is open to divergent renderings that favor different political camps, it is hard to ascertain the degree to which any given judge is either following legal principle or pursuing political goals.

Thus Spargo's protestation that he had "not had a political thought" since joining the bench seems so difficult to believe, not only because he ran in partisan elections, but also because we lack broad agreement about what constitutes faithful legal interpretation in contentious cases. One man's just legal settlement has become another man's politically motivated judicial ruling, and the public is left with a "deep skepticism about the impartiality of state courts and their ability to administer justice even-handedly."[42]

Law and Politics in the Federal Courts

Are federal judges in a different position than their state counterparts? Federal judges do not stand for popular election at all. Once nominated by the president and confirmed by the Senate, federal judges, including Supreme Court justices, hold office during good behavior—a requirement that effectively ensures life tenure on the bench.[43] The Framers of the Constitution believed that such lengthy judicial terms would work to guarantee impartiality. Alexander Hamilton claimed, for example, that lifetime judicial tenure not only would erect "an excellent barrier to the encroachments and oppressions" of the legislature but also would shield the courts from those "ill humors" of the people that had the tendency "to occasion dangerous innovations in government, and serious oppressions of the minor party in the community." The grant of lifetime tenure to federal judges was, Hamilton insisted, "the best expedient which can be devised in any government to secure a steady, upright, and impartial administration of the laws."[44] There would appear to be neither the need nor the opportunity for Spargo-style politicking here.

But the Framers' view of lifetime judicial tenure was questioned in its own day. Opponents of the Constitution feared the political power that could be wielded by permanently ensconced members of the Supreme Court: "independent of the people, of the legislature, and of every power under heaven," the justices were ultimately bound to "feel themselves independent of heaven itself."[45] Anti-Federalists worried that lifetime tenure, rather than guaranteeing impartiality, would create vast opportunities for judicial elites to pursue their own interests under the guise of unbiased adjudication.

The Anti-Federalists' basic concern—that the law, on its own, would be insufficient to constrain the political reach of federal judges—is essentially the same concern at the heart of the predicament facing state judges. Does this concern apply to the federal courts today? The federal docket is, if anything, more crowded with politically charged constitutional disputes than are the state court dockets, and there is little consensus on how the law should guide federal judges as they sort through such disputes. As Sanford Levinson has observed, "American constitutional lawyers, whether practitioners, academics, or judges, seem to feel relatively few genuine constraints in the kinds of arguments they are willing to make or endorse. It is, I am convinced, harder to recognize a 'frivolous argument' in constitutional law than in any other area of legal analysis."[46] Laurence Tribe echoed this observation when he announced he was suspending work on the third edition of his celebrated treatise

American Constitutional Law.[47] According to Tribe, a synthetic statement of constitutional law cannot be produced today because profound divisions in constitutional interpretation "have become too plain—and too pronounced—to paper over by routine appeals to the standard operating procedures of the legislative-judicial division of authority, the routine premises of the federal-state allocation of power, and the usual methods of extracting meaning from notoriously ambiguous texts."[48] To a degree that would please the original legal realists, Tribe seemed to be suggesting that federal judicial decisionmaking was less often a matter of "timeless legal principle" than "an evolving enterprise . . . imbued (even riddled) with contemporary political, social, and economic considerations."[49]

With federal constitutional law fractured by deep disagreements, one might expect federal judges to be plagued by the suspicion that they harbor political motives, regardless of the fact that they are altogether freed from the political demands of popular election. Indeed, the notion that federal judges are political actors is not only a suspicion permitted by the unsettled state of constitutional law but also an inference positively encouraged by the process of judicial appointment.[50] The selection of Supreme Court justices today is a highly politicized affair, with elected officials intentionally picking nominees in order to advance issues of importance to political parties and prominent interest groups.[51] The selection of judges for lower federal courts typically generates less drama and receives less press coverage than Supreme Court appointments. Even so, lower federal court appointments are shot through with political considerations. Judicial confirmations are routinely delayed and occasionally derailed as partisans compete for control over the selection process and attempt to fill the lower federal courts with ideologically congenial appointees.[52]

The identification of federal judges with politics does not stop with confirmation. The media regularly identifies federal judges by the president who nominated them and consistently tags judges as either "liberal" or "conservative," implicitly suggesting that judicial actions are best understood as a form of partisan policymaking.[53] The political insinuations purveyed by the media are reinforced by the practice of judicial decisionmaking, particularly at the level of the Supreme Court. The level of discord on the high bench has skyrocketed over the course of the twentieth century.[54] Over 80 percent of the full opinions announced by the

Supreme Court in the 1920s were unanimous; by the final years of the twentieth century, a little over 35 percent of the full opinions were joined by all the justices. The high degree of disagreement does not project an image of the Court as an impartial arbiter settling individual disputes by enunciating fixed and certain principles of law. On the contrary, the high incidence of splintered decisions makes the Court look more like a fractious political body squabbling over governance of the legal system. Rather than speaking with a single voice, the justices appear to be governed by a "norm of individualism" that actively encourages the public expression of policy disagreements.[55] When the Court regularly decides hotly contested cases by closely divided votes, often featuring stinging dissents, it is little wonder that observers, including the media, cast Court decisions in partisan terms.[56] Indeed, scholars have argued that the modern decline in consensus on the Supreme Court provided the initial impetus for studying the Court's decisionmaking as an essentially political enterprise.[57]

The public nonetheless demands that federal judges, like state judges, be neutral arbiters. Polls indicate that large majorities of Americans expect federal judges to apply the law impartially and distrust federal judges who advance narrow ideological interests.[58] Studies have shown that the Supreme Court in particular has received a good deal of public goodwill because it is generally thought to be an even-handed guarantor of basic democratic values for all.[59] On the whole, Americans seem to believe that the federal judiciary uses its independence to make fair decisions. Sixty-four percent of Americans surveyed in 2006, for example, trusted the Supreme Court to operate in the best interests of the American people either a "great deal" or "a fair amount."[60] When asked whether federal judges should be subject to greater political control by elected officials, over two-thirds of those surveyed said no.[61]

Federal judges understand the public's views, and they frequently echo the popularly held belief that federal courts should decide cases on a fair hearing of the arguments and evidence. In the opening remarks of his Supreme Court confirmation hearings, for example, Judge Samuel Alito said that good judges are "always open to the possibility of changing their minds based on the next brief that they read or the next argument that's made by an attorney" in court.[62]

All of this leaves federal judges boxed into a version of the same predicament that bedevils so many state judges. On the one hand, federal judges are subject to highly political processes of selection; have partisan affiliations routinely underscored by the media; work with legal materials open to conflicting political interpretations; and, at the level of the Supreme Court, commonly bicker with one another over how legal policy ought to be made. On the other hand, federal judges, including Supreme Court justices, are conventionally expected to reach their decisions through the impartial application of pre-existing legal principles without depending on political ideology or preference. Thus federal judges, like state judges, seem to play both political and legal roles, appearing to confirm and to refute the claims of legal realism as they go about their business.

The evidence suggests that, in spite of its belief in the impartiality of the federal bench, the public perceives federal judges to be playing political roles just as state judges do. When asked whether federal judges "rise above politics and hand down fair decisions" or "hand down decisions that reflect [the judges'] own political leanings," over 60 percent of those surveyed agreed that federal court decisions generally reflect political preferences.[63] Matters are not much different for the highest federal court. A large portion of the public believes that the Supreme Court operates with too little regard for either legal principles or impartiality; national surveys regularly find a near majority of respondents agreeing that the Court is "too mixed up in politics."[64] With the Court widely viewed as a political institution, the public often rates the Court's performance in partisan terms. Polls show that Americans routinely evaluate the Court from the perspective of their own individual party affiliation.[65] Positive opinions of the Court have fallen among Democrats and conservative Republicans because the former have found leading decisions to be too conservative while the latter believe that the Court has not been conservative enough.[66] And when asked what sort of judge is most likely to let personal beliefs influence legal decisions, 40 percent of those polled said liberal judges, 39 percent said conservative ones, and 13 percent thought that both were equally likely to do so.[67] For many members of the public, the legal ritual and rhetoric of the Court looks like a sideshow; it is politics, pure and simple, that seems to hold center stage.[68]

Federal judges and state judges both are well aware of the public's tendency to view the judiciary in political terms: 87 percent of all judges surveyed agree that courts are under increasing pressure to be directly accountable to public opinion.[69] In this context, it is not unusual to find federal judges responding to the public's political appraisals by tearing a page out of Justice Spargo's playbook: they insist that their decisions, contrary to appearances, are entirely free of political concerns.[70] Ninth Circuit Court of Appeals Chief Judge Alex Kozinski, for example, has described the notion that judges "engraft their own political philosophy onto the decisionmaking process" as so much "horse manure." It is true, Judge Kozinski conceded, that the siren song of political judging can be seductive. "It is frequently very difficult to tell the difference between how you think a case should be decided and how you hope it will come out. It is very easy to take sides in a case and subtly shade the decision-making process in favor of the party you favor, much like the Legal Realists predict." But judges ultimately have too much self-respect to betray popular ideals of legal principle and judicial impartiality. "Judges have to look in the mirror at least once a day, just like everyone else; they have to like what they see. Heaven knows, we don't do it for the money; if you can't have your self-respect, you might as well make megabucks doing leveraged buyouts."[71] At its core, impartial judging is a matter of "internal fortitude" entirely independent of the question of whether judges appear to act without political bias.[72]

Similar, though less colorful, denials of political judging can also be found at the level of the Supreme Court. The day after the Court decided *Bush v. Gore*, for example, Justice Clarence Thomas met with a group of high school students touring the Court building and announced that "I have yet to hear any discussion, in nine years, of partisan politics" among the justices.[73] Of course, an observer looking in on the Court might be tempted to see *Bush v. Gore* as an example of partisan politics. The five most conservative members of the Court (among them Justice Thomas) had stopped the recount process and handed the presidency to the conservative Republican candidate George W. Bush. The Court majority based its ruling on a novel constitutional claim that seemed to have been invented solely for the purposes of the case at hand—a fact that only heightened the appearance of partisanship. Justice Thomas nonetheless urged his audience to disregard appearances. "I plead with you that, whatever you do, don't try to apply the rules of the political world to this institution; they do not apply. The last political act we engage in is confirmation."[74] Justice Spargo could not have said it better himself.

Public Views of the Courts in General

Since both federal and state courts find themselves in similar positions, one might suppose that the public opinion of the courts in general is divided into contradictory political and legal elements.[75] This does indeed seem to be the case. Individuals gather impressions of the courts not only from conventional news sources but also from experience (including encounters with the architecture of court buildings and with the rituals of court proceedings) and from popular culture (including movies, novels, "reality" courtroom television shows, and wall-to-wall tabloid coverage of "trials of the century"). Scholars have suggested that this broad constellation of impressions yields conflicting images of the courts as institutions of principle and as arenas of bias.[76] These are the very same sort of conflicting images that characterize the public understanding of state and federal judiciaries.

We can obtain a clearer sense of the public's overall views by examining surveys designed to map general perceptions. In 2005, Syracuse University's Maxwell Poll posed a battery of court-related questions as part of a nationwide survey. The poll was set up to measure general public opinion about the courts; poll questions used the terms *judge* and *courts* generically without specifying federal or state level.

The Maxwell Poll provided a detailed rendering of a by-now familiar picture. According to the poll, 82 percent of the American public thought that the partisan background of judges influenced court decisionmaking either some or a lot.[77] This political perception was widely held. The poll found that an overwhelming majority of liberals (88 percent), conservatives (83 percent), people who attend religious services several times a week (84 percent), and people who never attend religious services (88 percent) all agreed that partisanship did not switch off when judicial robes were put on.

Given the widespread agreement that partisanship skews judicial decisionmaking, one would expect large segments of the public to view judicial selection in political terms. The Maxwell Poll confirmed this expectation. Among those surveyed, Republicans were eight times more likely than Democrats to trust the president and Senate to pick good federal judges (at the time of the survey, Republicans controlled the Senate and held the presidency). Moreover, three-quarters of survey respondents rejected the idea that fewer judges should be subject to popular election. A large majority appeared to see judicial selection as a political process and, as a result, they seemed to think that it made sense to organize judicial selection in a political way.[78]

What about the idea that judges are nonpartisan actors bound by legal principle? According to the Maxwell Poll, the belief that judges should be considered impartial arbiters was almost as common as the belief that judges were influenced by politics. Seventy-three percent of those surveyed agreed that judges should continue to be shielded from outside pressure and allowed to make decisions based on their own independent reading of the law. This majority in favor of shielding judges from politics held straight across party lines: three-quarters or more of Democrats and Republicans agreed that the courts should continue to be independent. The same was true of self-described liberals, moderates, and conservatives. The results were also no different when responses were broken down according to frequency of church attendance. Americans who go to church several times a week supported maintaining the ideal of judicial independence in the same large numbers as Americans who never attend church at all. In fact, even among those respondents who *disagreed* with the statement "you can generally trust public officials to do the right thing," the idea that judges should be insulated from outside pressure received a high level of support.[79]

The widely shared desire to preserve judicial independence that was captured by the poll clearly reflects a popular aspiration—and it also reflects a broad-based recognition that, whatever else might be said about the politics of judging, a wide variety of citizens rely on the courts to resolve disputes. When asked why so many conflicts end up in the courts, only a small percentage of Americans blamed politicians for failing to deal with the controversies in the first place and an even smaller percentage blamed judges for actively reaching out to decide hot-button issues.[80] Instead, almost half of those surveyed said that courts were at the center of so many conflicts because the people themselves demanded that the judiciary get involved. Many Americans appear to believe, in other words, that the courts faithfully respond to the citizenry as a whole. In light of this belief, judicial independence makes good sense: it is by allowing judges to make decisions without pressure from specific groups or parties that the judiciary is able to preserve the trust and interests of its broad public.

Thus, at the end of the Maxwell Poll we arrive once again at a remarkable ambivalence. A large majority of the public appears to believe that the courts are principled institutions where political pressure and partisan rivalry have no place; at the same time, a large majority of the public also appears to believe that partisanship influences the judicial process. The very same set of ambivalent opinions was also registered by the Annenberg Judicial Independence Survey in 2006.[81] On one hand, the Annenberg Survey found that large majorities of Americans (1) trust the judiciary to operate in the best interests of the people and (2) believe state courts and the U.S. Supreme Court have the right amount of power. On the other hand, the Annenberg Survey also found (1) that 75 percent of respondents believe that judges are influenced by their personal political views to either a great or moderate extent, and (2) that over two-thirds of those surveyed consider the influence of judges' personal political views to be either "not too appropriate" or "not appropriate at all." Whether the subject of discussion is the state courts, the federal courts, or courts in general, most Americans seem to share the same conflicting mix of legal and political perceptions, leading them to view judges as fair arbiters and political agents all at once.

The Nature of the Problem

I have argued that a substantial portion of the American public expects its judges to resolve disputes by reasoning impartially on the basis of legal principles, and that American judges regularly explain their decisions in terms consistent with public expectations of impartiality. At the same time, a substantial portion of the American public also believes that the judicial process is permeated with politics, a belief that seems to be amply supported by the country's highly political mechanisms of judicial selection and by the lack of agreement over how the law ought to be interpreted in politically charged cases. In public discourse, legal realism seems to be both dead and alive.[82] This contradictory condition in turn creates the appearance of judicial hypocrisy, stoking suspicions that judges may be affecting an air of legal impartiality in order to disguise the pursuit of political goals. And as the indicators of political judging grow more apparent, the suspicions of judicial hypocrisy will only multiply.[83]

How should this state of affairs be understood? Perhaps the most straightforward way to answer this question is to say that the public's conflicting views and attendant suspicions pose a growing threat to judicial legitimacy. American courts periodically have been subject to political attacks in the past, with liberals and conservatives each raising questions about judicial power at different times. But the current period—with political perceptions of the judiciary shared by a large majority of the public—may well present new risks. As Charles Geyh writes, "The more that the public and their representatives think that judges generally—not just a particular judge or panel of judges in isolated cases—follow their political leanings instead of the law, the more likely it becomes that long established [judicial] independence norms will be challenged with increasing intensity and will ultimately yield to calls for greater judicial accountability from Congress."[84] With a large segment of the public increasingly skeptical about the sincerity of the courts' legal pronouncements, it seems that the judiciary's standing as an independent, authoritative arbiter of disputes is in danger, raising the specter of a coming age "where political officials tell judges how to decide cases."[85]

This is not the only possible way to understand the ambivalent status of legal realism. I will spend the remainder of the book developing a substantially different interpretation of current conditions, an interpretation that explains how existing perceptions may at once threaten judicial legitimacy *and* enable legal power.

Yet before I begin to articulate my alternative approach, it is worth exploring the idea that the prevailing opinion may undermine the judicial process. There are at least three objections that can be raised against the argument I have to made to this point—and thus at least three reasons to doubt that the legitimacy of the courts faces growing danger. First, one might doubt that the public really suspects judges of hypocrisy. Second, one might question whether public perceptions of judicial behavior should be taken seriously. Finally, even if one agrees that the public suspects judges of being hypocritical and that such suspicions may have important short-term consequences, one might nonetheless maintain that public opinion is simply wrong. If popular perceptions of the courts are mistaken, then one could argue that concerns about judicial legitimacy will disappear as soon as the genuine nature of the judicial process becomes known to the public at large.

I shall take up each of these objections in the following sections. As I do so, I shall highlight the ways in which the current state of affairs may be said to threaten judicial legitimacy.

Hypocrisy, Insincerity, and Other Forms of Pretense

I have argued that the public frequently suspects judges of being hypocrites, of affecting a reliance on legal principle that they do not actually have. At the outset, one might question the choice to identify hypocrisy as the target of public suspicion. Hypocrisy is commonly understood to be a particularly serious and deplorable form of dissembling—a reflection of the fact that hypocrisy is historically associated with the feigning of religious belief.[86] Why suggest that the public suspects the worst of judges when the public may only be worried about insincerity, selective withholding of information, or some other more mild form of less-than-complete forthrightness?[87]

I use the term *hypocrisy* because it more precisely expresses the substance of public suspicion than alternative terms. *Insincerity*, for example, refers to a general type of dishonesty or lack of genuineness, the "assuming of a false guise in speech or conduct." *Hypocrisy*, by contrast, denotes a more specific kind of pretense: the hypocrite is "one who pretends to have feelings or beliefs of a higher order than his real ones."[88] An insincere person can feign kindness or cruelty, but the hypocrite, by definition, is more constrained. To be a hypocrite, one must pretend to be better than one actually is.

Hypocritical behavior, so understood, does seem to be what the public suspects. In 2005, the Maxwell Poll asked a representative sample of Americans whether they agreed or disagreed with the following statement: "Judges always say that their decisions are based on the law and the Constitution, but in many cases judges are really basing their decisions on their own personal beliefs." A solid majority of respondents agreed. Moreover, this view was shared by majorities in a wide range of different groups. Democrats (60 percent) and Republicans (59 percent), those who generally trust public officials to do the right thing (55 percent) and those who generally distrust public officials (59 percent), those who always vote (58 percent) and those who never vote (60 percent), those who approve of the president (60 percent) as well as those who disapprove of the president (58 percent)—all agreed that even though judges may consistently invoke high legal principle, they are often deriving their decisions from more mundane preferences.

The Maxwell Poll results were confirmed by a panel survey conducted in 2005 and 2006.[89] The panel survey asked respondents whether they agreed or disagreed with the identical statement used in the Maxwell Poll: "Judges always say that their decisions are based on the law and the Constitution, but in many cases judges are really basing their decisions on their own personal beliefs." Just as was the case in the Maxwell Poll, the panel survey found that a significant majority of respondents (nearly 62 percent) agreed.[90] Opinions were similar when questions specifically mentioned the Supreme Court. The panel survey found that a majority disagreed with the statement, "Judges' values and political views have little to do with how they decide cases before the Supreme Court."[91] The survey also asked respondents whether or not they agreed with the statement, "Since the Constitution must be updated to reflect society's values as they exist today, Supreme Court judges have a great deal of leeway in decisions, even when they claim to be 'interpreting' the Constitution." Over 70 percent of respondents agreed. Thus when asked whether the description that Supreme Court justices offer of their own decisionmaking should be accepted, almost three-quarters of the public said no.[92]

Such broadly shared skepticism may have dangerous consequences. When litigants doubt the impartiality of judges, defeat in court may look less like the rendering of justice than like the victorious litigant and the judge ganging up against the losing party.[93] Suspicions of judicial hypocrisy may thus discourage individual litigants from using and obeying the courts—and the effects of such suspicions may not stop there. Democratic government in general depends on the capacity of citizens to evaluate and control the performance of public officials. To the extent that citizens suspect judges of misrepresenting the way in which they arrive at their decisions, citizens may believe that they lack the information necessary to assess the operation of a powerful institution.[94] Skepticism that begins with the judiciary may ultimately spread, leading the citizenry to doubt the trustworthiness of government in general.

Indeed, some commentators believe that we are already at the threshold of "a war of all against all within and through the law." Without a shared belief that the judiciary serves a common purpose or is limited by fixed principle, law is becoming "little more than the spoils that go to winners in contests among private interests who, by their victory, secure the prize of enlisting the coercive power of the legal apparatus to enforce their agenda." Those who end up on the losing side of this bleak system will comply only because of fear of punishment and "out of the hope that they might prevail in future contests to take their turn to wield the law."[95]

The Importance of Appearances

Although one might concede that many Americans suspect judges of being hypocritical, one could nonetheless argue that the existence of suspicion does not mean judges are necessarily guilty of any actual inauthenticity or double dealing. Public beliefs about judges may bear little relation to how judges are really acting. Why should popular opinion be taken seriously when it may have no direct correspondence to the facts of concrete behavior?

I agree that the suspicion of judicial hypocrisy and a reality of judicial hypocrisy are not the same things. The former may or may not be indicative of the latter; without more direct information about how particular judges decide particular cases, one cannot say whether popular suspicions of hypocrisy accurately identify judges who instrumentally deploy legal principles or whether these suspicions misread judges who sincerely grapple with competing legal commitments. Indeed, even with more direct information about particular cases in hand, we should still expect that it will be hard to verify acts of judicial hypocrisy. Since the law is wide open to different partisan interpretations in contentious constitutional cases, it will often be difficult to prove that a given judge has used legal principle as a fig leaf for political interest.

Consider the judge who is conscientiously committed to basing her decisions on legal principle and the judge who is conscientiously committed to basing his decisions on political preference.[96] Both judges will publicly frame and explain their decisions in legal terms. In fact, both judges may not only produce opinions that look alike, but also may arrive at the same holding. Under such circumstances, it will be difficult for the public to identify which judge is being faithful to legal principle and which is being influenced by partisan commitments. Even specialists may find themselves plagued by uncertainty. As Lawrence Baum has argued, scholars have not arrived at a definitive explanation of judicial goals and motivations, and they are unlikely ever to do so. The fundamental difficulty derives from the fact that the "patterns disclosed by research typically are consistent with multiple explanations." Thus the "empirical findings that scholars use to support a particular interpretation of judges' behavior typically are consistent with other interpretations as well."[97] Justice Spargo may *look* like a "partisan hack lawyer" to some, but that does not mean he actually *is* a partisan hack lawyer nor does it mean that his rulings cannot be explained by anything other than political preference. When it comes to public suspicions of judicial hypocrisy, a whiff of smoke will not necessarily indicate the presence of fire.

Yet I would argue that the smoke is nonetheless important. Scholars have found that public confidence in the judiciary depends not only on the actual results of court rulings but also the ability of judges to convey the impression that their decisions are driven by the impersonal requirements of legal principle.[98] The avoidance of actual judicial improprieties is necessary to secure judicial legitimacy but it is not sufficient; judges must also visibly appear to play the role of neutral arbiter in order to reduce the probability of actual bias and to maintain popular support.[99] Indeed, due process in the Unites States has been understood to require judges not only to be fair and impartial but also to appear to be fair and impartial. Appellate courts enforce the due process requirement and have held that the "appearance of bias alone is grounds for reversal even if the trial judge is, in fact, completely impartial."[100] In substance and on the surface, judges are expected to decide cases on the basis of the law, facts, and arguments presented in the controversy before them.

The concern with judicial appearances has deep roots in the United States.[101] In an influential address to the American Bar Association in 1906, Roscoe Pound called attention to the perils of adverse public perceptions. The ensuing debates in the legal profession over the public standing of the courts and the appropriate standards of judicial behavior eventually led to the creation of the first Canons of Judicial Ethics in 1924. Like Pound, the Canons paid a great deal of attention to questions of appearance. As Charles Geyh notes, one canon declared directly "that a judge's official conduct should be 'free from . . . the appearance of impropriety,' [while] eleven other canons cautioned judges to avoid conduct that could create 'suspicion' of misbehavior or 'misconceptions' of the judicial role that might 'appear' or 'seem' to interfere with judicial duties, or that could 'create the impression' of bias."[102]

The 1924 Canons were advisory. But over the course of the twentieth century the Canons were revised into a Code of Judicial Conduct and ultimately made mandatory. By 1981 official judicial conduct commissions devoted to the enforcement of the Code had been established in all fifty states. The old concern over judicial appearance remained central to the modern Code. As a consequence, the sanctioning of judges for both the appearance and actuality of impropriety is a familiar feature of the legal landscape today.[103]

All of this suggests that public opinion should not be set aside simply because it is based on assessments of how judges look while carrying out their duties. Although appearances are fleeting, public judgments about appearance are hardly insubstantial. It may be that judges are not actually behaving "like partisan politicians: trading votes, brokering deals, or forming coalitions." It may be that judges really do take legal principles seriously, listen carefully to the arguments and facts in each dispute, and then decide "the cases before them in light of their own more or less coherent jurisprudential ideas about what the law requires." Even so, if judges *seem* to be deciding on the basis of political ideology, then this appearance encourages others not only to "treat court decisions as political events" but also to try "to shape and influence [court decisions] for their own political reasons."[104] Public impressions of judicial performance may place a political patina on the courts that is both influential and difficult to remove.

Public Ignorance and How to Eradicate It

One might agree that judicial appearances have been important and yet insist that it would be better if appearances did not carry such weight. In this vein, one could argue that it is insufficient to acknowledge, as I have, that public suspicions of judicial hypocrisy may not be right in any given case. It may be more accurate to say that public suspicions will be wrong in virtually *every* case. After all, many of the same polls that illustrate the public's conflicting views of judicial decisionmaking also often demonstrate the public's ignorance of the most basic facts about the judiciary. For example, half of all Americans, including nearly a third of college graduates, erroneously believe that Supreme Court cases decided by 5-4 votes are "too close to carry legal force and require subsequent review by either the lower courts or the Congress."[105] A majority of Americans do not know that federal judges are appointed and serve for life.[106] Indeed, most Americans appear to be more familiar with the names of Snow White's Seven Dwarfs than they are with the names of the justices serving on the Supreme Court.[107] The public's lack of detailed information about the courts is also evident at the state level. In Colorado, for instance, where there is a well-established judicial performance evaluation system designed to inform citizens about the records of sitting judges, over half of those voting in judicial elections nonetheless consider themselves to be uninformed about their own choices. Among this large body of uninformed voters, the most popular voting strategy is simply to vote to retain all judges seeking re-election; the second most popular voting strategy is to vote "for" or "against" judges completely at random.[108]

Perhaps the public's ambivalent half-politics-half-law understanding of the courts is simply another sign of ignorance. Although ill-informed public perceptions may be a significant short-term force, at the end of the day one might argue that these perceptions are mistaken impressions in need of correction. Isn't the appropriate response to point out the public's errors and to explain how the courts actually work?

In fact, scholars have written books explicitly designed to dispel common misunderstandings about the intersection of law and politics in the judicial process. Ronald Cass has argued, for example, that erroneous political perceptions of judicial decisionmaking are fostered by legal academics.[109] Part of the problem is that legal scholars tend to focus their scholarship on the most contentious Supreme Court cases, in which disagreement among the justices is at its height. More generally, legal scholars routinely assess judicial decisions on the basis of their own normative commitments, measuring the worth of a decision on the basis of how closely it conforms to the scholars' own political ideals rather than on how well the decision adheres to the law. Legal academics thus systematically exaggerate the importance of political claims and create the misleading impression that judges operate on the basis of mere preference. The justices are not political; it is the scholars who study the Court that are, and their slanted scholarship has obscured the true role of legal principles. "The rule of law acts in society much as a large body of water acts on weather patterns," writes Cass. "The ocean does not guarantee warm or constant temperatures, but it dramatically moderates the changes brought on by other forces. . . . [The rule of law] pulls society in the direction of knowable, predictable, rule-based decisionmaking, toward limitations on the power entrusted to government officials, toward alignment of power with legitimacy."[110] If the rule of law is rightly understood, Cass argues, then the judiciary's pervasive reliance on legal principle becomes clear. Even when considering the most contentious cases on the Supreme Court's docket—including cases like *Bush v. Gore*—the proper perspective allows one to see how the law dictates the outcome of controversy after controversy.[111]

In direct opposition to Cass, Terri Peretti has insisted that a law-centered view of judicial process is flatly wrong. Focusing on the Supreme Court, Peretti celebrates "the reality [that] the justices' personal political preferences strongly influence their interpretations of the Constitution."[112] Many commentators demonize the Court's essentially political nature because they fear politics and therefore incorrectly believe that a political judiciary is necessarily out of control. Peretti argues that the actual truth of political judging is quite different. Governing majorities intentionally place their preferred candidates on the high bench so that they will predictably decide cases on the basis of their political values. Thus the Court is explicitly designed to be just another policymaking venue among the many such venues in American politics, one more place in which policies made by other political institutions can be tested against a specific set of interests. It is not politics *per se* that undermines the courts, but only the "low politics" of "mere partisan favoritism" that does so. Properly understood, the Court's "high politics" of "consistent ideological policy making" is a genuine benefit that produces a representative and legitimate judicial process.[113] Problems emerge only when judges appear to decide on the basis of petty partisanship, forsaking high politics for low.

The contest between Cass and Peretti encourages one to choose sides. And, in fact, one can readily find studies written after Cass and Peretti that may be aligned on one side or the other, producing more ammunition for the battle over how legal or how political the judiciary may be said to be.[114] Yet rather than declaring one scholar or the other victorious, I would argue that both capture an element of the truth.[115] Cass is right to say that the rule of law is organized around legal principle, and Peretti is right to say that partisan preference plays a critical role in judicial decisionmaking. The mistake is to believe that either Cass's or Peretti's argument is sufficient standing on its own.

Consider Peretti's celebration of Court politics. In defending the political nature of judicial decisions, Peretti seems to ignore the fact that participants in the judicial process work hard to demonstrate that their actions have nothing to do with politics at all. Political partisans do, of course, frequently compete to install ideological fellow travelers on the bench. But political partisans do not typically explain their actions in terms of ideology; instead, they regularly deny that they are applying any kind of political "litmus test" and insist that they are simply supporting judicial nominees that will faithfully interpret the law.

Sitting judges are even less likely to describe their actions as expressions of political commitment, high or low. Whatever political factors may be at work in judicial decisionmaking, the typical judicial opinion presents itself as a declaration of what the law is. Judges do not describe or justify their votes in political terms, nor does the general public expect them to do so. Judges do not say, "I was put on this court because I am a conservative person who believes affirmative action programs should be dismantled and that is what I intend to do." Instead, they say "affirmative action is unconstitutional."[116] Judges lay claims to impartiality, neutrality, independence, and legal principle to demonstrate that they have weighed the arguments and evidence without regard to politics, not to indicate that judicial decisionmaking is a special form of politics.[117] While politics can appear to be either "high-minded or self-serving," the law strives to be free of political appearance altogether. "Politics—revolutionary or mundane—may not intrude into the rule of law. If it does, law becomes the illegitimate rule of men; it becomes merely the form, without the substance of law."[118]

The issue here is not that the distinction between "low politics" and "high politics" is meaningless. The corrosive effects of low politics have been a concern in many judicial systems and, as a result, the protection of the courts from petty bias has been central to the most basic understandings of judicial independence (I elaborate on this point further on). Clearly, one can coherently distinguish between mere partisan favoritism and consistent ideological policymaking. The point is that participants in the judicial process do not rely on such a distinction themselves; in actual practice, judicial decisions are justified without reference to any kind of political terms at all. Judges often come to the bench with decades of education and experience that habituate them to reasoning in legal terms. It seems unlikely that judges would abandon their training "the moment they don their robes" so that they could "satiate their political appetites without regard to their views of applicable law."[119] In her effort to describe the plain "reality" of judicial decisionmaking, Peretti seems to overlook this critical feature of actual judicial behavior.

Cass's argument is similarly incomplete. Cass credits the skewed, value-laden work of legal scholars with creating misleading political perceptions of the courts, but his argument seems to ignore deep structural connections between the judiciary and politics. Martin Shapiro's path-breaking work provides a useful corrective. In a sweeping analysis of courts across time and around the world, Shapiro notes that judicial independence means at minimum that the judge has "not been bribed or [is] not in some other way a dependent of one of the parties" in litigation. In most societies, such basic judicial independence has been achieved by making judges into government officials whose authority and compensation do not rely on the parties before them. Yet "when we ensure [basic] independence by creating the office of judge within some government structure, in a far more important sense [the judge] is not independent, for he is a dependent of those for whom he holds office."[120]

In other words, Shapiro's study demonstrates that the most common solution to the most basic problem of judicial independence everywhere introduces a new problem of its own, raising the possibility that judges may be driven less by a desire to do justice than by an interest in advancing the claims of the governing group. Political perceptions of the courts thus grow directly out of the judiciary's fundamental design. Judges may defend themselves against such perceptions by claiming to be independent of politics. Yet judicial defenses will always be measured against—and often undermined by—the fact that judges do indeed owe their positions to political figures. "When two parties must go to a third who is an officer," Shapiro concludes, "it is as evident to them as to the observer that they are no longer going to a disinterested third. Instead, they are introducing a third interest: that of the government, the church, the landowner, or whoever else appoints the official."[121] Rather than being a consequence of value-driven scholarship, the suspicion that judges are deciding cases on the basis of political interest appears to be generated by the basic structure of judicial institutions.

If the truth of the matter lies somewhere between the poles occupied by Cass and Peretti, one would expect the public to have an ambivalent view of the judicial process, a view that includes conflicting legal and political components. The arguments and evidence I have presented confirm that this is the case. And so, too, does the seminal research on popular legal consciousness performed by Patricia Ewick and Susan Silbey.[122] Based on a series of in-depth interviews with 430 individuals, Ewick and Silbey's work demonstrates that ordinary Americans typically define, use, and understand law in conflicting ways: on one hand, law "is imagined and treated as an objective realm of disinterested action . . . operating by known and fixed rules," and, on the other hand, law "is depicted as a game, a terrain for tactical encounters through which people marshal a variety of social resources to achieve strategic goals."[123] The same people hold these contradictory conceptions at the same time. Law is popularly understood to be "both sacred and profane, God and gimmick, interested and disinterested" all at once.[124]

This is not to say that one cannot try to synthesize either the public's contradictory perspectives or the competing arguments made by Cass and Peretti into a seamless view of judicial decisionmaking.[125] For example, one could argue that politics is actually part and parcel of legal interpretation on the Supreme Court and, as a result, that the justices "rarely experience overt conflicts between their political desires and their interpretive views" because such desires and views are constitutive parts of the same decisionmaking process.[126] As a matter of individual psychology, there may be no dissonance to be resolved. Members of the Court may quite "sincerely tell themselves that they fulfill their institutional duty or obligation to follow the rule of law, even as they simultaneously follow their political preferences."[127]

Some judges may understand their own actions in this smoothly integrated way and not personally experience any friction between the claims of legal principle and political preference that permeate the system. But this is not the only mode of decisionmaking that the judicial process allows (as I have indicated, there are many opportunities for judges to rely on legal principle, to use law as a cover for political preference, or to undertake some blend of the two). Moreover, the possibility that an individual judge may not feel any conflict between legal rules and political commitments does not mean that such conflicts do not actually exist. The scholarship I have reviewed indicates that the tensions between law and politics in the judicial process are indeed genuine, and the empirical evidence I have discussed suggests that most Americans see something like the same set of tensions that scholars do.[128]

Of course, to say that public opinion captures something important about the way in which the courts operate is not to say that the public is actually more informed about the details of the judicial process than polls suggest. As I have noted, the gaps in public knowledge are real. It strains credulity to claim that average citizens derive their conflicting views of the courts from a detailed understanding of judicial performance. It is true, for example, that the arguments presented in judicial opinions support the idea that judges decide on the basis of legal principle, while the increasing dissent rate among Supreme Court justices lends credence to a political view of the judiciary. Taken together, these two factors certainly suggest that a muddled, half-politics-half-law view of courts is accurate.

Yet there is no reason to believe that ordinary Americans are intimately familiar with either the contents of judicial opinions or the century-long trend away from Supreme Court consensus.

Acknowledging that Americans simply do not have a detailed understanding of the courts, one may still ask whether the lack of detailed knowledge prevents the public from making meaningful judgments. Scholars who study American elections have found that voters' lack of comprehensive factual knowledge about candidates tells us less about the quality of voter judgments than it does about the small incentives voters have to amass detailed information.[129] Gathering information about candidates is costly and, in view of these costs, citizens are likely to rely on the most readily available information (as opposed to most detailed information) as a guide.[130] Reasoning along these lines, one should expect many Americans to have views about the courts that are based on the information that is least onerous to acquire. One of the most easily obtained pieces of court-related information is that judges are impartial actors bound by legal principle (as I have indicated, this is the conventional understanding that is, among other things, endorsed by the American Bar Association and extolled by judges themselves). Another easily obtained piece of court-related information is that the judges operate on the basis of politics (this view is, for example, conveyed by highly political means of judicial selection and frequently encouraged by the media).[131]

These two pieces of readily available information about the courts are clearly in conflict. Do those individuals who gather easily accessible court-related information in turn develop conflicting views of the judiciary? Survey results suggest that they do. According to the Maxwell Poll, individuals who say that they follow news about court decisions are more likely than those who do not follow the news to believe (1) that the partisan background of judges influences court decisions and (2) that judges should continue to be shielded from outside pressure and allowed to make their decisions on the basis of an independent reading of the law.[132] The Maxwell Poll findings were confirmed in 2009. Surveying a nationally representative sample of Americans for their opinions about state courts, Princeton Survey Research Associates International found that those who closely follow news about their state are substantially more likely than those who do not closely follow the news (1) to believe that state courts are too often mixed up in politics, and (2) to have confidence in the job that their state courts are doing.[133]

Thus it seems that the more one keeps up with the news the more likely one is to believe that judges are influenced by politics *and* that judges are impartial arbiters.[134] The body of information that supports such an ambivalent understanding is unlikely to be very detailed—but that does not mean that this body of information is therefore without value.[135] The material I have presented here suggests that readily available information about the courts accurately portrays different elements of judicial behavior. As a consequence, it should not be too surprising to find many citizens arriving at opinions that faithfully reflect the uneasy mix of political and legal factors in the judicial process.

Conclusion

Large majorities of the American public seem to believe that all judges are political actors—except when they are not. This ambivalent point of view fosters the suspicion that judges often do not mean what they say; and this suspicion, in turn, threatens to erode public confidence in court authority and eat away at the judiciary's standing as an impartial arbiter of individual disputes.

In view of these circumstances, one might argue that the solution is to encourage judges simply to acknowledge the tension between law and politics openly.[136] Rather than insisting that their actions are driven by legal principle alone, judges could admit that political considerations are inevitably a part of judicial decisionmaking. Perhaps the honest and humble judge, who explains her reasoning in exploratory, less declarative terms, might pre-empt suspicions of hypocrisy by candidly discussing the ambiguities of legal language and the necessity of relying on political values. "If judicial law has lost the certainty associated with the myth of static, apolitical legal principle," William Popkin writes, "then litigants, the legal profession, and (perhaps) the public will be more reconciled to what courts do if they perceive a process in which judges openly appear to debate the results. When people know that the law is uncertain, a facade of certainty is an affront to the audience's intelligence and sense of fair play."[137]

Unfortunately, it is by no means certain that a new brand of judicial honesty would actually yield the promised results.[138] Nor is it clear that the assumptions behind this approach are sound. To call for more judicial candor in the first place is to presuppose that suspicions of judicial hypocrisy must be cleansed from the system if the rule of law is to remain intact. This underlying assumption may only capture part of the truth. As I have argued, suspicions of hypocrisy may well be signs of political pathology and harbingers of institutional collapse. In certain contexts, however, scholars have found that hypocritical behavior—both suspected and actual—may also work to sustain important social and political practices.[139] Thus popular skepticism about the real determinants of judicial decisionmaking may at once undermine and underwrite the exercise of legal power. I will begin to explore this line of thinking in Part II.

Part II
Elements of Common Courtesy

HYPOCRISY IS UNQUESTIONABLY A PEJORATIVE TERM. To call someone a hypocrite is to allege bad faith, to suggest that an individual's actions or arguments contradict what he or she actually believes. People consequently bridle at the accusation of hypocrisy and consider it to be a serious vice worth avoiding at all costs. As one scholar of the subject has observed, "I am no more likely to identify myself as a hypocrite than I am to call myself a cannibal."[1]

It is thus easy to see why public suspicion of judicial hypocrisy might be damaging to judicial legitimacy. As I argued in Part I, a large majority of Americans at once consider judges to be impartial and believe judicial rulings to be politically motivated. The tension between the two views naturally leads many to wonder whether judicial appeals to law are anything more than a fig leaf deployed to obscure partisan purposes. With a significant segment of the public dubious about the sincerity of court pronouncements, it seems that the judiciary's standing as an independent, authoritative arbiter is at risk.

Yet if it is generally true that hypocrisy is always negative, I would argue that it is also true that hypocrisy is not *only* negative. The suspicions of double dealing fueled by the public's half-politics-half-law understanding of the courts may erode judicial legitimacy, but these contradictory perceptions and suspicions may also form essential parts of the current legal order. The possibility that judges do not always mean what they say may function as a kind of *pharmacon*, simultaneously exhibiting the properties of a poison and a cure.[2]

How can this be? How can public skepticism about judicial decrees be corrosive and, at the same time, be part of a dynamic that enables legal power? In Part II, I begin to explore the constructive capacities of hypocritical behavior by analyzing the workings of common courtesy. I argue that common courtesy is, like law, a collection of rules. Moreover, I argue that the law-like rules of courtesy are frequently attended by suspicions of hypocrisy—suspicions that at once underwrite critiques of courtesy and identify the very means by which courtesy successfully operates. With an understanding of how an ever-present opportunity for hypocritical behavior actually helps sustain courtesy, I argue that we can turn back to the judicial process and consider how the possibility of hypocrisy may play a similar sustaining role in the legal context.

Of course, in using courtesy as a basis for explaining law I am not suggesting that the two rule-based systems are identical. Courtesy is decentralized and informally enforced while law is hierarchically organized and backed by state power. Courtesy also tends to be occupied with seemingly small matters of social interaction while law is concerned with an enormous range of issues including the most momentous disputes of the day.

Courtesy and law are distinct, and I do not suggest that they should be thought of as being completely the same. I make a different claim. On the basis of certain similarities between courtesy and law, I argue that they are similar in other key respects as well. The strength of my argument depends on the validity of the similarities I identify and on the new insights my comparison yields, not on a strict identity between courteous behavior and legal action. To put the point differently, I do not rely on courtesy as a legal microcosm, but as an analytical model—as a way of understanding more clearly how a rule-based system may function because of the possibility of pretense (rather than merely in spite of it).

What, then, does the study of courtesy tell us? My analysis suggests that courtesy depends on hypocrisy as a means for managing the stubborn facts of human disagreement and difference. For people to get along, courtesy does not require personal goals to coincide or good feelings to prevail; on the contrary, regardless of what people actually think about one another, courtesy asks only that they be well mannered. One might wish that people were capable of interacting with each other on the basis of genuine mutual respect, but such a wish is unlikely to be realized given the narrow interests and strong passions that often drive behavior. Taking people as they are, courtesy works to secure social coordination in a sea of divergent beliefs and competing attachments by creating a means by which individuals can forge usefully thin false friendships.[3] Giving everyone a chance to engage in hypocrisy by conforming to an artificial code of decent behavior, courtesy permits mutually advantageous interactions to occur in a thousand different situations when conflict would otherwise result.

The reliance on hypocrisy makes courtesy useful, but my account of courtesy does not stop with considerations of utility. If people valued courtesy solely because it helped enlist the cooperation of others, then they would stop being courteous the moment a more promising mode of behavior recommended itself. Once the widespread disdain for hypocrisy is considered, the abandonment of courtesy seems even more likely. Why would anyone risk looking like a hypocrite when there may be other means of getting along? Indeed, courtesy is often said to be in decline, with fewer and fewer individuals conforming to the dictates of decent behavior.

Although there is something to the courtesy-in-crisis view, I argue that courtesy is actually a fairly robust system for governing individual action—a system that persists for reasons in addition to its value as a hypocritical *modus vivendi*. In part, courtesy endures because its basic elements are introduced to most people when they are young. The method of introduction is not based on persuasion: children are usually habituated to courteous behavior through a prolonged program of repetition enforced by the inflexible say-so of parents. The continuous drill of courtesy lessons during childhood produces adults who are disposed to follow the conventions of good manners and who can be shamed whenever they stray from the path of politeness. Adults schooled in this manner may be truly virtuous, but they need not be. Courteous adults are committed to particular forms of conduct and need not actually accept the substantive notions of concern and respect that may be communicated through these forms. Thus, even though courtesy is artificial, thin, and a matter of outward behavior, properly trained adults remain attached to it as a routine for negotiating social interaction. Courtesy is not a matter of morality, but it nonetheless has a kind of normative significance for the well-bred.

Courteous behavior is further bolstered by pleasure. I argue that courtesy serves as an agreed-upon means for granting respect and giving praise to truly deserving individuals, providing a way of satisfying the legitimate desire to recognize and reward exemplary individuals. But this is not all. Courtesy also serves to gratify the desires of the undeserving. The artificial rituals and fake pleasantries of courtesy appease vanity in a multitude of small ways, allowing everyone in polite society to feel more honorable and worthy of respect than they actually may be. In either case, whether it is a matter of respecting the deserving or flattering the unworthy, politeness is enjoyable. The reciprocal practice of courtesy thus ties the affections of every individual in polite society to the conventions of good manners.

Finally, I argue that courtesy is a durable practice because it typically supports the existing hierarchies. Courtesy is not the handiwork of generic individuals confronted with the abstract problem of coordinating their action; instead, specific forms of courtesy are the consequence and hallmark of particular social orders. It is true that the accommodations between people facilitated by courtesy are mutual and yield mutual benefits. Yet mutuality is by no means a guarantee of equality. Although everyone can derive some benefits from living in polite society, some people systematically reap a larger share. Codes of courtesy mark off and counter-pose social groups, deploying distinctions between polite and rude behavior that work to reinforce hierarchies across classes. Those who profit the most from politeness have every incentive to preserve a system that keeps everyone in their proper place.

In sum, I argue (1) that courtesy is a law-like set of rules that relies on the possibility of hypocrisy in order to ensure smooth social interactions, and (2) that courtesy's reliance on hypocrisy is bound up with habit, pleasure, and the inequalities of the existing order.[4] As this list makes clear, some of courtesy's constituent components are not particularly admirable. Moreover, the system of social accommodation secured by courtesy is neither necessarily fair nor just: a polite person can be cruel and a society characterized by highly polished manners can be hierarchical and rigid. Courtesy is flawed—and yet it endures. The task of Part II is to explain why courtesy can be fruitfully compared to law and to explain how courtesy is able to function; the task of Part III is to extend my analysis to the judicial process.

How Can Courtesy Be Compared to Law?

It is helpful to begin with a definition. To be courteous—just as to be civil, polite, chivalrous, or gallant—is a matter of observing the rules required by good manners.

The differences between the various modes of enacting good manners are ones of emphasis and orientation. Civility typically refers to the bare minimum of good manners, suggesting little more than the avoidance of overt rudeness. Politeness, by contrast, connotes polish and sophistication, implying a relationship to the interests and pursuits of advanced culture. Courtesy, at its origin, drew its name from princely courts and referred to the graciously complaisant behavior of courtly gentlemen. Courtesy has since taken on a more democratic cast (becoming "common courtesy") and refers to an everyday form of good manners, at once less dignified than politeness and more attentive than civility. Chivalry and gallantry are both somewhat old-fashioned forms of good manners directed especially toward women. Gallantry suggests dashing deeds and ornate expressions of antique courtesy, while chivalry implies high-minded and self-sacrificing action.[5]

Although I will refer to politeness and civility, my primary interest is in courtesy, the most ordinary form of good manners in contemporary society.[6] As my initial definition indicates, courtesy is at its core a matter of observing rules or "etiquette," as the specific dictates and procedures of conventional good manners are known. Courtesy handbooks and guides are literally crammed with etiquette's specific directives covering everything from table manners ("Don't encircle your plate with your arm") to grieving the loss of a loved one ("One cannot refuse an invitation to be a pallbearer except for illness or absence from the city").[7] In fact, the focus on etiquette is so pronounced that one can find treatises on courtesy that consist of nothing but lists of rules.[8]

It is this commitment to rules that provides the initial impetus for thinking about courtesy and law together. Both courtesy and law are regulatory systems designed to shape, guide, and control individual behavior. The organization and application of the two sets of rules differ (I will have more to say on that subject shortly). Yet since they are both ways of governing action, it seems reasonable to compare the demands of law to the detailed requirements of etiquette.

I will consider in the following how law and courtesy have been most frequently weighed in relation to one another. I will then discuss the somewhat different approach to comparing law and courtesy that I plan to take.

Law and Courtesy in Symbiosis

One of the most common ways of relating law and courtesy to one another is in terms of symbiosis. For example, the nationally syndicated columnist and preeminent etiquette guru Judith Martin, known to her readers as Miss Manners, has argued that legal rules and etiquette work together in a mutually beneficial way to secure social peace, with law addressing the most serious breaches of order and courtesy managing everything else. Miss Manners puts it this way:

> Both the law and etiquette provide rules for the promotion of communal harmony, according to the principles of morality and manners, respectively. The law addresses the most serious conflicts, including those threatening life, limb, and property, and dispenses such fierce sanctions as fines, imprisonment, and loss of life for the violation of its rules. With only the sanction of shame at its command, etiquette addresses conflicts for which voluntary compliance is generally attainable, and thus serves to avert antagonisms that might escalate into violations of law.[9]

Miss Manners contends that the cooperative relationship between courtesy and law depends on each being given its due. To maximize "communal harmony," we must recognize that there are conflicts which courtesy cannot handle and disagreements which the law ought to leave alone. This beneficial division of labor is threatened when law (which is, after all, the more powerful system) intrudes into social disputes that courtesy should govern. Such intrusions should be avoided. It is true, Miss

Manners writes, that the law "can compel where Miss Manners can only wheedle." But to cede courtesy's domain to law is to generate needless expense and exacerbate "anger by giving formal attention and dignity to petty differences."[10] The rules of courtesy and law work best when they work in balance.

This same symbiotic understanding of law and courtesy is shared by a large number of legal practitioners. As the Committee on Civility of the Seventh Judicial Circuit found in its survey of professional conduct, many legal professionals believe there has been a decline in cordiality between lawyers, between lawyers and judges, and among judges themselves. The interactions between professional participants in the legal process are, of course, governed by a host of legal rules. Even so, the proliferation of legal strictures has been insufficient to prevent legal practice from becoming a forum for aggressive jockeying and plain rudeness. The declining use of common courtesy in legal circles has made it increasingly unpleasant to work as a lawyer or judge and has undercut the legal system's capacity to manage conflict as constant confrontations between legal practitioners prolong disputes between clients. According to the Committee on Civility, the administration of justice is "a truth-seeking process designed to resolve human and societal problems in a rational, peaceful, and efficient manner." Without the consistent practice of courtesy, avoiding behavior that "may be characterized as uncivil, abrasive, abusive, hostile, or obstructive," the goals of the legal process simply cannot be realized.[11] Even in the company of lawyers and judges, legal rules cannot promote peace and order unless courtesy is also allowed to do its job.

To help legal practitioners mind their manners, the Committee on Civility developed a code of courteous conduct for all legal proceedings in the Seventh Circuit. Many other courts and bar associations around the country have done the same: courtesy and civility codes can now be found in Arkansas, California, Colorado, the District of Columbia, Florida, Hawaii, Idaho, Maryland, Massachusetts, Michigan, Mississippi, Missouri, New York, North Carolina, Pennsylvania, South Carolina, Tennessee, Texas, Utah, Virginia, Washington, and Wisconsin.[12] As one might expect given her own views of the law-courtesy symbiosis, Miss Manners has applauded all these "little Miss Mannerses" working to restore the equilibrium between law and courtesy in "what should be a gentlemanly and ladylike, albeit vigorous, profession."[13]

This symbiotic view of law and courtesy, endorsed by courtesy experts and legal practitioners alike, rests on the idea that organizational differences between legal rules and etiquette suit them for interlocking roles. Courtesy is generally learned and applied on a decentralized basis, with the constraints of good manners initially imprinted on children by their parents and then enforced by courteous individuals casting shame on rude conduct whenever they happen to come across it.[14] The lack of centralized instruction and the individualization of enforcement make the practice of courtesy uneven; parental instruction is assiduously pursued by some and given less attention by others. As an off-setting advantage to such unevenness, the decentralized organization of etiquette also makes courtesy flexible and easily applied in a wide variety of settings without the formality and expense of an official proceeding. Courtesy is free and available to all, and can be readily and continuously deployed by individuals to negotiate the small interactions and disagreements that make up ordinary life.

Legal rules are structured in a substantially different way that suits them to handling more deeply conflict-ridden matters. To begin with, legal rules are backed by state power—a fact that allows law to claim priority over other rules and standards in society. The shame used to enforce etiquette can certainly be formidable (Miss Manners claims that her own "look of disapproval has been known to sizzle bacon"), and contemporary legal reformers have attempted to incorporate shaming into legal punishments.[15] Yet state power is more formidable still, and it is the alliance with state power that helps make legal rules the preeminent instruments for controlling individual behavior and resolving disputes.

Technically speaking, legal rules are also arranged as a true system rather than as a mere set (as is the case with etiquette). That is, the body of legal rules not only features rules that directly govern individual conduct, but also contains legal rules that order and manage other legal rules.[16] There are legal rules that specify how other legal rules are to be applied in cases of dispute, how legal rules are to be updated, and how legal rules are to be recognized as authoritative. Courtesy altogether lacks this secondary layer of governing rules. Rather than being resolved by institutions and official practices, questions about how proper etiquette is to be authoritatively known, applied, and changed are typically taken up by self-appointed figures such as Miss Manners or Emily Post. Such etiquette experts have no "official" credentials for their position and depend entirely on the active "assent of those being led"—a sign of the fact that manners is a highly decentralized field in which everyone feels they have something to contribute.[17] Law, with its special rules establishing the procedures for legislation and adjudication, operates in a far more hierarchical and certain fashion, creating a more stable set of structures for handling thorny issues of political control and social peace.[18]

The symbiotic understanding of law and courtesy posits that the two differently organized sets of rules—one decentralized and informally enforced, and the other hierarchical and backed by state power—will together pull the sum total of social relations in the same direction. There is no guarantee, of course, that the two systems will in fact complement one another.[19] Still, the very differences in organization suggest the possibility that law and courtesy may be able to work in a coordinated way, just as the differences between biological species allow dissimilar organisms to live together in symbiosis. Courtesy provides a particularly constructed means for managing social interactions; law, with its different configuration, may take over where courtesy leaves off. Rather than impeding cooperation, the organizational differences between the two systems may give each their appropriate role and facilitate mutually supportive effort. As Karl Llewellyn noted in his classic series of law lectures, "law did not create the order, but law attempts to guarantee its continuance." The "great core of order" in society is generated by a range of processes, many of which are not law-like in structure or operation. When these processes "fail to produce a workable result," Llewellyn argued, law draws on its own distinctive resources "to offer machinery to settle particular disputes and give us all a new foundation for getting on."[20]

Courtesy as a Basis for Understanding Law

The widely held symbiotic view of law and courtesy helps make a case for examining legal rules and etiquette together. Yet the symbiotic view does not quite point in the direction that I wish to take here. Symbiosis describes a cooperative relationship between courtesy and law, but my goal is to use an analysis of one system to better understand the operation of the other. Instead of considering how courtesy and law may work in combination, I want to explore what the functioning of courtesy can tell us about the functioning of law.

My approach is not common, and one could argue that the differences between law and courtesy expressed in the more conventional symbiotic view actually undercut the kind of comparison that I wish to draw. Consider, for example, that the symbiotic view of law and courtesy assigns the responsibility for managing small, everyday interactions to courtesy. Can a practice that is concerned with seemingly insignificant matters of deportment really tell us very much about a system of legal rules designed to handle serious conflict? Thomas Hobbes, for one, did not think so. In setting forth his political philosophy Hobbes dismissively swept aside manners as inconsequential directives focused on "how one man should salute another, or how a man should wash his mouth, or pick his teeth before company." When it comes time to consider "those qualities of man-kind, that concern their living together in Peace, and Unity," there is simply no place for trivial questions about decent behavior and "other points of the *Small Moralls*."[21]

The symbiotic view also relies on courtesy being organized and enforced on an individual, decentralized basis. I have suggested that this structure makes the development and implementation of courtesy somewhat irregular (even as it also makes courtesy flexible and easy to adapt to a wide range of situations). Yet a number of observers today, including many ardent advocates of good manners, would characterize my description of courtesy's patchy application as a tremendous understatement. In their view, it is more accurate to say that courtesy is on the point of collapse.[22] Ordinary people and courtesy experts alike often lament the boorish behavior of individuals who prefer to act "naturally" rather than politely, who stubbornly adhere to the retrograde courtesy codes of a bygone era, who wish to invent their own personal "style" of manners, or who seem to have no idea that there is such a thing as polite behavior in the first place. To many, the most striking thing about common courtesy is that it no longer appears to be common. Can a practice that is itself on the threshold of extinction really help explain how the legal system works?

These objections—that courtesy is trivial and dying out, and thus cannot serve as a means for understanding something as significant and enduring as law—do have some foundation. For example, the handwringing today about the death of common courtesy echoes long-standing complaints about the sorry state of American manners. Visiting the United States in the first part of the nineteenth century, the Englishwoman Fanny Trollope excoriated Americans for their lack of refinement.[23] The American faith in equality and practice of commerce had destabilized the rank-ordered society inherited from England; in place of the old hierarchy of inferiors and superiors, Americans increasingly found themselves crowded into teeming cities and relating to one another through the new, dynamic means of mass democracy and market capitalism.[24] Trollope thought it impossible for good manners to prevail in a society where traditional markers of breeding and status had lost their meaning. Although she admitted that the American belief in equality meant that individuals could overcome their origins ("Any man's son may become the equal of any other man's son; and the consciousness of this is certainly a spur to exertion"), she argued that the benefits were far outweighed by a "positive evil": belief in equality bred a "coarse familiarity, untempered by any shadow of respect, which is assumed by the grossest and the lowest in their intercourse with the highest and most refined." As Trollope tartly concluded, "the theory of equality may be very daintily discussed by English gentlemen in a London dining-room, when the servant, having placed a fresh bottle of cool wine on the table, shuts the door, and leaves them to their walnuts and their wisdom; but it will be found less palatable when it presents itself in the shape of a hard greasy paw, and is claimed in accents that breathe less of freedom than of onions and whiskey."[25]

Since Trollope decried the barbarism of Americans nearly two hundred years ago, complaints about the condition of domestic manners have continued more or less unabated. Social commentators have chalked up the deterioration of manners to new immigrants, the vulgar rich, the insolent poor, and the conditions of city life, as well as to "the First World War, Prohibition, jazz, the movies, the automobile, radio, the Depression, the Second World War, television, permissive child-rearing techniques, rock music, contraceptive pills, the Vietnam War, student radicalism, the women's movement, psychological therapies, and fast food."[26]

The long history of complaining about the state of American manners demonstrates that those who worry about the levels of rudeness today have plenty of company. But it also shows that common courtesy
is more durable than contemporary criticism would otherwise suggest:
no matter how dire the warning about the precarious condition of good
manners, the practice of courtesy has always managed to persist, providing each succeeding generation with a basis for new complaints about the
imminent disappearance of civility and politeness from American life.
It is worth remembering that courtesy is a decentralized system that is
learned and enforced at the level of the family and the individual. Such
a system clearly will have difficulty sustaining itself in times of social
change and growing diversity—a difficulty that is amply documented in
the history of laments about decaying manners.[27] Yet the repeated assaults
on courtesy take place alongside the ongoing work of those attempting to
preserve and adapt standards of decent behavior.[28]

For example, the nineteenth century witnessed an explosion of etiquette manuals written by authors who shared Trollope's assessment of
American manners and yet also believed that new codes of courtesy could
be tailored for the country's "fluid, pluralistic, and often aggressively
egalitarian" society. These new "apostles of civility" strived to "establish
order in a restless, highly mobile, rapidly urbanizing and industrializ-
ing democracy. . . . They redefined issues of social conflict to questions
of personal governance, social propriety, and 'good taste.' The rule of
etiquette would extend the laws and teach each individual his social duties."[29] Rather than plunging Americans into a state of savagery, the presence of bad manners encouraged the reformation and reassertion of good
manners with the hope of transforming into a new kind of gentility the
"coarse familiarity" that offended Trollope.

The efforts of nineteenth-century etiquette manual writers would
inevitably be undone by the dynamic society that they wished to regulate.
But others in turn would take up the work of refashioning and sustaining courtesy in new circumstances. In the early 1920s, Emily Post began
drafting her book *Etiquette* in a conscious effort to provide guidance in
the period of rapid change after World War I. The editor who helped
inspire Post spoke to her at length about the pressing need to instruct
people how to behave: "all those new war wives desperate to know how

to write a thank-you note, all those immigrants who had made it to our country before the rules tightened, all those new-money people, ashamed to admit they had no idea how to behave in society." Although the editor's take on social trends was couched in offhand terms, his general vision was unerring, and Post astutely developed it. She tirelessly strove to remain in tune with new generations confronting new conditions, and her efforts earned her a large audience. From the date of publication in 1922 until Post's death in 1960, *Etiquette* would go through ten editions (after Post died, the Emily Post Institute would continue to crank out more editions along with a variety of spin-off works). During World War II, *Etiquette* was the book most often requested by GIs, and for the bulk of the twentieth century, Post's manual on manners would consistently rank second on the list of books most commonly stolen from public libraries (the number one spot was held by the Bible).[30]

Post met with tremendous success during her time—and she was not alone. Published in 1952, Amy Vanderbilt's *Complete Book of Etiquette* would sell nearly one million copies in its first six months on the market.[31] The twentieth-century demand for advice on manners would grow not only to accommodate blockbuster books like those by Post and Vanderbilt but also to find a place for hundreds of minor works by journalists and other authors outlining the rules of appropriate behavior (when Deborah Robertson Hodges attempted to catalogue all the writing on etiquette published in the United States from 1900 to 1987, she ended up producing a bibliographic volume nearly two hundred pages long).[32]

Today, with society now more heterogeneous and mutable than ever before, there are etiquette consultants who advise Americans on everything from the conduct of weddings and funerals to the handling of workplace relations and the management of domestic life. Good manners still matter. Journalistic surveys indicate that common courtesy is widely practiced, while more rigorously scientific studies demonstrate that the absence of basic manners makes a measurable (and highly negative) difference in how a person is perceived.[33] The fact is that amid the complaints about declining standards of decency and rising levels of rudeness, many strive to be courteous even under the most difficult conditions. This dynamic is evident in American cities where studies show that Jewish, Korean, and African-American merchants all work hard to inject courtesy into their daily interactions with customers, even as shifting racial tensions and class differences continually jostle each other and periodically ignite violent riots.[34] Critics justifiably point to the areas in which good manners are being undermined, but we should not forget that good manners are also at the same time constantly being revised and reinforced.[35]

All of this suggests that the effort to use courtesy as a basis for understanding law cannot be dismissed on grounds that good manners are on the verge of disappearing. But what of the claim that courtesy is trivial? Even if courtesy is a more robust system for governing behavior than contemporary criticism would lead one to believe, can rules that address trifling points of personal conduct really tell us very much about something as important as law?

Courtesy does indeed encompass many small concerns. But smallness should not be confused with insignificance. As Norbert Elias demonstrated in his magisterial work on manners and their evolution, the emphases and orientations of etiquette bear witness to the overall state of human relations in a given society. Consider table manners. Appropriate eating behavior may seem to be a relatively unimportant concern, at most connected to prevailing beliefs about hygiene. Elias argued to the contrary that ways of eating actually are part of "the totality of socially instilled forms of conduct."[36] The Middle Ages, for example, was an era when passions were freely expressed and individual behavior was subject to only a few blunt controls. The table manners of the time reflected the general lack of constraint: "Eating from the same plate or dish as others [was] taken for granted. One must only refrain from falling on the dish like a pig, and from dipping bitten food into the communal sauce."[37] The gradual development of rules for using spoons, forks, individual plates, and napkins (so that mealtime became a less free-wheeling affair and more of an occasion for delicacy and refinement) was part of the slow growth of more finely calibrated and comprehensive social controls governing the full range of individual behavior. Rules for dining were not then, and are not now, merely a matter of cleanliness; instead, they were and are indicative of an entire mode of existence. And what is true of table manners is also true of manners as a whole: etiquette in all its forms is an attempt to place "the imprint of society on the inner self," directing individual actions into socially preferred channels.[38]

This is not to say that courtesy is always followed or that everyone agrees on what constitutes proper behavior. As I have indicated, there is an impressive history of criticism in the United States that suggests manners are often a locus of substantial debate. Yet manners may remain socially significant indicators while disagreement about them continues.[39] Even in the context of dispute, the rules discussed in etiquette manuals do, as Erving Goffman argued, describe some of the "norms that *influence* conduct."[40] In a given social gathering, there may be some dissensus about the appropriate way to act, but courtesy remains a reference point for how public behavior ought to unfold and provides a set of guidelines for determining who is likely to make a safe partner for social interaction. After all, if a person does not attempt to fit into a gathering by conforming to etiquette, how can one be sure that such a person, having committed an infraction against one norm, might not be capable of other infractions? As Goffman noted, the role that manners play in identifying individuals with whom one may productively interact means that those influenced by "a particular involvement idiom are likely to sense their rules for participating in gatherings are crucial for society's well-being."[41] It is true that good manners are (merely) a matter of minor restrictions and small behavioral modifications. Nonetheless, it is "out of such unpromising materials that the gossamer reality of social occasions is built."[42] Or, as Erasmus put it in his enormously popular and influential "On Good Manners for Boys" written in 1530, "I do not deny that decorum is a very crude part of philosophy, but in the present climate of opinion it is very conducive to winning good will and to commending those illustrious gifts of the intellect to the eyes of men."[43]

If courtesy is actually important and durable, as I have argued, then the initial objections to using courtesy to understand law—objections that were rooted in claims about how courtesy is trivial and disappearing—lose much of their force. Of course, one could still object to my approach. Even if courtesy is more significant and enduring than some might believe, it remains the case that law and courtesy are separated by fundamental differences in organization and application. Doesn't the fact of such differences necessarily frustrate my attempt to use one system as a basis for understanding the other?

I do not think so. My goal is to use courtesy as an analytical model in order to understand how a rule-based system may function because of the possibility of hypocritical behavior (rather than simply in spite of it). The question to ask of an analytical model is not whether it is identical to the phenomenon to be explained, but whether the model is similar enough to be used for the purposes of explanation. Analytical models, like maps, are "not reality, nor are they isomorphic to reality. Rather they are representations of reality."[44] The usefulness of models and maps is determined by how well they serve their intended purposes, and not by how perfectly they reproduce the entire topography of the terrain to be explored. Thus, in the case at hand, we can say that the value of courtesy as an analytical model depends on the quality of explanation that the model yields. The fact that courtesy and law differ in some ways does not mean that a productive comparison between the two rule-based systems cannot be made.

Courtesy as a Useful Pretense

To draw the kind of comparison I have argued for, it is necessary to move beyond a general outline of courtesy's structure and look at its workings more closely. As we shall see, the first thing that closer examination reveals is that courtesy's usefulness depends on the many opportunities it presents for hypocritical behavior.

To begin, consider the example of the United States Congress. Congress is home to one of the most enduring practices of courtesy in American public life. The congressional commitment to "decorum in debate" can be traced back to the procedural rules adopted by the House of Representatives in 1789 for the sake of preserving order and comity in deliberations.[45] These rules direct members of the House to address "the topic under consideration rather than the advocates themselves," depersonalizing debate so that "speakers do not address each other but rather the chair ('Mr. Speaker')" and so that "they speak of each other as representatives of a state ('the gentlelady from . . . ') not as spokespersons for a party or a position."[46] The goal is to establish a "norm of reciprocal courtesy" based on the understanding that "the differences between Members and parties are philosophical, not personal, that parties to a debate are entitled to the presumption that their views are legitimate even if not correct, and those on all sides are persons of good will and integrity motivated by conviction."[47]

Congressional courtesy is noteworthy in two respects. First, congressional courtesy is remarkable because it is underwritten by rules that may be enforced by majority vote.[48] The centralized structure of congressional courtesy has made it more stable than its everyday cousin—at least so long as congressional majorities have remained committed to sustaining the established forms of decorum. In recent decades new majorities organized around personal re-election efforts and perpetual campaigning have controlled Congress, and their interest appears to be less in maintaining old principles of reciprocal courtesy than in advancing their political fortunes through hard-nosed partisanship and personal attack.[49] The resulting decline in congressional good manners has spurred many efforts to revise and reinvigorate congressional comity. This cycle of crisis and revival resembles the cycle of decline and reinvention that has characterized the history of common courtesy in modern times. The difference is that congressional efforts to reinstate decorum have been more organized: rather than relying on a hodgepodge of self-appointed etiquette advisors, members of Congress have staged bipartisan retreats, commissioned special studies, and convened public hearings designed to restore and reinforce the institution's basic terms of civility.

The second notable—and, for my purposes, more important—feature of congressional courtesy is its artificiality. Members of Congress organize themselves into partisan camps on the basis of strongly held views; when these views are debated, decorous expressions of admiration often appear to be mere window dressing that fails to conceal how representatives really feel about one another. As one advocate of congressional courtesy stated in his testimony before the House of Representatives, the use of polite language in the context of partisan disputing often "sounds awfully hypocritical." "When you are listening to a debate and someone says, 'My distinguished and eloquent and learned colleague from the great and productive State of Minnesota makes some unverified basic assumptions,' I am not sure whether I should believe the form of address or the challenge you made about the Member."[50] There is, of course, still opportunity for the expression of authentic admiration in congressional debate, for the rules of decorum do indeed provide members of Congress with a means of communicating genuine respect for one another. Yet the same rules are also a means for communicating the pretense of mutual respect, and in the actual practice of congressional deliberation it often seems as if phony esteem is far more plentiful than the real thing.

It may not be surprising to learn that the words politicians use often ring hollow. But in this instance elected officials faithfully represent ordinary people. The everyday practice of common courtesy, just like the formal practice of more elaborate courtesies in the halls of Congress, often appears false. Many common courtesies involve showing respect for others—with the emphasis placed on "showing."[51] As Miss Manners notes, the respect called for by good manners is a matter of "outward form," an exhibition of "consideration toward everyone and a showing of special deference to those who are older or in a position of authority." The requirement of respectful display works as a behavioral minimum: although one might have "genuine admiration" for "someone who has proved himself to be worthy of it," all one need do in order to be courteous is go through the conventional motions of showing respect.[52] Real feeling and deep conviction are certainly compatible with common courtesy, but they are not essential. Good manners may reflect true personal decency or they merely may reflect the desire to appear truly decent; the genuinely gracious soul and the unrepentant rogue may both be unfailingly polite.

Whether in the context of formal congressional debate or mundane personal interactions, there are clear difficulties with courtesy's openness to hypocrisy. Because very different sorts of people may exhibit good manners, it is hard to tell when courtesy is actually meant and when it is a sham, leaving one unsure whether a given individual is a "solid gentleman" of good standing or a mere "social counterfeit" out for himself.[53] Genuinely upright people may be suspected of bad faith while swindlers may be esteemed—all because good manners are a matter of external appearance and conventional form. Just as advocates of congressional courtesy are aware of its potentially duplicitous uses, the possibilities of double dealing are no secret to proponents of everyday politeness and civility. As Miss Manners acknowledges, the rules of etiquette can easily be used instrumentally, and it is often the case that "really mean people get the advantage of practicing ingratiating behavior."[54]

How does common courtesy manage to soldier on under the constant threat of hypocritical exploitation? Why do we continually work to revise and reinforce systems of polite behavior in which well-intentioned people may be suspected of not really meaning what they say while con artists may be given more credit than they deserve?

Ruth Grant's study of hypocrisy suggests the beginnings of a response: common courtesy does not survive in spite of the potential for hypocrisy, but because of it.[55] Within the ideal world of true intimates, where everyone who depends on one another has perfectly aligned interests, hypocritical posturing would be thoroughly destructive. In the actual world of community life, however, where the people who depend on one another often have conflicting interests, hypocritical behavior helps "false friends" make collectively useful arrangements without requiring deep agreement or genuine affinity.[56] People in polite society "are not treated according to their individual merits or their just desserts, nor according to one's true feelings toward them as individuals, but according to conventional forms." These conventional courtesies "allow civic public relations between people who are not friends," offering a standardized way for people to interact without requiring the terms of each meeting to be negotiated from scratch or obliging individuals to be connected by true affection.[57] Courtesy endures because it does not require personal goals to coincide or good feelings to prevail. Regardless of what individuals actually think about one another, courtesy holds out the promise that people will live in harmony simply if they are well mannered. The suspicion that polite tokens of respect are fake (either in Congress or in ordinary life) may be an indication that someone is trying to exploit courtesy for their own selfish advantage. Yet the same suspicion is also an indication of courtesy successfully operating to secure communal peace—a matter of individuals going along for the sake of getting along.[58]

The idea that hypocrisy helps make courtesy useful depends on a specific understanding of the human condition. First of all, to accept that polite pretense provides a way of ensuring social coordination, one must believe that the differences in individual beliefs and interests are significant and irreducible. If everyone could somehow be trained or persuaded to adopt the same views and advance the same interests, then there would be no need to seek any techniques for managing diversity and disagreement.

Beyond accepting heterogeneity and conflict as unalterable facts, one must also believe that ordinary people are governed by an inextricable mix of high principle and low passion. On the one hand, one must see moral standards as an essential part of social life. Such standards form the basis of communal ties, provide a means for restraining destructive impulses, and furnish a set of ideals to which community members aspire. "A political community cannot exist without some shared morality and some common standard for honor and respectability," Grant writes. "Public discourse is conducted in moral terms, and that shared language is itself part of the constitution of any particular public."[59] Thus one must consider it to be impossible for people to permanently set aside moral principle for the sake of interactions anchored solely in self-interest. The moral standards that give shape and meaning to the community do the same for individuals, and few will willingly settle for social relations that are completely without moral bearings. As individuals go about their business, they not only "want to be thought of as good," but also "want to think of themselves as good."[60]

Yet, on the other hand, one must also believe that public life cannot ultimately be run on the basis of morality. People are often motivated by ambition, pride, and vanity; as a result, they will never be completely able to practice the high principles that they preach. Public moral standards remain important, as does the inclination to follow them. Individuals are, however, typically too consumed with self-love to live up to these moral standards and will seek shortcuts whenever they can. As Grant puts it, "because society requires morality but men are not always moral, hypocrisy is inevitable."[61] Rather than actually being good, individuals will strive for the appearance of goodness in the hope of creating impressions that allow them to look better than they are.

Grant traces this mixed portrait of human proclivities to Machiavelli. Elements of the same understanding also can be found in the maxims of La Rochefoucauld (who wrote that "hypocrisy is a tribute that vice pays to virtue" and "social life would not last long if men were not taken in by each other") and in the writings of Edmund Burke (who praised "pleasing illusions" of sentiment and tradition that cover "the defects of our naked, shivering nature" so that "the fierceness of pride and power" may be subdued and "the different shades of life" may be harmonized).[62]

Echoes of the same thinking can also be found deep within American history.[63] James Madison believed that individuals were capable of some goodness, that there were "qualities in human nature which justify a certain portion of esteem and confidence." But Madison also believed that there is a "degree of depravity in mankind which requires a certain degree of circumspection and distrust." Because man's "reason and self-love" are bound up together "his opinions and his passions will have a reciprocal influence on each other." The result is a "zeal for different opinions" that has "divided mankind into parties, inflamed them with mutual animosity, and rendered them much more disposed to vex and oppress each other than to co-operate for their common good." Thus Madison argued that any plan to establish a new political order must take people for the intensely passionate, highly self-interested, and only occasionally virtuous creatures that they are.[64]

If we follow this line of thinking from Machiavelli to Madison and accept that ordinary people are at once ethically attuned, willful, and vain, then courtesy becomes valuable because it allows individuals to trade on significant yet often unobtainable moral standards, permitting them to call for expressions of concern and mutual respect without necessarily requiring very much in the way of actual virtue. Courtesy does not attempt to untangle the threads of principle and passion that run through each person. Instead, courtesy provides a code of behavior and a set of conventions that channel human contradictions in socially productive directions, making possible cooperation and mutual benefit where one would otherwise expect empty moral gestures, self-seeking actions, and conflict. Courtesy offers a kind of "coping mechanism for the problem of vice," furnishing forms of concealment that permit people "to be better than they might be" by giving them the opportunity to pretend to be better than they are.[65] In a word, courtesy is useful precisely because it allows for hypocritical posturing.

Advocates of good manners have long argued along these very lines. Lord Chesterfield, the great eighteenth-century champion of etiquette, admitted that "the strictest and most scrupulous honour and virtue alone can make you esteemed by mankind." And yet such moral rectitude will not make an individual "liked, beloved, and sought after in private life." Why is this so? Since people value virtue, one might say that it is reasonable to assume that good morals should be sufficient for personal success. This assumption turns out to be unwarranted, Chesterfield argued, because reason does not firmly govern the passions and appetites embedded in human nature. "Reason ought to direct the whole, but seldom does. And he who addresses himself singly to another man's reason, without endeavoring to engage his heart in his interest also, is no more likely to succeed, than a man who should apply only to a King's nominal minister, and neglect his favorite." Courtesy is therefore "absolutely necessary to adorn any, or all other good qualities or talents." Good manners create a pleasant facade that allows life to proceed without irritation or conflict—a fact made plain by the practice of politesse among European aristocrats. Royal courts "are, unquestionably, the seats of politeness and good-breeding," Chesterfield wrote, and "were they not so, they would be the seats of slaughter and desolation. Those who now smile upon and embrace, would affront and stab each other, if manners did not interpose; but ambition and avarice, the two prevailing passions at courts, found dissimulation more effectual than violence; and dissimulation introduced the habit of politeness."[66]

In our own day, Miss Manners has similarly claimed that courtesy obscures and softens the strife produced whenever individuals try to live side by side. Miss Manners frequently reminds her readers that people do not naturally get along. To argue that they will get along if they just get to know one another "trivializes intellectual, emotional, and spiritual convictions by characterizing any difference between one person's and another's as no more than a simple misunderstanding, easily resolved by frank exchanges or orchestrated 'encounters'."[67] It is the hypocrisy of courtesy—the insistence that individuals conform to an artificial code of decent behavior whether or not they actually like one another—that is necessary to make social peace and smooth interaction possible, without unrealistically attempting to reconcile stubborn conflicts and without romantically wishing away deep disagreements. Honest communication has far less promise of producing social coordination, even though "hardly anyone would dispute the proposition that morals are more important than manners."[68] Were the virtue of truth telling to be widely practiced, everyone would have license to hurt one another's feelings and we would end up with people shouting at each other in the streets. "It turns out," Miss Manners concludes, "that dear old hypocrisy, inhibitions and artificiality, daintily wrapped in a package called etiquette, were protecting us from forms of natural behavior that even the most vehement opponents of etiquette find intolerable."[69]

Courtesy as a Habit and as a Pleasure

The idea that manners rely on the potential for hypocrisy moves us toward a deeper understanding of how courtesy operates and endures. There are questions that remain, however. Hypocritical good manners have value, but hypocrisy is still reviled. Even though one can say that the possibility of using courtesy to conceal real feelings helps enlist the cooperation of others, why would anyone risk looking like a hypocrite in the first place when there may be other, less compromising means of getting along? Are people willing to invite the perception of bad faith simply because courtesy is useful?

One response to these questions is to insist that considerations of utility alone are ultimately sufficient because the hypocrisies of good manners can be easily managed and contained. As Chesterfield argued,

> In the course of the world, a man must very often put on an easy, frank countenance, upon very disagreeable occasions; he must seem pleased when he is very much otherwise; he must be able to accost and receive with smiles those whom he would much rather meet with swords. . . . All this may, nay must be done, without falsehood and treachery; for it must go no farther than politeness and manners, and must stop short of assurances and professions of simulated friendship. Good manners, to those one does not love, are no more a breach of truth than, "your humble servant" at the bottom of a challenge is; they are universally agreed upon and understood, to be things of course. They are necessary guards of the decency and peace of society; they must only act defensively; and then not with arms poisoned with perfidy. Truth, but not the whole truth, must be the invariable principle of every man who hath either religion, honour, or prudence.[70]

According to Chesterfield, the hypocrisies required by politeness may be readily controlled, permitting the well-bred man to avoid opprobrium even though he, "like the Chameleon," must "be able to take every different hue."[71] With the suspicions of double dealing held in check by gentlemanly skill, good manners will be clearly desirable because they are plainly useful.

Unfortunately, the limits that Chesterfield identified are quite difficult to maintain in practice. Individuals with the requisite breeding and training may try to ensure that a pose struck for the sake of cordiality does not raise doubts about the excellence of their true character. Yet, as I argued earlier, manners are a matter of external display, and there is no barrier to courtesy being deployed by the unregenerate to create an illusion of genuine decency. There is, by extension, no barrier to the suspicion that good manners are "a breach of the truth," even when the well-bred person scrupulously follows Chesterfield's advice. In fact, scholars have found that significant suspicions about the hypocrisy of good manners surfaced as early as the sixteenth century, when authors such as Erasmus began to extol civility as a valuable form of "outwarde honesty" that made inner virtues publicly visible and more effective. "Erasmus did not concern himself with the vicious or talentless man who uses such a representational technique to project absent merits," Anna Bryson writes. "Yet once manners are conceived of as representational, they can also be regarded as theatrical and even dissimulatory."[72] Manners may be used to express authentic virtue or they may be used to create the mere appearance of good character; the gap between external courtesies and internal motivations inevitably allows movement in both directions, creating suspicions about the true nature of individual motives that cannot be dispelled by the most impeccable breeding.

Conceding that good manners will often look hypocritical, Chesterfield's position might still be defended by arguing that the suspicions aroused by courtesy will actually never be too serious. Courtesy is an everyday form of pretense, after all. Even though the display of good manners may unavoidably raise doubts about a person's true motives, one could argue that these doubts will never amount to much because they will be tempered by the knowledge that almost everyone is playing the same game. One might even say that a certain amount of hypocrisy is inescapable in contemporary life.[73] Modern society demands that we each enact many different roles and, in doing so, inevitably opens up many opportunities for contradiction and phony behavior. If we are all in the same boat, then perhaps the threat of well-mannered hypocrisy is not too worrisome and Chesterfield's goal of carefully restricting dissimulation to matters of mere politeness may still be realized.

The difficulty with this defense, however, is that it overestimates the likelihood of forgiveness.[74] People do not easily get along and, as David Runciman observes in his historical analysis of hypocrisy, the pretenses that are coolly discussed in the abstract often turn out to be very touchy subjects when conflict-prone individuals bump up against each other. "[H]owever much one might recognize [hypocrisy's] essential triviality as a vice," Runciman writes, "it is impossible to avoid its potential significance as a motor of political conflict, given its capacity to provoke people beyond measure."[75] Pretenses that are neither particularly egregious nor malicious may nonetheless elicit a torrent of criticism when the pretending is done by individuals we dislike. Thus the question remains: Are people willing to risk the appearance of hypocrisy that attends courteous behavior simply because good manners are useful?

Rather than claiming that utility alone is sufficient, one could argue that utility helps sustain courtesy by operating in concert with moral obligation. That is, instead of asserting, as Chesterfield did, that the separate domains of manners and morality can be made to co-exist without any perception of conflict, one could argue that courtesy itself should be treated as an authentic virtue. If manners and morality are not separate, and if courtesy is understood as a matter of moral commitment, then it will not be utility on its own that overcomes the taint of suspected hypocrisy and keeps people polite. Individuals will conform to the rules of etiquette because it is useful *and* because it is the right thing to do. It is in this spirit that some nineteenth-century etiquette writers cited Jesus as the model gentleman and proclaimed the Golden Rule to be the central tenet of good manners.[76] More recently and in the same vein, a variety of scholarly commentators have argued that courtesy and civility are fundamentally moral issues (P. M. Forni, for example, defines civility as "a form of goodness," and Stephen Carter calls it "an attitude of respect, even love, for our fellow citizens").[77]

The treatment of courtesy and civility as moral virtues does not, of course, prevent individuals from hypocritically deploying manners for their own selfish purposes. But it does allow those asserting courtesy's moral status to claim that hypocritical manners are not really good manners at all. "If politeness is a quality of character (alongside courtesy, good manners and civility), it cannot be a flaw," Forni writes. "A suave manipulator may appear to be polite but is not."[78] In a similar vein, Edward Shils argues that genuine "substantive civility" self-consciously places the interests of the whole society above the interests of the part.[79] It is "a belief which affirms the possibility of the common good; it is a belief in the community of contending parties within a morally valid unity of society. It is a belief in the validity or legitimacy of the governmental institutions which lay down rules and resolve conflicts. Civility is a virtue expressed in action on behalf of the whole society, on behalf of the good of all members of the society to which public liberties and representative institutions are integral."[80] On this view, to be truly civil, just as to be honest or just, requires clear convictions about the rightness of specific values.

Given the understanding of human nature on which my account of manners relies, this moral view of courtesy and civility is at once understandable and unrealistic. The moral view is understandable because, as I suggested, ordinary people want to be thought of as being good. Public moral standards matter, and few individuals will engage in a mode of behavior that is openly advertised as being entirely without any moral dimensions. Manners respond to this basic impulse. Rules of etiquette make available an agreed-upon way of expressing true respect for others, a way of acknowledging the moral worth and dignity of those with whom we live.[81] Manners may thus serve as a template for how to treat others as ends rather than as mere means; in doing so, manners may help communicate "moral attitudes to fellow inhabitants of our moral world."[82]

At the same time, however, the view of human nature on which manners rest suggests it is unrealistic to envision courtesy as operating either solely or fundamentally on a moral plane. People do indeed want to be thought of as being good. Yet, as I have also noted, passions and appetites prevent most people from following moral dictates. This means that those who wish to communicate moral attitudes are often not particularly moral themselves. If courtesy is to be common and apply to all the small interactions that make up ordinary life, then it must take into account the willfulness, self-love, and ambition of ordinary individuals and not be left as the preserve of the rare moral virtuoso who actually manages to live by society's normative standards. From this perspective, the most sensible voice in the recent scholarly discussions of civility and courtesy belongs neither to Forni, Carter, nor Shils, but to Judith Shklar.

As Shklar observed (using terms that echo Machiavelli and Madison), American society is an irreducibly diverse and unruly assemblage of passionate, conflict-prone individuals: "We do not agree on the facts and figures of social life, and we heartily dislike one another's religious, sexual, intellectual, and political commitments—not to mention one another's ethnic, racial and class character." Social peace and mutual accommodation are nonetheless possible in such a context, not because the populace will actually be moved by a common set of moral convictions, but because there are opportunities for acting in ways that mask our true beliefs and interests. "The democracy of everyday life, which is rightly admired by egalitarian visitors to America," Shklar wrote, "does not arise from sincerity. It is based on the pretense that we must speak to each other as if social standings were a matter of indifference in our views of each other. That is, of course, not true. Not all of us are even convinced that all men are entitled to a certain minimum of social respect."[83] The reliance on pretense does not sit easily with the importance assigned to public moral standards, and many people may prefer not to dwell on the artificial posturing that facilitates social interaction.[84] Even so, the reliance on pretense remains whether or not individuals are comfortable acknowledging it.[85] Rather than being a corruption of true civility or politeness, hypocrisy is the means by which good manners become useful in a society in which almost no one can live up to collective ideals.

To suggest that manners are not essentially moral, as Shklar did, is to underscore the proposition that manners are primarily an activity of outward display. Intentions matter a great deal in morality, and they hardly matter at all in manners. A person performing a moral action for the wrong reasons is considered to be immoral. By contrast, a person acting courteously is considered to be courteous regardless of her motives. Courtesy is as courtesy does. For this reason, etiquette is able to provide a routine for negotiating social interaction, helpfully putting "a decent cover over ugly feelings" while generally leaving the feelings themselves intact.[86] Indeed, as Goffman noted, it is the person who conforms to the conventions of good manners—by striving "to fit in and act as persons of his kind are expected to act"—who reveals the "least amount of information about himself" in a gathering.[87] Courtesy permits public action while screening private beliefs, allowing everyone to be polite regardless of their underlying desires or character. The opportunity for concealment is not an incidental feature of etiquette; on the contrary, it is the "fact that information about self can be held back in this way" that provides a "motive for maintaining the proprieties."[88] Again, it is the very avenue through which good manners prove themselves to be valuable that also opens them to the charge of being hypocritical.

We thus return once more to the question with which this section began: Are people willing to expose themselves to suspicions of hypocrisy simply because courtesy is useful? As I have noted, the desire to avoid being seen as hypocritical is powerful. If this desire cannot be satisfied either by skillfully controlling appearances or by insisting that manners are fundamentally moral, then does the viability of courtesy depend only on its practical value as a means of securing social coordination? The answer to this question, I would argue, is that courtesy remains appealing because habit and pleasure often work alongside considerations of utility, cementing attachments to courteous behavior in ways that are consistent with the jumble of principled beliefs and strong passions that characterize human nature.[89]

Consider the role of habit. Good manners rest to a significant extent on habituation—a fact that is illustrated by the profusion of etiquette manuals directed at parents and the subject of child rearing.[90] Childhood is the ideal time to inculcate polite behavior precisely because the young need not be persuaded about the inherent rightness of any particular values; the goal is simply to make them act courteously. As Erasmus wrote in his manners manual for boys, "Young bodies resemble young shoots, which come to maturity and require the fixed characteristics of whatever you determine for them with a pole or trellis."[91] Or, as Miss Manners put the point more recently, etiquette is "best taught at the start of life, when learning without conviction is easiest."[92]

The cultivation of courteous habits in children is chiefly a matter of parental guidance and repetition (Miss Manners refers to these elements, respectively, as "example" and "nagging"). Elders must first model polite conduct, giving the young a pattern of behavior to observe and imitate. Once exemplary behavior has been enacted, parents must then repeatedly exhort and admonish children to perform like adults. This sustained, often frustrating program of training eventually instills habitual responses: "Exasperating as it is to have to keep repeating things . . . the reward is that after six thousand four hundred and twelve times of prompting a child to say 'Thank you,' he or she will shock you, and probably himself too, by saying it before he has had a chance to think about what he is doing."[93]

It is possible, of course, that the continuous drill of courtesy lessons enforced by parental say-so might eventually lead to something like the sincere embrace of substantive virtues. The idea that repeated action might produce some elements of genuine conviction is a common one, endorsed by figures from Thomas Jefferson ("In truth, politeness is artificial good humor, it covers the natural want of it, and ends by rendering habitual a substitute nearly equivalent to the real virtue") to Miss Manners ("If you write enough thank-you letters, you may actually come to feel a flicker of gratitude").[94] Benjamin Franklin advocated this idea of virtue-via-habit throughout his life. Consistent with the notion of human nature I have explored here, Franklin saw the self as "a constellation of passions and interests," a disorderly composite of impulses and appetites that made it unlikely that individuals would act on the basis of pure and virtuous motives. Given these circumstances, the best bet was to shape the self "into a productive whole through good habits." Thus Franklin was, as his biographer notes, committed to a simple proposition: "*do* the right thing, and in time you will learn to *want* to do the right thing."[95] Or, as Franklin himself put it, "It was a wise counsel given to a young man, *Pitch upon that course of life which is most excellent, and* CUSTOM *will make it the most delightful.*"[96]

Yet even though one might say that authentic goodness is the ultimate goal of good habits, it remains the case that good manners do not depend on individuals actually becoming more or less who they are pretending to be. The habits of courtesy are, at base, habits of action. Childhood training produces adults disposed to follow the conventions of etiquette and who can be shamed whenever they stray from the path of politeness. Such adults are committed to particular routines of conduct and need not actually accept the substantive ideas of concern and respect that the routines may be used to express. Habit conditions individuals to adhere to form, preparing them for a practice of courtesy that is (as we have already seen) largely a matter of outward display rather than an issue of inner intentions. Motives may be altered by long habitual practice, but they need not be for politeness to prevail. Indeed, in some instances, acts of courtesy may even be said to work best because the force of habit leaves no space at all for intentionality. "The deepest beauty of [saying] 'Excuse me'," writes Mark Caldwell, "is exactly that is not a true apology, indeed implies no real emotion at all. Its rote vacuity is precisely what makes it so useful. It helps us steer daily between countless social reefs, without effort or even thought, much less a crisis of conscience."[97]

Courteous behavior is also sustained by pleasure. As I have noted, courtesy is capable of serving as a means for granting respect and giving praise to truly deserving individuals. Operating in this register, courtesy provides a way of satisfying the desire to breathe life into moral standards by recognizing and rewarding exemplary individuals. The joys associated with giving the deserving their due are important, but they do not account for the bulk of courtesy's pleasures. As I have argued, courtesy is not at root a moral enterprise; good manners are directed primarily toward maintaining appropriate appearances for those who cannot actually live up to moral ideals. As a consequence, the main pleasures of courtesy are, like the main business of courtesy itself, concerned with appearance and outward display.

Courtesy softens and smoothes the surfaces of personal interaction and, in doing so, it not only helps make social coordination possible but also helps make social life more pleasing and enjoyable. Burke had the beautifying effects of refined manners and "ancient chivalry" in mind when he mourned the great losses wrought by the French Revolution: "It is gone, that sensibility of principle, that chastity of honor which felt a stain like a wound, which inspired courage whilst it mitigated ferocity, which ennobled whatever it touched, under which vice itself lost half its evil by losing all of its grossness."[98] Manners lend a veneer of grace and sophistication to life, appealing to our feelings and our attachment to attractive display. (Arguing in a similar vein, Oscar Wilde would later observe that "what is interesting about people in good society . . . is the mask that each one of them wears, not the reality that lies behind the mask."[99]). Burke could not support the revolutionaries because they had stripped the public sphere of its tasteful and elegant gilding, and in doing so had eliminated a critical means of engaging citizen affections.[100] "There ought be a system of manners in every nation which a well-informed mind would be disposed to relish," Burke wrote. "To make us love our country, our country ought to be lovely."[101]

Like Burke, Chesterfield also understood the surface pleasures of good manners. Indeed, Chesterfield understood that the appearance-related satisfactions of courtesy and politeness could speak directly to one of the most powerful human passions: self-love. A "mistaken self-love" is harmful, Chesterfield conceded, because it induces individuals to "take the immediate and indiscriminate gratification of a passion, or appetite, for real happiness." Yet the sensible indulgence of self-love is the defining characteristic of polite society. "If a man has a mind to be thought wiser, and a woman handsomer, than they really are, their error is a comfortable one to themselves, and an innocent one with regard to other people; and I would rather make them my friends by indulging them in it, than my enemies by endeavoring (and that to no purpose) to undeceive them." Chesterfield argued that it was of no use lamenting the fact that self-love drives people to place so much stock in such shallow talk, for the "world is taken by the outside of things, and we must take the world as it is; you or I cannot set it right." Besides, the way of the world makes the pleasures of politeness available to everyone. The reciprocal practice of courtesy allows all to appease the vanities of each, binding the heart of every individual in polite society to the conventions of good manners. Thus it is not only useful to be courteous, it also feels good. "Pleasing in company," Chesterfield noted, "is the only way of being pleased in it yourself."[102]

Taken together, the acquisition of habitual good manners and the pleasures of politeness help relieve individuals of the burden of genuinely respecting others for themselves as they really are, and thus help sustain the practice of courtesy even though this practice is subject to hypocritical manipulation. This is not to say that habit and pleasure play their manners-supporting roles perfectly. As we have seen, the decentralized structure of courtesy makes it difficult to adapt manners to shifting social circumstances. The pull of habit and pleasure compounds the problem, sometimes wedding individuals to past practices that no longer help secure social peace. Old habits and old pleasures both die hard, and systems of behavior that rely on them will not be easy to update.

Keeping such limitations in mind, we can nonetheless say that habit and pleasure both provide ways of investing people in etiquette. When the mechanisms of habit and pleasure are paired with the usefulness of courtesy, it becomes easier to see why individuals are willing to court suspicions of hypocrisy by being polite. Hypocrisy remains an object of scorn; even so, people may nonetheless embrace a social practice that is open to the possibility of hypocrisy because the force of habit, the appeal of pleasure, and considerations of utility give them incentives to do so.[103]

Courtesy and Hierarchy

There is a final reason why individuals are willing to engage in the pretence of good manners: courtesy typically supports established hierarchies. Manners mark off and counter-pose the groups that compose a given polity, deploying distinctions between polite and rude behavior that work to reinforce pecking orders across classes.[104] "Civility facilitates communication," Virginia Sapiro observes, "but it can also choke it off, especially among those who are of relatively low status or those whose communication might call particular attention to themselves or their needs, or might be considered inappropriate by other people."[105] Those who profit the most from courtesy have powerful reasons to preserve a system that keeps everyone in their proper place.

How can courtesy be common and at the same time serve the interests of specific groups? The habits and pleasures that underwrite good manners do not pose a barrier to hierarchy; indeed, history shows that such habits and pleasures can be shaped to suit many different schemes of dominance. This is so because, as Foucault demonstrated, the exercise of power may not only exclude and coerce, but also produce and create, generating behaviors, gestures, and discourses that in turn support and reproduce existing inequalities.[106] Thus courteous habits and polite pleasures often reflect prevailing patterns of social control.

We can see this dynamic at work in the nineteenth-century United States, where women were habituated to, and expected to take pleasure in, forms of etiquette that plainly supported male authority. Conventions of the period required women to remain dependent on men as their guardians in public spaces.[107] In this context, there was almost no way in which women standing alone could publicly advocate their own interests without being considered indecent (as one etiquette manual for women from 1837 explained, "Contending for your rights stirs up the selfish feelings of others; but a readiness to yield them awakes generous sentiments.").[108] For women of this era, to be polite was also to be politically powerless.[109]

In a similar fashion and for long stretches of American history, African Americans were enmeshed in codes of courtesy that perpetuated their subordination. The statutes that set up the basic terms of Jim Crow segregation were surrounded and sustained by well-established rules of racial etiquette that relegated blacks to a lower status than whites. As Martin Luther King Jr. described this system of etiquette, "your first name becomes 'nigger,' your middle name becomes 'boy' (however old you are) and your last name becomes 'John,' and your wife and mother are never given the respected title of 'Mrs.'."[110] In this environment, the well-mannered African American was a person who kept to his appropriate station in the racial order and avoided the rudeness of being "uppity."

Like women and African Americans, members of the LGBT community have also found themselves embedded in schemes of manners that ensure their marginal status. In their efforts to spur stronger governmental responses to the AIDS crisis in the 1980s, activists were expected to work within prevailing forms of courtesy that not only deemed displays of grief and anger in public proceedings to be disruptive but also disparaged the public discussion of non-heterosexual practices as shameful.[111] Members of the LGBT community could "respectfully" push for more proactive AIDS policies by conforming to prevailing understandings of decent behavior. But in following the path of respectability gays and lesbians ran the risk of reaffirming the shame that conventional standards of politeness attached to homosexuality. AIDS activists were thus left with the choice of either fighting "cruelty and oppression" or "being nice."[112]

These examples suggest that courtesy is highly plastic, that the habits and pleasures that sustain courtesy can be molded to serve the purposes of different governing groups. How is this understanding of courtesy as a flexible tool of the powerful consistent with courtesy's social usefulness? As we have seen, courtesy furnishes a valuable means of social coordination, allowing individuals to arrive at mutually beneficial arrangements without necessarily having to like or respect one another. I have focused on the possibility of hypocrisy that allows courtesy to facilitate such coordination, but one might also call attention to the egalitarian commitments seemingly implicit in courtesy's role as a guarantor of social peace. Reasoning in this vein, one might claim that courtesy's creation of mutually beneficial arrangements introduces elements of equality and fair treatment that undercut efforts to organize good manners for the advantage of the few. It is true, of course, that any assurance of equal treatment within polite society offers little protection for anyone who is altogether excluded from such society (it could be said that such pariahs have been denied "the right to be hypocritical" because they have been prohibited from participating in the pretenses of good manners and the advantages such pretenses permit).[113] Yet, at least for those to whom etiquette does apply, one might argue that the practice of mutual accommodation—a practice that requires both parties to a courteous exchange to find some benefit to conducting their business according to good manners—necessarily protects the weak from exploitation by the strong. And so one might ask, Do the same factors that make courtesy useful also work against inequality and domination?

Polite society does indeed offer something to all its members. Even so, I would argue that the doling out of mutual benefits hardly prevents courtesy from being used to sustain status quo hierarchies. This is so for two reasons. First, as we have seen, people are drawn to courtesy by factors other than utility. Good manners are appealing in part because parents drum the rudiments of good behavior into their children's heads and in part because adults take pleasure in the artificial pleasantries and rituals of polite society. These two factors furnish motives to remain courteous independent of the usefulness of having an agreed-upon means of coordination. Since habits and pleasures can be attached to a variety of etiquettes that promote a range of power structures, we can expect that there will be forces within any given system of manners that may work against whatever egalitarian guarantees mutual accommodation provides.

Second, there is reason to think that mutual accommodation itself is not actually very egalitarian in the first place. A requirement that the benefits of an interaction be jointly distributed is not equivalent to a requirement that benefits be symmetrically distributed. Mutuality is not necessarily the same as equality, and in principle it is just as possible to have a system of shared accommodation that rewards all equally as it is to have a system of shared accommodation that gives a larger share of rewards to some parties rather than others. To be useful as a means of coordination, courtesy must confer at least *some* benefits on everyone in polite society; it need not confer *the same* benefits on all.

If we return to the example of nineteenth-century etiquette for women, we can see how the asymmetries of mutual accommodation operate. Although the conventions of courtesy unquestionably placed women of the time in a subordinate position, there was also more to the story. In practice, courtesy both gave and took away, presenting women with new opportunities to interact in public spaces while perpetuating gender hierarchies at the same time.[114] As Jenny Davidson notes, the development of "tact" as a distinctly female form of courtesy during the nineteenth century gave women new social leverage. The tactful woman was equipped with the tools necessary for the "management of inequality," giving her the ability to negotiate a variety of social situations and leaving her better off than those without any position in polite society at all.[115] But even though the exercise of self-control and delicate diplomacy conferred advantages, women were not equal to men. Nineteenth-century women clearly benefitted from being courteous—it is just that men of the period benefitted from their own good manners still more.

The experience of polite women in the nineteenth century illustrates a general principle: good manners require individuals to accept the conventions of appropriate behavior (along with the hierarchies that such conventions support) as they are. Far from being a timeless code of behavior or an abstract solution to a generic problem of social coordination, courtesy is the consequence and hallmark of individual social orders. Good manners are framed within existing sets of power dynamics, and the social peace ensured by a particular scheme of courtesy has historically been a social peace that exists on specific terms, serving the interests of some more than others.

This is not to say that courtesy is a collection of rules that *exclusively* promotes the fortunes of the powerful. In exchange for accepting the existing conventions of appropriate behavior, good manners provide all individuals with the means and opportunity to manipulate prevailing etiquette to one's own advantage. As I have suggested, however, courtesy's opportunities by no means present an obstacle to inequality. Indeed, the allocation of at least some measure of benefit to all members of polite society actually works to stabilize prevailing patterns of dominance, giving all individuals a reason (in addition to reasons provided by habit and pleasure) to abide within the hierarchical order established by courteous behavior. Working through the refined channels of etiquette, the strong need not adopt aggressive tactics to help hold down the weak. On the contrary, it is through their participation in the small hypocrisies of polite society that the weak help hold up the strong.[116]

The existence of a link between courtesy and hierarchy does not, of course, prevent one from optimistically insisting that this link can be broken. One might argue that the ongoing cycle of decline and renewal that has characterized modern manners presents opportunities to create more egalitarian forms of courtesy, offering a chance to shed the hierarchy-sustaining conventions of the past and develop a new etiquette that truly dispenses equal benefits to all. Miss Manners champions this approach, and has written at length about how manners ought to be restructured to suit the contemporary "American idea of equality of treatment," an idea that she defines as a matter of everyone "being recognized as being 'as good as anyone else'."[117] Alternatively, and independent in any effort to rebuild manners from scratch, one might claim that mere access to polite society puts individuals in a position to challenge the entrenched interests that such society shelters. Mark Caldwell reasons in this vein when he writes that the true power of good manners "is to maneuver delicately and hesitantly in the right direction, without provoking controversy—it being prudent to postpone the sermon until the prospective convert has been lured into the chapel."[118] This is more than just a matter of tactically managing inequalities. Whatever patterns of control good manners may support, Caldwell's claim is that egalitarian reform may be courteously engineered from inside the system.

These optimistic accounts of courtesy's egalitarian possibilities suggest that in an ideal society manners will serve as guardians of a just and fair status quo. Unfortunately, all actual societies have fallen well short of the ideal—and thus, as I have argued, manners have historically served to protect a status quo that is far from being just and fair. Whatever changes some future revolution in manners might someday bring, the courteous have traditionally adhered to existing conventions in order to spare feelings and appease small vanities. When given a choice between behaving courteously and expressing the "bare truth" about a situation, the well-mannered usually have, as Emily Post regularly advised, picked courtesy every time.[119]

Those struggling to overturn established hierarchies often experience such polite attitudes as obstacles to change, ways of deflecting attention away from issues that raise fundamental questions about existing structures of domination. "Civilitarians," as Randall Kennedy calls those who champion courtesy and respectability today, "have fits over 'coarse language,' but homeless families and involuntary unemployment only get a shrug. They focus more indignation on the raunchy lyrics of gangsta rap than the horrific indifference that makes possible the miserable conditions that those lyrics vividly portray." When politics is a matter of maneuvering within existing forms of inequality and unfair treatment, the gentle methods of courtesy may provide a model for behavior. But when politics is an open battle against forms of injustice, then courtesy is "deeply at odds" with the "willingness to fight loudly, openly, militantly, [and] even rudely" that activism often requires.[120]

When rights are demanded in impolite tones, those making unvarnished claims for recognition may appear unalterably opposed to the gentle ways of courtesy. This appearance may be reinforced by champions of the existing order who, like Burke decrying the destruction of the

French Revolution, claim that brash bids for new privileges and status will push society to the brink of barbarism. Such appearances can be misleading. New rights claims are often ill-mannered, it is true. But such claims are "rude" only with respect to prevailing conventions of courtesy. Martin Luther King Jr. and other civil rights activists grossly violated the racial etiquette of Jim Crow segregation, but in doing so they acted (at least in part) in the name of a new kind of politeness that showed the same respect to individuals regardless of race. As the Civil Rights Movement demonstrated, discourteous behavior aimed at changing the treatment of some group will often lead to the establishment of new forms of politeness, not to the abandonment of manners altogether. These new codes of behavior may move a society a step closer to the ideal state in which manners preserve justice. Absent a total transformation of human relations, however, some inequities will remain and the new courtesies will, like the system of etiquette they have displaced, work to maintain a ranking among classes.

Conclusion

Courtesy is a rule-governed form of behavior that is often dogged by suspicions of hypocrisy. Because different sorts of people may act according to the conventions of polite society, it is difficult to know whether a well-mannered individual is a person of genuinely good character or a con artist exploiting etiquette for the sake of self-advancement. The ever-present possibility of hypocrisy in polite society exacts a price: truly decent people always run the risk of being perceived as rogues who are trying to pass themselves as being better than they actually are, and duplicitous people always have a chance of being unfairly esteemed. This same possibility of hypocrisy also pays a dividend: by allowing people to conform to an artificial code of decent behavior, courtesy permits individuals to make mutually useful arrangements without requiring deep agreement or real affinity. In this way, courtesy makes it possible for passionate, conflict-prone individuals to achieve social peace, letting individuals who want to be good (and yet who are usually only capable of appearing to be good) turn the pretense that they are better than they are into a practical means of getting along.

Courtesy's constructive use of hypocrisy is bound up with and supported by other powerful factors. Individuals are courteous not only because it is useful, but also because it is habitual. Children are schooled from a young age in the rudiments of appropriate behavior. The repeated performance of courteous actions may lead some to inwardly embrace substantive values that well-mannered actions outwardly exhibit. But such inner conviction is not necessary for habit to take hold, nor is possession of the appropriate intentions necessary for behavior to be polite. This habitual commitment to the forms of courtesy is strengthened by pleasure. Courtesy provides an agreed-upon way of satisfying the impulse to recognize moral goodness and praise those truly worthy of respect. Moreover— and more often—courtesy also gratifies less lofty desires. Good manners refine and soften the surfaces of social life, engaging our affections and our attachment to beautiful display. The fake rituals and pleasantries of good manners also appeal to self-love, allowing each member of polite society to feel more honorable or worthy of praise than they may actually be.

Finally, the practice of courtesy is also underwritten by prevailing hierarchies. In any given society, courtesy is typically a bulwark of the established order, defining appropriate behavior in terms that serve the interests of the most powerful groups. History shows that habit and pleasure can readily be enlisted in the project of protecting the status quo, leading the great mass of people to support conventions of courtesy that systematically favor the interests of the few. The possibilities for using courtesy as means of social coordination can also be turned to the same status-quo-maintaining purpose: when all members of polite society gain some measure of benefit from the conventions of good manners, then all have some interest in working within the power structures perpetuated by such conventions.

Courtesy is far from perfect. Etiquette produces a scheme of behavior that emphasizes appearance over substance, creates endless opportunities for hypocrisy, and promotes existing hierarchies over fairness. And yet courtesy endures. Moving through cycles of decay and resurgence, good manners engage our interests, habits, and affections in no small part because of the opportunities that manners present for pretense and double dealing.

My aim in presenting this analysis of courtesy is to set the stage for evaluating another rule-based system of behavior: the judicial process in the United States. In Part I, I indicated the various ways in which suspicions of judicial hypocrisy can eat away at perceptions of judicial legitimacy. With my assessment of courtesy in hand, we are now in position to consider how such corrosive suspicions might also feed into and sustain the current legal order. I turn to that consideration in Part III.

Part III
The Rule of Law as the Rules of Etiquette

"WHAT IS LESS REASONABLE THAN TO CHOOSE the eldest son of a queen to rule a State?," Pascal once asked.[1] Since pedigree is no guarantee of talent or skill, it seems absurd to select individuals for such an important position on the basis of lineage. Surely we should choose those people with the best character and experience rather than picking those who happen to have the right parents.

And yet, according to Pascal, the seeming absurdity of hereditary monarchy makes a certain amount of sense. "For whom will men choose, as the most virtuous and able? We at once come to blows as each claims to be [the best]. Let us then attach this quality to something indisputable. This is the king's eldest son. That is clear and there is no dispute."[2] Bloodlines are indeed poor predictors of leadership ability, and this fact can generate serious difficulties for those governed by royalty. But given the fractious tendencies of human nature, selection by kinship also has the great advantage of securing civil peace. "The most unreasonable things in the world become most reasonable," Pascal concluded, "because of the unruliness of men."[3]

Pascal's observation about the reasonableness that may arise from unruliness applies to good manners. As I argued in Part II, common courtesy can be criticized on several fronts. To begin with, courtesy is an artificial code of behavior that is always open to hypocritical manipulation;

thus polite society is a place where well-intentioned people may be suspected of not really meaning what they say while dissemblers may be given more credit than they deserve. Moreover, courtesy is rooted in habits and pleasures that historically have been shaped to suit the interests of the few. The steady pull of routine, the appeal of flattery, and the allure of beautiful display have helped tie the great majority of people to polite conventions that systematically reward some classes more than others. These features of courtesy are undeniably negative. Yet if we consider the disorderly jumble of principle and passion that defines the human condition, then we can see that there is also a certain logic to courtesy's design.

As thinkers since Machiavelli have argued, people are propelled by a volatile mix of ardent zeal, focused self-interest, and moral aspiration. Members of the same community usually share at least some significant normative ideals, but they also are driven by competing interests and impulses, and remain incapable of actually conducting public life according to the ethical principles they value. Courtesy provides a way of managing the welter of human interactions, permitting individuals to trade on moral standards without requiring them to overcome personal appetites or to develop much in the way of actual virtue. Relying on the wish to be esteemed, the pleasures of attractive appearance, the comfort of habit, the longing for power, and the interest in obtaining the fruits of cooperation, courtesy runs with the grain of human nature, making possible a measure of peace and mutual benefit where one otherwise would expect only self-serving assertions and strife.

The disadvantages of such an arrangement are real. But so too are the advantages. Courtesy secures beneficial social coordination while also emphasizing form over substance, creating endless opportunities for hypocrisy, and promoting existing inequalities over fairness. It is a scheme of behavior that at once improves upon and broadcasts the flaws and inconsistencies of human nature.

What do the workings of common courtesy suggest about the rule of law? Law, like courtesy, is a body of rules designed to shape, guide, and control individual behavior. What follows if the analogy between the two bodies of rules is extended and courtesy is used as a model to help understand how law operates? Can the legal process, like the practice of courtesy, be said to function because of the possibility of hypocrisy rather than merely in spite of it? Can the exercise of legal power be understood to depend on routinized behavior and the gratification of desire? Can the considerations of utility, habit, and pleasure that feed into the legal order be said to simultaneously facilitate mutually beneficial accommodations and sustain hierarchies?

In this final section of the book, I present an argument that allows us to see how these questions can be answered in an unconventional way. My analysis is grounded in the Janus-faced context that envelopes the American courts. As I argued in Part I, the American judiciary finds itself in an environment in which the claims of legal realism are both dead and alive. On one hand, a significant portion of the public expects its judges to resolve disputes by reasoning impartially on the basis of legal principles, and judges regularly explain their decisions in terms consistent with the public's expectations. On the other hand, a substantial portion of the public also believes that the judicial process is permeated with politics, a belief that seems to be amply supported by the country's highly political mechanisms of judicial selection and by the lack of agreement over how law ought to be interpreted in politically charged cases. The contradiction between the two dimensions of the legal process creates the appearance of judicial hypocrisy, stoking suspicions that judges may be affecting an air of legal impartiality in order to disguise the pursuit of political goals. I have explained how the public's conflicting views and attendant suspicions threaten judicial legitimacy. Using my analysis of courtesy as a guide, I now explain how existing conditions may also help enable legal power.

I address a range of works in the following pages, moving across the fields of legal theory, empirical analysis, and sociolegal scholarship. I identify the basic components of my argument in different areas of study and then use these components to outline an understanding of our half-politics-half-law court system that differs markedly from standard views. My goal is to articulate the general contours of a new approach, showing how it is possible to think about the rule of law in a novel way.[4]

I begin with an examination of scholarly work that treats law as a set of facilitating procedures, a collection of formal rules and tests that the courts use to manage disputes without addressing the fundamental roots of conflict. This proceduralist understanding presents law, like courtesy, as a means of securing engagement and coordination between people who otherwise disagree about substantive ends. Extrapolating from the example of courtesy, I argue that the proceduralist view of law may be adapted and extended so that we can think of judicial dispute management as relying on the possibility of pretense. Impartial judgment is an important legitimating ideal for courts, but if we believe that people are not only ethically attuned but also willful, ambitious, and vain, then we must recognize that that ideal of impartial judgment will not always be achieved. A judicial process that permits actors to be principled as well as merely to appear to be principled is a process that truly appeals to all, allowing opposing parties to commit to law as a language for framing claims and brokering acceptable settlements. The judicial process, so understood, is a kind of game that everyone can play.

Having developed an account of how the possibility of hypocritical behavior is a fundamental characteristic of law, I then consider the sustaining roles played by habit, pleasure, and hierarchy. Again reasoning from the example of courtesy, I argue that the public's allegiance to law depends on more than just the broad interest in securing the benefits of dispute management and the wish to appear to be principled and impartial (without necessarily being so). Historically, the rule of law has always depended on habituation, the slow accretion of practice into customs that orient a people toward law's procedures and methods. Americans in particular have developed a strong habitual attachment to law, an attachment that has been noted since the early decades of the country's existence and that remains an important part of public culture today. Law also depends on pleasure. Although legal procedures are undoubtedly formal and dry, these same procedures stylize conflict and in doing so serve as a pleasant refuge from the harsher realities of life. Law also publicly declares victors, and offers these victors the enjoyable prospect of advertising their successes to the community at large. Beyond the pleasures of sanctuary and winning, law offers individuals the gratification of being treated like rights-bearing subjects. The judicial process confers status and gives people the satisfying feeling that they deserve to be listened to, whether or not they actually do deserve to be heard. Finally, law also depends on the interest in maintaining power. The judicial process is open to all and provides benefits to all—but the distribution of benefits is hardly equal.

The rules and procedures of law are structured so that their ordinary operation systematically rewards some more than others, creating a system that is in everyone's interest yet disproportionally advantageous for those who already hold important resources. Those who benefit the most have strong incentives to keep the system in place.

In sum, I suggest that pervasive public suspicions about judicial sincerity, far from being indicators of imminent collapse, are an expression of how our system now functions. The American judicial process is a flexible form of politesse, and is used to manage and soften conflict as well as to shield larger inequalities from serious challenge. The rule of law produced in this way is neither particularly fair nor free of paradoxical tensions. Yet it is durable and persists by reliably enlisting our interests, habits, and affections.

Legal Procedures and Useful Pretenses

I have argued that one of the central features of courtesy is that it turns hypocrisy to constructive use. In ordinary community life, in which individuals depend on one another and yet remain divided by different interests and passions, courtesy creates possibilities for cooperation by offering an artificial code of behavior. Genuine respect and mutual affection are not required for the "false friendships" of polite society to form; courtesy offers social coordination and civil peace so long as everyone simply agrees to be well-mannered.[5] This offer is widely accepted, in part, because most individuals are capable of only appearing to live up to community ideals. The opportunity for polite pretense is valuable in a world where people strive to keep up appearances because it permits everyone "to be better than they might be" by giving them a chance to pretend to be better than they are.[6]

As I noted in Part II, courtesy and law are often connected in terms of symbiosis: manners mavens and legal professionals alike both argue that courtesy and law work together to maintain communal harmony. In this vein, for example, Justice Ruth Bader Ginsburg has called on judges to avoid intemperate and abrasive language in their opinions (and especially in their dissents) in order to promote the judiciary's capacity and standing as an authoritative, dispute-resolving institution. It is by speaking in a polite "judicial voice" that courts may become more effective at performing their official duties.[7]

Although the symbiotic view has its merits, my approach to the relationship between courtesy and law is somewhat different. Rather than examining how courtesy and law may work in combination, I wish to explore what the functioning of courtesy can tell us about the functioning of law. Unlike Justice Ginsburg, I do not intend to consider how the judicial voice can be made more decorous; instead, I plan to assess the ways in which judicial action itself may be a form of decorum.

To see how dynamics that drive courtesy might also be at work in the judicial process, we should first, for the sake of analysis, accede to the proposition that the same understanding of human nature out of which courtesy grows also provides the context in which law must function. That is, we should accept, as a working premise, that differences between individuals are significant and irreducible; thus we should view disagreement as an obstinate fact of community life, never to be finally overcome but only to be more or less successfully managed. Moreover, we should accept that humans are governed by an inextricable mix of high principle and low passion. As a result, we should stipulate that most people take public moral standards seriously yet remain too filled with ambition and vanity to actually practice what they preach.

As I noted in Part II, I recommend this somewhat pessimistic view of human nature, along with the understanding of courtesy that flows from it, as a way of explaining how the American judicial process works. I do not claim that this view of human nature perfectly represents how people are nor do I claim that courtesy and law are identical. My claim instead is that an analytical model built on these ideas serves the purposes of explanation by generating new insights into how the rule of law currently operates.

What, then, does courtesy tell us about law? To begin to develop an answer to this question, consider that law, like courtesy, has often been thought to serve a facilitating function. A number of scholars have argued that courts effectively manage disputes by pursuing acceptable settlements without altering the fundamental factors that generate the disputes in the first place. Law, on this understanding, is an artificial medium in which otherwise opposed parties may jointly find ways of moving on.

A leading example of such thinking can be found in the classic discussion of legal reasoning by Lief Carter and Thomas Burke.[8] Carter and Burke argue that the rule of law, in its essence, is a matter of requiring people to "look outside [their] own will for criteria of judgment."[9] Whatever the specific features of a given political order may be, the rule of law directs individuals to adopt independent, publicly shared principles outside the sphere of personal attachments and private beliefs. Highly charged conflicts will certainly tempt people to evaluate competing claims by their own feelings and convictions. But the rule of law asks us to push beyond individual preferences. "The whole point of the rule of law," Carter and Burke write, "is to set standards of governance that transcend individual moral feelings. If all we have are our moral feelings, we are no better than Islamic or other religious fundamentalists who insist that *their* moral scheme justifies destroying other incompatible moral systems."[10]

According to Carter and Burke, one great advantage of having such independent standards of governance is that they create a highly useful language of dispute management for the courts. The rule of law sets aside the "dramatic and emotional work of poetics and theatrics" and commits the judiciary to "the logic of ideas."[11] Unlike the world of electoral politics, in which "smart participants know that they should obfuscate, change the subject, [and] hurl mud" to achieve their goals, the rule of law requires judges to work out their arguments openly and to furnish reasons for their rulings.[12] It is a deliberate process that relies on "elaborate mechanisms for sequencing questions" and structured frameworks that dictate how each sequenced question is to be addressed.[13] The payoff of such "slow and stately (and often boring)" legal procedures is that they help broker community peace, channeling hotly contested questions into a forum in which they can be more easily handled.[14]

Judicial proceedings offer this chance for managed resolution because the painstaking formalities of law leave the roots of disputes largely untouched. It is unnecessary for the contending parties to be personally transformed or genuinely reconciled because the goal of the judicial process is not to arrive at an objectively correct or perfectly just conclusion so much as it is to employ a method for coping with conflicts, a way of negotiating limited areas of consensus while allowing great regions of disagreement to remain intact. The essential work of courts, Carter and Burke write, is "about getting an answer that is good enough to settle the matter in a way that people can accept."[15]

The idea that the judicial process is configured to produce "good enough" settlements allows us to see law, like the conventions of good manners, as an adaptable means for managing the enduring disputes of social life. To put this same point differently, Carter and Burke allow us to see law, like courtesy, as a procedural system: a set of formal rules that facilitate engagement and coordination between people who otherwise disagree about substantive ends.[16] Given this shared basis, can we also say that the public support for law rests on the same hypocritical foundations as polite society?

There are, of course, differences of state power and structure to be considered.[17] Law, unlike etiquette, is backed by force; as a consequence, legal rules can claim priority over all other rules in society and individuals may be compelled to obey judicial dictates. Moreover, law, unlike etiquette, is organized as a true system, with a primary layer of rules that directly controls individual conduct as well as a secondary layer of rules that governs other legal rules. This complex structure makes law more durable and ordered than courtesy, with identified procedures for applying legal rules to disputes, for updating legal rules, and for determining which legal rules are authoritative. In short, law works through highly organized institutions and official practices, whereas the maintenance of polite society is left to the uneven and usually unorganized efforts of individuals.

Acknowledging these differences, one may still sensibly ask about the nature of public support for the judicial process, for no legal system can survive without a substantial degree of voluntary compliance. People must agree to bring their conflicts to the courts rather than seeking resolution in some unofficial dispute-processing venue.[18] Moreover, once disputes have landed in the judicial system, judges often count on parties to conform to court decisions without coercion. Policymakers have long understood that the judiciary depends on public support, and their recognition is evident in the web of regulations designed to ensure that judges preserve the public's confidence.[19] Thus, even though law is a complex language of dispute management that the state enforces, it is ultimately the population as a whole that must commit itself to this language for the rule of law to be effectively established. As Brian Tamanaha concluded in his sweeping review of the history, politics, and theory surrounding rule-of-law ideals, "[p]ervasive social attitudes about fidelity to the rule of law" are "the *essential* ingredient" in developing and sustaining a law-governed system.[20]

And so we return to the question posed by the similarities between proceduralist understandings of law and the example of courtesy: Is the public acceptance necessary for the rule of law rooted in the possibility of hypocrisy?[21] If we think of law as a special language that courts use to reframe conflict in more tractable terms, then we can say law is always open to hypocritical manipulation since its tests and procedures may readily be used to mask actual intentions. When judges and lawyers transpose a dispute into a legal idiom, they inevitably create a space between the judicial rendering of the issues and the forces driving the original disagreement. This space between law and ordinary fact constantly presents legal actors with the opportunity to obscure their motives and argue contrary to their beliefs.[22]

To say that law is open to hypocrisy is not, however, the same as saying that it somehow depends on hypocrisy. One may agree that law is an artificial, versatile mode of managing disputes and at the same time argue that the public's allegiance to the judicial process is not connected to the ever-present possibility of double dealing. Carter and Burke claim, for example, that the courts actively earn public confidence by making impartial judgments. They argue that when a judge successfully "harmonizes" the facts of the case, legal standards, background social norms, and moral principles in a written opinion, then the judge shows that she has resolved the dispute at hand in a way that the public can trust.[23] The harmonious decision remains a thoroughly legal one, bound up in and defined by the formal procedures of the judicial process. At the same time, the harmonious decision also communicates "an image of a viable community" containing fair "forums in which decision and action replace indecision and drift."[24] Finding community-sustaining impartial judgment in the artificialities of judicial process is, Carter and Burke write, just like finding impartial judgment in the artificial arenas of games and sports. "You may root passionately for one side, but when a referee's call goes against your team, you don't automatically condemn it. You ask if you trust it, whether the facts on the field fit the call."[25] A judge's legal reasoning does not win public acceptance because it provides a useful way of obscuring and softening interests and passions (as the example of courtesy would suggest). Instead, the well-crafted judicial opinion gains support because it ultimately persuades us that "the possibility of trust and impartiality [is] alive."[26]

With their invocation of trust and impartiality, Carter and Burke strike a familiar chord. As I noted in Part I, judicial legitimacy is conventionally understood to depend on principled and impartial judicial decisionmaking. From this perspective, any skepticism about whether judges actually mean what they say can only be harmful, undermining the basic claim that courts have for public support. It is true that Carter and Burke treat law as a contrived language, a specialized way of arguing about disputes that is not directed at "figuring out what [actually] happened" but at "analyzing what facts the [legal] rules allow us to seek and what to do with these facts once we 'know' them."[27] It is also true that law, understood as a set of artificial procedures, can easily be deployed in ways that raise suspicions about the sincerity of legal actors. But for Carter and Burke, as for many scholars and commentators, such suspicions are signs that the system is failing.[28] The strength and stability of the judicial process is to be found in the quality of the reasoning displayed in the opinion. It is by impartially harmonizing the elements of a case that a judge demonstrates how "the facts on the field fit the call" and proves he can be trusted with the dispute-managing power that he possesses.

It is certainly reasonable to call attention to the role of impartiality as Carter and Burke do. As we saw in Part I, judges at every level routinely present their decisions as being objective and fair, and a large majority of the public accepts the judicial displays of evenhandedness as true. This belief in impartiality is supported by scholarship that shows the judicial process to be infused with legal principle. Clearly, judicial impartiality is a central component of judicial legitimacy.

And yet, in addition to believing that judges are impartial arbiters, a large majority of the public also believes that judicial decisionmaking across the board is influenced by political preference. This belief is supported by scholarship that shows the judicial process to be permeated by political claims and commitments.

The example of courtesy, contrary to the claims made by many observers, suggests that *both* of the public's views feed into the legal order. How does this work? Recall that the rules of etiquette not only provide a means of expressing genuine concern and respect for one another, but also a way of merely "showing" concern and respect for those whom we do not authentically admire. As a result of its dual nature, courteous behavior inevitably breeds suspicions about the real motives of anyone who is being polite. It is this same duality, however, that also allows courtesy to serve as a code of behavior for all, appealing to the truly decent as well as to those who wish simply to appear decent. Applied to the judicial process, the example of courtesy suggests that law, in order to be a language of dispute management for everyone, must appeal to those honestly seeking principled and impartial adjudication as well as to those who merely want to drape themselves in the mantle of principled impartiality. People value the ideal of objective reasoning and fair judgment, but they usually remain too filled with self-love to live up to this ideal and will seek shortcuts where they can. As a result, many individuals will merely dress up their claims and preferences in the formal language of law in the hope that this will allow their cause to look better than it actually is. The presence of so many poseurs in the system naturally leads the public to suspect that the judicial process is subject to instrumental manipulation. Yet even though such suspicions chip away at judicial legitimacy, they also point to the very mechanism that attracts people to judicial dispute management. It is the possibility of hypocrisy that at once threatens public support for the judiciary and makes the courts appealing.

Limits of Rational Argument and the Game of Law

The revision of the proceduralist view of law that I am suggesting may be developed further by examining the limitations of rational argument and the idea that law is a kind of game.

Consider first the role of rational argument. The courtesy-based approach to the judicial process shares with Carter and Burke the understanding that law is a set of facilitating procedures. The courtesy approach is also compatible with Carter and Burke's claim that individuals may be persuaded to accept court rulings on the basis of well-crafted arguments. Just as good manners, for all of their artificiality, remain a vehicle for expressing genuine respect and admiration, so too law remains a medium in which truly impartial reasoning may occur.

It is important to note, however, that Carter and Burke do far more than merely allow the possibility of impartiality and reasoned persuasion: their argument critically depends on "the assumption that *someone* actually reads judicial decisions, and that the quality of the reasoning will assuage the feelings of even those who disagree with the outcomes."[29] The fact that the courtesy approach permits rational suasion while Carter and Burke require it reflects a basic difference. Carter and Burke place a great deal of weight on the persuasive power of reasoned judgment (and, as a consequence, the observation that much of the public has little detailed knowledge of judicial actions poses problems for their argument).[30] Courtesy asks reason in law to carry a far lighter load.

As I noted in Part II, rational arguments may be deployed in an effort to produce social coordination and mutually useful accommodations, but such arguments cannot serve as the primary form of appeal since reason does not firmly govern our impulses and appetites. "Rationality is a bond between persons," the philosopher Stuart Hampshire has observed, "but it is not a very powerful bond and it is apt to fail as a bond when there are strong passions on two sides of a conflict."[31] This failure of rationality is bound to occur on a regular basis because we live in communities with great diversity and intense disagreement. Our different needs, histories, ambitions, and vanities all conspire to keep us zealously engaged in endless disputes ("One needs to see," Hampshire writes, "that one's own way of life and habits of speech and thought, not only seem wrong to large populations, but can be repugnant in very much the same way in which alien habits of eating, or alien sexual customs, can be repugnant."[32]). Rather than simply trying to argue us out of this condition, courtesy relies on a suite of alternative mechanisms to keep people loyal to the pacifying methods of politeness.

Courtesy's strategy is, as I have noted, an old one. Machiavelli's work marked the beginning of an argument that reason was insufficient to cabin and control human passions.[33] This argument touched off a search for more effective constraints that ultimately led to what Albert Hirschman calls the "principle of the countervailing passions": to "fight fire with fire" by using "one set of comparatively innocuous passions to countervail another more dangerous or destructive set."[34] The discovery that desires and drives could be used to play a countervailing role was hailed as a great advance, a "message of hope" that there was a way to thread the needle between the "destructiveness of passion and the ineffectuality of reason."[35] Courtesy operates in this tradition of thought and steers deleterious passions into polite channels by employing a range of offsetting interests, appetites, and routines.[36] In this way, courtesy, like all schemes of countervailing passions, helps create predictability and peace in an inconstant, conflict-ridden world.

The example of courtesy suggests that the quality of judicial reasoning is of secondary importance in establishing and maintaining the rule of law. Of greater significance is that law is a means of dispute management that takes people more or less as they are (where "the way people are" is understood in terms of the view of human nature I am using here). Individuals are neither required to abandon their partisan passions at the courthouse door nor asked to realize their significant yet ordinarily unobtainable normative ideals; instead, they must only agree to couch their conflict in legal terms. This system has the advantage of making possible civil peace when the cacophony of competing interests and appetites in the community would otherwise defeat efforts to manage conflict. Everyone, including judges, is given the chance to clothe their claims in law's independent tests and procedures, lending their views an appearance of importance and impartiality that may not have much of a connection to underlying substance. It is an arrangement that is geared to all those with a greater capacity to seem than to be. Rather than relying on honest, rational, and direct communication—an approach that would only serve to make the differences between people more plain—the judicial process fashions a forum for dispute management with "flexibility, compromise, negotiation, and a measured dose of hypocrisy."[37]

It is true that legal training and judicial rulings alike are steeped in the impersonal language of logic, but as Oliver Wendell Holmes warned, that does not mean we should believe that impartial reason is the most important force at work.[38] The lawyer's goal is to represent her client, to frame arguments in the most advantageous terms in order to prevail—or, failing that, to at least "give the losing party, and his friends and sympa-thizers, as much satisfaction as any loser can expect."[39] For legal counsel, then, there arguably is no "such thing as intellectual impartiality" since the imperatives of advocacy "require a lawyer to begin with something to be proved."[40] Logic, in the hands of legal advocates, is often simply an instrument that may be used to attack or defend partial interests. Judges do not have clients, but this does not mean that they are therefore exem-plars of impartial reason. The evidence I reviewed in Part I suggests that judges at all levels are likely to bring a variety of partisan interests to the bench. Although such interests do not pose an insuperable obstacle to fair reasoning and judgment, their presence suggests that judges may often value goals other than the production of well-crafted opinions. Indeed, as Judge Richard Posner has argued, the basic task of articulating reasons for their decisions may not matter very much at all to many judges.[41] "When judges got busy," Posner notes, "the first thing to be delegated was opinion writing."[42]

The image of all participants in the judicial process making use of law for their own purposes corresponds to a dynamic we observed in Part I: at both the state and federal level, there appears to be little agreement about what constitutes faithful legal interpretation, at least with regard to the highly charged constitutional disputes that compose an impor-tant segment of the judicial docket. Instead of a shared understanding of what law requires in contentious cases, there is a proliferation of legal arguments ranging across the political spectrum. The sheer number of divergent claims accommodated by the system suggests that many people are enthusiastically taking advantage of their chance to mold law to suit their interests.

One might well wonder how this situation can possibly comport with the rule of law. I began my discussion of Carter and Burke with their basic definition of the rule of law as a matter of requiring people to "look outside their own will for criteria of judgment." Yet instead of an account of how individuals seek an independent standard of judgment, we seem to have arrived at an understanding that envisions participants in the judicial process having ample opportunity to advance their per-sonal agendas under the cover of law. In my efforts to adapt and extend the proceduralist views of Carter and Burke, have I in fact transfigured their rule-of-law argument into an argument about the rule of men? Not quite. I claim that individual interests and passions make their way into the judicial process, and I also maintain that there is a substantial public faith in the impartiality of judges. On one hand, there is always the possibility for law to be used to suit the agenda of interested parties, and, in the actual practice of judicial decisionmaking, there frequently may be no straight line of causation leading from abstract premise to concrete ruling. On the other hand, legal principle and impartial reason still matter and remain key components of judicial legitimacy.

How can this be? The pretense and instrumentalism of the judicial process do not foreclose a meaningful role for legal principle and impartial reasoning in two senses. First, as I have already noted, courts may still produce truly impartial reasoning and genuine fair judgment, just as courtesy can still be used to convey authentic concern and respect. As Carter and Burke argue, a judge may reach an acceptable settlement because her arguments actually persuade the parties that she has fairly applied independent standards of governance to the dispute before her.

Moreover—and, as the example of courtesy would suggest, more often—principle and impartiality are significant in a different register.[43] Individuals value collective ideals even though they often cannot always live up to them, and systems of principle remain important ordering mechanisms even if no one can consistently conform to their terms. Law will often be treated like a tool and be made to function in the interests of its users,[44] and yet this tool will be accepted by and have value for people only if it is enveloped by overarching principles that convey a message of unity and impartiality, independent of law's diversity of partisan uses. The resulting system endures not in spite of the contradiction between instrumental action and impartial principle, but because this contradiction suits law to the individuals who are governed by it. In other words, it is because individuals have a need to advance their own particular interests and a need to feel they are meeting impersonal, coherent standards that law operates on two conflicting planes at once. People insist, Judith Shklar once noted, that "the impartiality of judges and of the [legal] process as a whole requires a dispassionate, literal pursuit of rules carved in spiritual marble."[45] This insistence on legal principle "may seem ridiculous" because "most thoughtful citizens know that the courts act decisively in creating rules that promote political ends."[46] Even so, the political use of the judicial process need not eclipse principled legal understandings. The mix of political and legal factors is "not at all socially or psychologically indefensible," Shklar wrote. "Indeed, if we value flexibility and accept a degree of contradiction, this paradox may even seem highly functional and appropriate."[47]

We can see this paradoxical confluence of political interests and impartial principles at work if we revisit and revise the comparison, made by Carter and Burke, between legal reasoning and sports officiating. Carter and Burke analogize the judge to the referee: both figures are charged with enforcing the rules and both are capable of making impartial judgments about the application of these rules in controversial circumstances. To extend the reach of this analogy, consider that beyond the specific claim that judges and referees have related roles, we can say more generally that both judges and referees are engaged in games. Referees do not play the same part as players on either team, and judges do not play the same part as litigants and lawyers. Nonetheless, referees and judges are both very much "in" the game, in the sense that they, like all the other game players, carry out roles that are dictated by the rules of play. Viewed from this perspective, the most noteworthy parallel to draw is not that judges look like a kind of referee, but that *everyone* in the judicial process, including judges, is involved in a kind of game.

The game analogy is helpful because it illuminates a particular way in which individuals may relate to legal principle. When people play a game, they need not accept the rules of the game as being objectively true or morally correct. It does not matter whether individuals playing the same game possess the same set of motives or substantive convictions; in order for the game to be played, the participants need only look on the rules of the game as standards for making the appropriate moves. Gaming is defined by observable performance, not by purity or sincerity of intention, and we know a person is playing by looking to see if his actions, explanations, and evaluative critiques of other players are presented according to the rules of the game.[48] As Hart recognized, the application of this gaming perspective to the judicial process suggests that people may participate in the game of law (for example, making claims couched in principle and calling for justifications as the rules of law require) for any number of reasons. Legal rules may conceivably be "accepted simply out of deference to tradition or the wish to identify with others or in the belief that society knows best what is to the advantage of individuals."[49] Indeed, judges "might apply the law in order to pick up their paychecks."[50]

The example of courtesy tells us that two of the key motivations for entering the legal game are the interest in securing the benefits of dispute management and the wish to appear to be principled and impartial. These motivations, like any motivation to play that is not exclusively rooted in beliefs about the moral rectitude of a game's rules, understandably prompt suspicion: How can we be certain that someone playing the legal game for such reasons won't try to cheat? In particular, how can we be sure that a judge won't decide a case on the basis of some personal preference and then merely pretend that legal principle and impartial reason led to the result?[51]

The answer is that we cannot be sure—especially when we consider that some important rules of the legal game, such as those determining what counts as faithful interpretation, are often ambiguous and open to sharp contestation.[52] The lack of certainty about how the game of law is being played is reflected in the broad public suspicion that judges often do not mean what they say. These suspicions are disabling and weaken the public confidence on which the judiciary relies. Yet the corrosive consequences of such suspicions are, I have argued, also paired with the system-empowering effects that come from allowing a great range of claims to be sheathed in appropriate legal form. People often speak and act as if they are using legal rules to plan and guide their actions; they move within law, appealing to principle and impartial reason as standards for their actions and as grounds for criticizing those with whom they disagree. The fact that so many choose to play the legal game is a remarkable achievement, even if the reasons that they have for playing also increase the odds that they may try to exploit the rules of the game for their own advantage.

To say that this system represents the rule of law rather than the rule of men is merely to recognize that there remains a real difference between requiring people to work through "a relevant body of rules" and simply permitting "them to do as they please or to do what they consider right without regard to rules."[53] The legal game retains measures of stability and predictability independent of personal will because "the *path* to the result" is ultimately constrained.[54] A participant in the judicial process may be able to slalom through a field of rules en route to a preferred conclusion, but her course will remain within certain bounds if for no other reason than because there is a particular set of rules she is "obliged to get around."[55]

Habit, Pleasure, and Hierarchy

Following Carter and Burke, I have argued that the signal contribution of the rule of law to community life is that it provides independent standards for judicial dispute management. I have sketched the outlines of a legal arrangement that meets the needs for independent dispute management, and does so in ways that at once appeal to broadly held interests and suggest a real risk of hypocritical manipulation. Law, as I have described it, has a push-me-pull-me relationship to pretense at its core.

Given how strongly hypocrisy is disdained, why would anyone accept a system with endemic opportunities for double dealing? Is the usefulness of the process—both as a means for securing social coordination and as a mechanism for satisfying the need to appear impartial and principled—sufficient to outweigh the opprobrium heaped on hypocritical behavior?

Expressions of distaste for law's thinness and manipulability are certainly easy to find, as the many contrivances of the judicial process tempt people to speak directly about the world as it is rather than the world as it is legally rendered. Observers may condemn the judicial confirmation process when they hear nominees repeatedly describing their approach to cases as simple "fidelity to the law" without engaging the underlying political claims that fuel the confirmation battle or that will influence decisionmaking on the bench.[56] Judges themselves may decry the artificiality of legal rules and procedures, and call for examinations of the real motives behind legal doctrines and the true impact of legal rulings.[57] Critical claims about the malleable unreality of legal reasoning may be particularly pronounced in judicial dissents, when judges on the losing end of a decision may accuse the majority of relying on a "sterile formalism" that obscures vital facts or of engineering a "massive disruption of the current social order" by developing a legal logic that bears no relationship to actual conditions.[58]

How does law withstand such criticisms about its inauthenticity and potential to mislead? I posed a similar question in my discussion of courtesy. In that context, I argued that the viability of courtesy depends not only on its usefulness but also on elements of habit, pleasure, and hierarchy that help cement attachments to polite behavior in ways that are consistent with the unruly mix of principles and passions in human nature. The possibility of hypocritical manipulation remains a highly undesirable aspect of good manners, yet we nonetheless embrace codes of courtesy because the force of ingrained habit, the appeal of small pleasures, and the lure of power all work alongside considerations of utility to give us incentives to do so.

The same factors are at work in the context of law. Consider first the role of habit. Apart from the interests in dispute management and principled appearances that generally attract people to law, a broad law-sustaining habit can be found within the larger community. Hart called it the "habit of obedience," a general disposition to follow law that manifests itself in daily behavior.[59] The habit is a reflexive response that can take the form of "unreflective, effortless, engrained" compliance when legal dictates are easy to follow, as in the case of automatically and unthinkingly driving on the right side of the road.[60] The habit is also a routine behavior that is evident in areas of life in which the demands of law are more exacting and following the rules "runs counter to strong inclinations."[61] When it comes to the payment of taxes, for example, the habit of obedience exerts influence as the fact of compliance "for some considerable time past" makes it likely that people will continue to comply in the future.[62]

As Hart noted, the habit of obedience requires "no general conception of the legal structure or of its criteria of validity."[63] Most people are inclined to follow law either out of deference to the way in which things have always been done or out of fear of being punished should they disobey. The habit of obedience is thus suited to the discordant amalgam of principles and passions within each of us: it breeds attachment to law by relying on the ease of inertia and the interest in avoiding penalty—all without requiring individuals to be persuaded by rational argument, to embody the normative ideals expressed in legal rules, or to possess much legal knowledge. Repeated compliance to law may in some instances lead an individual to consciously embrace the values expressed in legal principles and to believe that in obeying, "what he does is the right thing both for himself and for others to do."[64] But this is not essential, for the habit of legal obedience, like the habit of courtesy discussed in Part II, is at root a habit of action. Habitual obedience conditions people to adhere to the forms of the legal game; motives may be altered by such sustained customary practice, but this is not necessary for conformance to law to continue.

In the historical experience of different societies, the habit of obedience that Hart described in general terms has evolved in the context of particular traditions, in each case providing support for the establishment and growth of the rule of law in specific places. In Europe, for example, the "rule of law tradition congealed into existence in a slow, unplanned manner that commenced in the Middle Ages, with no single source or starting point."[65] This diffuse process of development was driven, in part, by the gradual spread of habitual obedience throughout the whole population, including subjects as well as the sovereign. The influence of the habit in this period was transmitted through the medium of a shared religious culture. Medieval European society as a whole was governed by "Christian justice," and monarchs, who were Christians like everyone else, regularly vowed to uphold Christian law.[66] The routine of "repeated oaths and voluntary affirmations" worked on kings and queens just as the repeated practice of obedience to Christian law worked on ordinary people, creating a "settled general expectation" that rulers and ruled alike would continue to follow the same rules in the future as they had in the past.[67] Thus the "weight of mundane regularized conformity" ensured that all felt bound by law.[68]

In the United States, the habit of obedience has developed in terms that are particularly favorable to the courts. American political tradition is deeply marked by a distrust of concentrated public power, a distrust that led early generations to adopt state and federal constitutions that "splintered government authority" among separate branches and across different political subdivisions.[69] Americans in the nineteenth century consequently steered away from the consolidated power of the national bureaucracies and strong legislatures that were developing throughout Western Europe and, instead, grew used to government by decentralized, locally staffed institutions. Chief among these decentralized institutions were the courts. Indeed, Americans became so thoroughly accustomed to and reliant upon the judiciary that by the 1830s Tocqueville found "legal language" to be "pretty well adopted into common speech," and "the language of every party-political controversy . . . borrowed from legal phraseology and conceptions."[70] The legal habit forged in the nineteenth century is still very much with us today, as Americans continue to experience the courts and litigation as a central "mode of governance," a source of authority that is so deeply embedded within the "unconsciously maintained patterns" of public life that any effort to import a differently configured legal system would be less a matter of "transplant surgery" than an exercise in "psychotherapy."[71]

In addition to being underwritten by habit, law, like courtesy, is also bolstered by pleasure. This reliance on pleasure may be somewhat difficult to see, since the judicial process looks like an unlikely place to find any kind of contentment or delight. Legal procedures often are, as Carter and Burke noted, slow, stately, and boring—and this appears to be so by design. The dullness of law serves the goal of dispute management, helping to create a rendering of events that is more tractable than the messy particulars of actual experience. The flesh-and-blood drama and details that make life interesting and entertaining "do little more than encourage law to trip over itself."[72] The arguments of lawyers and judges therefore attempt "to transcend differences, finding the relevant links in a chain of potentially unrelated episodes," and the successful legal narrative presents "just enough material to make its case, paring down encumbrances lest they distract from the overall grasp of precedent and principle."[73] To find pleasure here would appear to require moving outside the system altogether, seeking out stories, perspectives, and experiences that the judicial process does its best to obscure and marginalize. Indeed, there may be great satisfaction to be found in resisting law, in performing small "tricks and deceits" that turn the tables on those attempting to play by the rules of the legal game.[74]

And yet law does have its pleasurable features. Recall that courtesy provides a means of giving respect and praise to truly deserving individuals; in doing so, etiquette helps satisfy the desire to live up to moral standards by recognizing and rewarding exemplary individuals. To the extent that the judicial process actually produces impartial decisions, it too fulfills the desire to see public life governed by important norms. By hearing both sides of a dispute and by operating on the basis of reason and principle, the judicial process creates a forum in which it is possible for "justice . . . to be done and be seen to be done."[75] When this occurs, the litigants experience the pleasure of "the moral affirmation bestowed upon [them] by the judge."[76]

Of course, the possibility that the claims of justice may be vindicated does not mean that they always will be. Even though courtesy may be used to convey authentic admiration and respect, I have argued that good manners are directed primarily toward maintaining appropriate appearances for those who cannot actually live up to moral ideals. Along these same lines, I have also argued that although the judicial process may produce genuinely objective and fair decisions, law is centrally concerned with creating appearances of principle and impartiality rather than producing their substance. Thus we should expect that the main pleasures of courtesy and law, like the main business of courtesy and law themselves, are necessarily bound up with surfaces and display.

What are the surface pleasures of law? Just as good manners lend a patina of elegance and grace to the drabness of ordinary life, law creates a kind of sanctuary in which the brutalities of a dispute may be given a stylized and intellectually refined gloss. In this way, the very legal procedures that induce boredom may also foster an appealing sense of shelter and relief. Law's "raw materials are the ugly realities of life, but they are transformed in the judicial game to intellectual disputes over rights and duties, claims and proofs, presumptions and rebuttals, jurisdiction and competencies."[77] This legal repackaging of reality provides respite for litigants buffeted by the blunt force of conflict, refuge for lawyers making arguments in which they do not believe, and a salve for judges meting out heavy punishments. This is not to say, of course, that law somehow fashions a completely idyllic space filled with sweetness and light. The advantages of law are relative: it is when compared to the "sinister realities" of "hatred, disease, crime, betrayal, [and] war" that the judicial process provides a measure of comfort.[78]

Law, like courtesy, also presents appearance-related pleasures that appeal to vanity and self-love. Playing the legal game offers satisfactions for triumphant litigants who can crow about their "meticulously orchestrated" strategies or brag about "the quality of legal talent" enlisted on their side.[79] It is fun to be publicly recognized as a winner, and the judicial process offers a number of opportunities for victorious parties to trumpet their success. More broadly, law also promises a degree of ego gratification for all participants, win or lose. In addition to providing a method for managing disputes, a means for keeping up appearances of principle and impartiality, and a way of sheltering people from harsh conditions, legal procedures also have another function: they assign and confirm status, conveying a public message about individual worth through the manner in which disputing parties are treated.[80] When the judicial process deals with litigants in a way that appears to be "polite, respectful, and unbiased," then people are more likely to accept judicial decisions and rate the legal system positively, more or less regardless of how their case is finally resolved.[81] To demonstrate solicitude for complaints and to allow individuals to relate their side of the story is to treat people like rights-bearing subjects that deserve to be valued. This legal showing of respect does not change the fact that one party in a dispute may end up getting the better of the other any more than polite flattery increases the actual beauty of a person's appearance or the true stature of his achievements. In both cases, the pleasure is in how things are said and how affairs are conducted, not in the ultimate outcome or in any concrete change in underlying conditions. Like the courtesies of polite society, respectful treatment at the hands of law has a powerful effect because it speaks to the desire to be treated with dignity, whether or not a person actually merits such concern and attention.

What of hierarchy? We have seen that one of the reasons that at least some people are willing to tolerate the hypocrisies of good manners is that courtesy is the handmaiden of the existing order. Those who gain the most from the prevailing patterns of dominance have every reason to support codes of courtesy that channel behavior in directions favoring the status quo. What is the relationship between law and the interest in maintaining power?

As a matter of historical fact, law has clearly been used to shore up hierarchies. In Part II, I examined instances in which etiquette played a role in maintaining the subordination of women, African Americans, and the LGBT community. In each one of these instances, law was used to solidify and maintain domination by enforcing restrictions on participation in important social and political institutions and by imposing narrow notions of equality and privacy to justify marginalization and powerlessness.[82]

As with courtesy, the question is not whether powerful groups will attempt to use law as a means to maintain their position, for there are many examples of such attempts. Instead, the question is one of fit: How does the desire to maintain power—a desire that manifestly attracts dominant groups to law—comport with the interests, habits, and pleasures that otherwise sustain the judicial process?

Several factors that I have considered clearly do not prevent law from operating in the interests of the few. The habit of obedience, for example, is quite passive and can attach itself to highly inegalitarian legal systems. In fact, Hart argued that a hypothetical "extreme case" society in which the majority of people relate to law exclusively through habits of obedience would be "deplorably sheeplike," and he warned that in such circumstances "the sheep may end up in the slaughter-house."[83] Habit helps invest people in the existing legal system and may well be an obstacle to those seeking change. But there is little reason to think that habit, on its own, can deter established law from serving the goals of specific classes. The same holds true for the wish to appear principled and impartial, the pleasure that comes from being treated as a rights-bearing subject, and the comforts of refuge. Admirable appearances, respectful treatment, and sanctuary are available to all participants in the judicial process, regardless of their social or political standing outside of law. These threshold-level benefits may easily be part of a legal system that ultimately rewards some more than others. Indeed, as is the case with courtesy, one can argue that the advantages available to all are more than merely compatible with a hierarchical system: universally conferred benefits may actually help stabilize the prevailing hierarchy because these benefits give everyone some reason to support the existing order even if that order skews in favor of certain groups.

Yet if these factors do not stand in the way of efforts to shape law in the interest of dominant classes, there are other elements of the courtesy-based approach that, at least at first blush, appear to work against making the judicial process into a tool of the powerful. Consider that the entire practice of dispute management is, as we have seen, geared toward the production of acceptable settlements. Why would litigants accept settlements that systematically advance the few? So long as the judiciary must elicit consent from contending parties, ensuring that they are willing to bring their disputes before the courts and obey judicial rulings, then the individual demands for acceptable resolutions must be taken seriously by the courts. Rather than tipping the scale in favor of governing groups, the necessity of attending to each party's range of preferred outcomes would seem to empower the weak to protect themselves from exploitation by the strong.

In response, one may argue that the need for acceptable settlements in law, like the need for mutual accommodation in polite society, does not necessarily offer much protection since in principle losing parties will find even substantially unfavorable resolutions to be "good enough" if they are convinced that some other possible outcome would have been worse. Mutual benefits need not be symmetric benefits, and one could claim there is simply no need to grant substantially equal gains to all for judicial dispute management to be effective.

This response is sufficient in the case of courtesy, but it is incomplete in the case of law. Law creates visible winners, and the satisfaction that comes from success increases the motivation that all parties have to zealously advance their claims. It is one thing to say that people will accept a system that disproportionately favors the few so long as everyone stands to gain something from the system's operation. It is another thing to say that people will tolerate a system of unequally distributed benefits when the victors reap pleasure from brashly broadcasting their success. When the joys of victory are great and publically expressed, then each and every disputing party has reason to consider the only acceptable settlement to be one in which they win.

Taken together, the requirement of acceptable settlements and the pleasures of winning would appear to frustrate efforts to use law as a shield for established hierarchies. And yet, on closer examination, the need for mutually acceptable settlements and the desire for victory turn out not to hinder the legal preservation of hierarchy very much at all. This is so because, as sociolegal scholars have long understood, there is more than one way to succeed in the judicial process. Most ordinary individuals have only "occasional recourse to the courts" and are invested in the outcome of their particular case.[84] For such "one shotters," the only result that matters is the disposition of the dispute in which they are involved. By contrast, "repeat players," with multiple and ongoing engagements in the judicial process, have smaller stakes in specific outcomes; they use their resources to manage their disputes with an eye toward influencing the rules of the legal game that will govern litigation in the future. Repeat players are consequently willing to settle when it makes strategic sense to do so, taking a loss in a specific case for the sake of preserving favorable rules in an entire run of cases. The individual, one-shotter litigant facing an organized, well-resourced repeat player may aggressively push for a preferred outcome and manage to claim the pleasure of winning her case. At the level of the specific dispute, such a result lends law "a flavor of equality," suggesting that differences in position between the two parties do not determine judicial decisions.[85] The resource differences are nonetheless reflected at the level of legal rules where the wise management of victories and defeats permits repeat players to structure the overall system to their advantage.[86] Two different senses of "good enough" settlements and two different kinds of winning are thus in play. The legal system may widely distribute acceptable results and feelings of victory, all the while ensuring that individual winners do not threaten the position of those organized, powerful groups with the wherewithal to shape their litigation with an eye toward the long term.[87]

This is not to say that repeat players have complete control of the legal system. The possibility that judges may use legal procedures as screens to obscure their own partisan interests suggests that the resources powerful groups pour into securing a favorable legal environment will not always be well spent. In spite of careful strategic management, the effort to secure an advantageous set of rules necessarily loses some of its value when one cannot be sure that decisionmakers will always follow the rule-book to the letter. Powerful classes are nonetheless drawn to law because of the degree of control it offers relative to alternative means. Just as law looks like a sanctuary when compared to the ferocity of open conflict, it also looks like an attractive method of retaining power when compared to the instabilities introduced by violent repression.[88]

Conclusion

I began this book with a problem of appearances. Large segments of the American public regard judges as impartial arbiters and at the same time believe judicial rulings to be politically motivated. The tension be-tween the two views leads many to suspect that judicial talk about the requirements and meaning of law is simply empty rhetoric designed to conceal the pursuit of partisan purposes. These conflicting public views and their accompanying suspicions are largely matters of perception: most Americans do not have direct experience with judges or courts, and they form their opinions by observing and reacting to the surface of the judicial process. Although one may complain about the folly of focusing on ap-pearances, the fact remains that popular perceptions matter a good deal.[89] Judicial legitimacy depends, among other things, on the ability of judges to convey the impression that their decisions are driven by the impersonal requirements of legal principle. When a significant majority of the public is dubious about the sincerity of judicial pronouncements, then the judi-ciary's standing as an independent, authoritative body is at risk, even if the majority's view is based merely on impressions of how the courts look.

Using my analysis of common courtesy as a guide, I have ended the book by arguing that law's problem of appearances also points toward a source of strength. Conflicting perceptions of the courts raise doubts about judicial legitimacy; at the same time, the same perceptions also indicate how the judicial process goes about serving the public's needs and winning its allegiance. If we assume that most Americans value the ideals of impartiality and principle expressed in legal procedures, and yet remain too consumed with self-serving passions to live up to these nor-mative ideals, then a legal system that gives everyone a chance to appear impartial and principled, without actually requiring them to be so, is a system that has broad appeal. Indeed, the opportunity to simulate desirable-yet-unobtainable ideals is not only attractive but also highly useful, for it creates a common language of dispute management that the courts may use to reframe conflicts in more tractable terms. The thinness and artificiality that open law to criticism also account for a substantial part of its allure and its practical value.

As with courtesy, law's constructive use of pretense is bound up with a range of additional factors. Steady habits of obedience, the thrill of victory, the pleasures of sanctuary and respectful treatment, and the abiding interest in maintaining power all help to strengthen legal attachments and help explain why people remain loyal to the judicial process in spite of the risk that actors within the process may not always mean what they say. Of course, not all of these additional factors play their law-supporting role without difficulty. Satisfaction may be found in resisting law, for example, and individuals may find it more gratifying to skip the joys of the established process for the sake of subverting its procedures and demands. The pursuit of pleasure may thus position people "against the law," leading them away from the majesty of law's aspirations as well as from the competition of interests that takes place under the cover of these aspirations.[90] Yet without denying the waywardness of desire, we can still say that habit, pleasure, and hierarchy on the whole help invest people in the judicial process, and do so in ways that are generally consistent with the impulses and appetites embedded in human nature.

Thus it is possible to see, contrary to conventional understandings, that law is not facing a grave threat to its stability. It is true that our system is beset by suspicions of hypocrisy generated by clashing public perceptions of judicial action. Almost everywhere one looks there seems to be cause to doubt that the judicial process is conducted in good faith: law is a practice of dispute management that always speaks in terms of logic and objective analysis, and yet does not always rely on reason; law is a formal arrangement that appeals to a sense of principle and right, but without necessarily being geared toward producing concrete manifestations of fairness; and law is a body of tests and procedures that asks individuals to seek standards of judgment outside their own will while creating an arena for the pursuit of personal interests and attachments. Our rule of law is far from perfect and may rightly be criticized for appearing unreasonable, unfair, and inconsistent.[91] And yet, in spite of just criticism and the fear that the current system will ultimately founder under the weight of its own contradictions, the judicial process continues to endure because it suits the individuals it governs—at least if we understand these individuals to be motivated by a messy mix of principled belief and passionate demands.

As I have argued, most people will not accept a scheme of adjudication that is merely a bare-knuckled battle between interests without any hint of normative purpose or objectivity, nor are most people capable of living up to a system that is strictly governed by principle and requires the realization of impartial judgment. An arrangement that gives both passions and principles their due, permitting talk of law to be paired with the pressures of politics, is the only kind of arrangement that will work. Under such conditions, the suspicions of hypocrisy that attend the judicial process do not indicate a looming crisis so much as they suggest that the process depends on a cluster of considerations that produce concerns about double dealing as part of their ordinary operation.

There are, to be sure, many different views of the human condition, and one might claim that some view other than the one I have employed provides a more accurate rendering of how people really are. That may very well be true—but my argument has been that it is the power of explanation, not the degree of resemblance, that counts. Different conceptions of human nature, like different maps, convey different levels of detail about a specific area to be explored. For my purposes, what matters is not whether any given concept or map is identical to the terrain to which it refers, but whether the concept or map helps us understand where we are.

In this spirit, I have presented a particular view of human inclinations and interactions, along with an accompanying understanding of courtesy, as a way of accounting for the American legal system as it is. We live in a world where most Americans believe that the judicial process is infused with politics at the same time that they believe judicial decisions are impartially determined on nonpolitical, purely legal grounds. My goal has been to explain how these conflicting beliefs may cohere, allowing people to view judicial decisionmaking as being anchored in something other than legal principle and yet to accept this decisionmaking as part of a legitimate legal process.

Reference Matter

Notes

Part I

1. Adam Liptak, "Judges Mix with Politics," *New York Times*, February 22, 2003, B1–B8. I am using a rough-and-ready definition of legal realism. The realists actually developed a complex range of related ideas and theories. For different accounts of legal realism's genesis and development in the United States, see Edward A. Purcell Jr., *The Crisis of Democratic Theory: Scientific Naturalism and the Problem of Value* (Lexington: University Press of Kentucky, 1973); Laura Kalman, *Legal Realism at Yale, 1927–1960* (Chapel Hill: University of North Carolina Press, 1986); Morton J. Horwitz, *The Transformation of American Law, 1870–1960: The Crisis of Legal Orthodoxy* (New York: Oxford University Press, 1992); John Henry Schelegel, *American Legal Realism and Empirical Social Science* (Chapel Hill: University of North Carolina Press, 1995); Neil Duxbury, *Patterns of American Jurisprudence* (New York: Oxford University Press, 1995); and Stephen M. Feldman, *American Legal Thought from Premodernism to Postmodernism: An Intellectual Voyage* (New York: Oxford University Press, 2000).

2. *Spargo v. New York State Comm'n on Judicial Conduct*, 244 F.Supp.2d 72, 79 (N.D.N.Y., 2003).

3. *Ibid.*, 80.

4. *Republican Party of Minnesota v. White*, 536 U.S. 765 (2002).

5. Liptak, "Judges Mix with Politics," B1.

6. Al Baker, "Partisan Pit Bull, but Not on the Bench," *New York Times*, February 22, 2003, New York and Region section. Spargo's belief that the district court may have gone too far was ultimately vindicated. In December 2003, the Second Circuit Court of Appeals vacated the district court decision on the grounds that Spargo's constitutional claims had been improperly raised in federal court. *Spargo v. New York State Comm'n on Judicial Conduct*, 351 F.3d 65, 85 (2d Cir. 2003). The disciplinary actions against Spargo subsequently resumed in New York with the additional charge that Spargo had solicited money for his legal defense from attorneys with cases pending in his court. In December of 2004, the state Supreme Court rejected Spargo's constitutional challenge to the state code of judicial conduct ("Decision of Interest: Restrictions on Judicial Speech in

Conduct Rules Are Not Unconstitutionally Vague," *New York Law Journal*, December 16, 2004, 19). As Spargo's legal fortunes turned, he suggested that the courts were now swinging too far in the other direction and failing to respect judicial candidates' freedom of speech: "You know, in my experience, under our restrictive and rather obtuse rules, it is much harder to become a judge than to do a good job once you are actually on the bench. Perhaps more judicial freedom of speech will result in more good judges being elected to the bench." See Thomas J. Spargo, *A Peripatetic View of Judicial Free Speech*, 68 ALB. L. REV. 629, 634 (2005). In March 2006, the New York State Commission on Judicial Conduct unanimously recommended that Spargo be removed from the bench. See John Caher, "Commission Calls for N.Y. Judge's Removal," *New York Law Journal*, April 3, 2006, http://www.law.com/jsp/article.jsp?id=1143812717567 (last accessed August 30, 2009). The Court of Appeals upheld the removal recommendation, thus ending Spargo's judicial career. In December 2008, Spargo was indicted by a federal grand jury for attempted extortion and soliciting a bribe. He was convicted on all counts in August 2009. In December 2009, Spargo was sentenced to twenty-seven months in federal prison.

7. In other words, Spargo appeared to lack what H.L.A. called an "internal" view of the law. See H.L.A. Hart, *The Concept of Law*, 2nd ed. (New York: Oxford University Press, 1994), 56–57, 89–91. For further discussion of Hart, see notes 116 and 121.

8. Compare the similar argument made by Justice Scalia. *Republican Party v. White*, 576 U.S. at 784. See also Judicial Elections White Paper Task Force, *Judicial Selection White Papers: The Case for Partisan Judicial Elections*, 22 TOL. L. REV 393, 393–409 (2002).

9. *White*, 536 U.S. at 803 (Justice Ginsburg dissenting, internal citations and quotation marks omitted). See also Terri Jennings Peretti, *In Defense of a Political Court* (Princeton, NJ: Princeton University Press, 1999), 11–35; and Richard A. Wasserstrom, *The Judicial Decision: Toward a Theory of Legal Justification* (Stanford, CA: Stanford University Press, 1961), 14–22.

10. Oliver Wendell Holmes, *The Path of the Law*, 10 HARV. L. REV. 457, 465–466 (1897).

11. Kalman, *Legal Realism*, 229. See also William Twining, *Karl Llewellyn and the Realist Movement* (Norman, OK: University of Oklahoma Press, 1985), 382.

12. The spread of public suspicion presents a potential problem for judicial legitimacy, but it does not necessarily present a problem for legal realism as a theory of legal behavior. Several legal realists argued that judicial decisionmaking could not openly and exclusively be anchored in something other than the law and, at the same time, easily remain a legitimate "legal" process. For example, both Jerome Frank and Thurman Arnold believed that the open acknowledgement of the role of non-legal factors in judicial decisionmaking would ultimately require the broad psychological transformation of many individuals. Frank and Arnold understood that the judicial process

could not be considered to be exclusively political—and nonetheless still be accepted as legally authoritative—unless we developed a new kind of person. Public doubt and uncertainty about judicial decisionmaking in the absence of such personal transformation would not have surprised either Frank or Arnold. See Thurman W. Arnold, *The Symbols of Government* (New Haven, CT: Yale University Press, 1935) and Jerome Frank, *Law and the Modern Mind* (Gloucester, MA: Peter Smith, 1970, reprint of the 1930 edition). As will become clear over the course of the book, I agree with these realists that the tensions between law and politics in the judicial process are not going away. See also my discussion of Arnold in Keith J. Bybee, "The Rule of Law Is Dead! Long Live the Rule of Law!," March 2009, http://ssrn.com/abstract=1404600 (last accessed August 30, 2009).

13. I use the term *rule of law* in fashion similar to Robert A. Kagan's use of *way of law* in his book *Adversarial Legalism: The American Way of Law* (Cambridge, MA: Harvard University Press, 2001). Although Kagan and I focus on different factors, our analyses are similar in the sense that we both ultimately direct our attention away from individual judicial decisions (and the specific legal principles at stake in those decisions) toward the political beliefs, habits of mind, and cultural practices that inform and sustain judicial decisionmaking. I argue that this cluster of beliefs, habits, and practices constitute the American rule of law.

14. An estimated 40 percent of state appellate judges are chosen by partisan election (at least for their initial terms); 43 percent of general jurisdiction state trial court judges are selected by partisan elections (at least, again, for their initial terms). See Kyle D. Cheek and Anthony Champagne, *Partisan Judicial Elections: Lessons from a Bellwether State*, 39 WILLAMETTE L. REV. 1357, 1357–83 (2003). See also G. Alan Tarr, "Politicizing the Process: The New Politics of State Judicial Elections," in Keith J. Bybee, ed., *Bench Press: The Collision of Courts, Politics, and the Media* (Stanford, CA: Stanford University Press, 2007), 52–74; and the essays collected in Matthew J. Streb, ed., *Running for Judge: The Rising Political, Financial, and Legal Stakes of Judicial Elections* (New York: New York University Press, 2007). For a survey of the ways states elect their supreme courts, see Chris W. Bonneau and Melinda Gann Hall, *In Defense of Judicial Elections* (New York: Routledge, 2009). The use of partisan elections for at least some judicial offices has declined since 1987. See Lynn Langton and Thomas H. Cohen, *State Court Organization, 1987–2004*, October 2007, Bureau of Justice Statistics, Office of Justice Programs, United States Department of Justice, 9.

15. Robert Barnes, "Judicial Races Now Rife with Politics," *Washington Post*, October 28, 2007, A01.

16. James Sample, Lauren Jones, and Rachel Weiss, "The New Politics of Judicial Elections, 2006" (Justice at Stake Campaign and The Brennan Center of Justice at NYU Law School: 2007), 5, http://www.justiceatstake.org/contentViewer .asp?breadcrumb=3,570,979 (last accessed August 30, 2009). At the same link, see also

"The New Politics of Judicial Elections, 2000," "The New Politics of Judicial Elections, 2002," and "The New Politics of Judicial Elections 2004." For a recent analysis of judicial elections in Ohio, see Adam Liptak and Janet Roberts, "Campaign Cash Mirrors a High Court's Rulings," *New York Times*, October 1, 2006, A1, A22–23.

17. For example, the Eighth Circuit Court of Appeals relied on *White* to invalidate the parts of the Minnesota judicial conduct code that had prohibited judicial candidates from attending political gatherings, from seeking political endorsements, and from personally soliciting campaign funds. See *Republican Party of Minnesota v. White*, 416 F.3d 738 (8th Cir. 2005). On January 23, 2006, the U.S. Supreme Court, without comment, turned down Minnesota's appeal to the circuit court decision. See *Dimick v. Republican Party of Minnesota*, 126 S.Ct. 1165 (2006). Similarly, on October 10, 2006, the federal district court in the Eastern District of Kentucky struck down two canons of judicial conduct in Kentucky that prevented judicial candidates from identifying themselves by political party and from personally soliciting campaign funds. See *Carey v. Wolnitzek*, 2006 U.S. Dist. LEXIS 73869 (E.D. Ky. Oct. 10, 2006). See also Charles Geyh, "Preserving Public Confidence in the Courts in an Age of Individual Rights and Public Skepticism," in Keith J. Bybee, ed., *Bench Press: The Collision of Courts, Politics, and the Media* (Stanford, CA: Stanford University Press, 2007), 21–51; Charles Geyh, *Why Judicial Elections Stink*, 64 Ohio St. L.J. 43, 43–79 (2003); G. Alan Tarr, *Rethinking the Selection of State Supreme Court Justices*, 39 Willamette L. Rev. 1445, 1445–1470 (2003); and Roy A. Schotland, "Should Judges Be More Like Politicians?," *Court Review* 39 (2002): 8–11. For surveys of *White*'s impact, see Richard Briffault, *Judicial Campaign Codes After Republican Party of Minnesota v. White*, 153 U. Pa. L. Rev. 181, 181–238 (2004); David Schultz, *Republican Party of Minnesota v. White and the Future of Judicial Selection*, 69 Alb. L. Rev. 985, 985–1011 (2004); and Rachel P. Caufield, "The Changing Tone of Judicial Election Campaigns as a Result of *White*," in Matthew J. Streb, ed., *Running for Judge: The Rising Political, Financial, and Legal Stakes of Judicial Elections* (New York: New York University Press, 2007), 34–58. For the argument that *White* has had no negative affect on the already political nature of state supreme court elections, see Bonneau and Hall, *In Defense of Judicial Elections*.

18. Greenberg, Quinlan, Rosner Research Inc., "Justice at Stake National Survey of American Voters, October 30–November 7, 2001," http://faircourts.org/files/JASNational SurveyResults.pdf (last accessed August 30, 2009). See also Deborah L. Hensler, *Do We Need an Empirical Research Agenda on Judicial Independence?*, 72 S. Cal. L. Rev. 707, 710–14 (1999).

19. Greenberg, Quinlan, Rosner Research Inc., "Justice at Stake National Survey of State Judges, November 5, 2001–January 2, 2002." http://faircourts.org/files/JASJudges SurveyResults.pdf (last accessed August 30, 2009).

20. *Caperton v. A.T. Massey Coal Co.*, 129 S. Ct. 2252 (2009). For the argument that the logic of *Caperton* ultimately calls into question the constitutionality of judicial elec-

tions, see Pamela S. Karlan, *Electing Judges, Judging Elections, and the Lessons of Caperton*, 123 HARV. L. REV. 80 (2009).

21. Briffault, *Judicial Campaign Codes*, at 211. The dissenters in *White* squarely endorsed this same understanding of judicial impartiality. See *White*, 536 U.S. at 797–821. The majority was more reserved in its judgment about the importance of what it called judicial "open-mindedness" or a "quality in a judge [that] demands, not that he have no preconceptions on legal issues, but that he be willing to consider views that oppose his preconceptions, and remain open to persuasion, when the issues arise in a pending case." *White*, 536 U.S. at 778. The majority ruled that it need not decide whether judicial open-mindedness constituted a compelling governmental interest because, as a threshold matter, a concern for judicial open-mindedness could not be effectively served by the specific restrictions on judicial campaign behavior at issue in *White*. Thus the majority concluded that it "may well be that impartiality in this sense, and the appearance of it, are desirable in the judiciary, but we need not pursue that inquiry." *White*, 536 U.S. at 778. Justice Sandra Day O'Connor, one of the justices that made up the five-member majority, later expressed regret for her decision. See Matthew Hirsch, "Swing Voter's Lament: At Least One Case Still Bugs O'Connor," *The Recorder*, November 8, 2006, http://www.law.com/jsp/article.jsp?id=1162893919695 (last accessed August 30, 2009). For an additional critique of the majority's position, and for the argument that the justices themselves all invoked the ideal of judicial open-mindedness in their own Senate confirmation hearings, see Geyh, *Why Judicial Elections Stink*, at 66.

22. American Bar Association Commission on the 21st Century Judiciary, "Justice in Jeopardy," July 11, 2003, 9, http://www.abanet.org/judind/jeopardy/pdf/report.pdf (last accessed August 30, 2009). Judicial impartiality is not only fair to individual litigants but also necessary to maintain the separation of powers among different branches of government. Where judges decide cases on the basis of party interest (rather than on the basis of the law and evidence presented in a given case), then they may become part of a single partisan coalition spanning governmental branches and chip away at the checks and balances necessary to make the separation of powers work. See Briffault, *Judicial Campaign Codes*, at 231–33; and Peter M. Shane, *Interbranch Accountability in State Government and the Constitutional Requirement of Judicial Independence*, 61 LAW & CONTEMP. PROBS. 21, 21–54 (1998).

23. Indeed, in the best Spargo-like fashion, participants in pitched political battles for judicial office are often critical of their very own political activity. See Adam Liptak, "Judicial Races in Several States Become Partisan Battlegrounds," *New York Times*, October 24, 2004, 1, 30.

24. This general finding is reported in David B. Rottman, "Public Perceptions of the State Courts: A Primer," paper prepared for presentation at the Third National Symposium on Court Management, Atlanta, Georgia, August 13–19, 2000; see also Hensler, *Do We Need an Empirical Agenda on Judicial Independence?*. Rottman reviews thirty-two

polls, but he does not report trends or specific percentages, nor does he control for question wording. With the thirteen polls in the upcoming discussion, I introduce more recent data and attempt to supply more precision in question selection.

25. Four of the polls drew from a national sample, and the other nine were conducted on a statewide basis (of these nine, two were conducted in Minnesota eight years apart). I thank Bert Brandenburg of the Justice at Stake Campaign for supplying the bulk of these polls. In chronological order, the polls are (1) Fleming and Associates, "An Analysis of Attitudes and Perspectives in the State of Rhode Island Towards the Rhode Island Court System for the Rhode Island Judicial Branch," April 1989; (2) The Survey Research Center, University of New Orleans, "Citizen Evaluation of the Louisiana Courts: A Report to the Louisiana Supreme Court, Volume I, The Survey," June 16, 1998; (3) Center for Research and Public Policy, "Statewide Public Trust and Confidence Study," prepared for the Connecticut Judicial Branch and the Connecticut Commission on Public Trust and Confidence, August 1998; (4) The National Center for State Courts, "How the Public Views the State Courts: A 1999 National Survey," presented at the Conference on Public Trust and Confidence in the Justice System, May 14, 1999, Washington, DC; (5) GMA Research Corporation, "How the Public Views the Courts: A 1999 Washington Statewide Survey Compared to a 1999 National Survey," prepared for Office of the Administrator of the Courts, State of Washington, 1999; (6) Shaening and Associates, Inc., "How New Mexicans View the State Courts: How Do We Compare to the National Picture and How Perceptions Have Changed Since 1997," prepared for the Administrative Office of the Courts, February 2000; (7) Anderson, Niebuhr and Associates, Inc., "1999–2000 Minnesota Supreme Court Public Opinion of the Courts Study," 2000; (8) Greenberg, Quinlan, Rosner Research Inc., "Justice at Stake National Survey of American Voters, October 30–November 7, 2001"; (9) Institute for Public Affairs, University of Illinois at Springfield, "2002 Illinois Statewide Survey on Judicial Selection Issues," prepared for Illinois Campaign for Political Reform, August 2002; (10) Princeton Survey Research Associates International, "2006 Annenberg Judicial Independence Survey," prepared for the Annenberg Foundation Trust at Sunnylands, August 2006; (11) James L. Gibson, "Judging the Politics of Judging: Are Politicians in Robes Inevitably Illegitimate?," paper prepared for the "What's Law Got to Do with It?" Conference, Indiana University School of Law, March 27–28, 2009—the survey discussed in the paper was conducted in 2006; (12) Justice at Stake, Minnesota Statewide Poll, conducted by Decision Resources, Ltd., January 2008; and (13) Princeton Survey Research Associates International, "Separate Branches, Shared Responsibilities: A National Survey of Public Expectations on Solving Justice Issues," conducted on Behalf of the National Center for State Courts, April 2009.

26. The impartiality questions and responses for each of the thirteen polls (following the order listed in note 25) are as follows. (1) If you had a case pending in court, you would be treated fairly. 69 percent agree. (2) Judges are fair and impartial. 57 percent

agree. (3) Connecticut courts are usually fair. 73 percent agree. (4) Judges are generally honest and fair in deciding cases. 79 percent agree. (5) Judges are generally honest and fair in deciding cases. 73 percent agree. (6) Judges are generally honest and fair in deciding cases. 73 percent agree. (7) Judges are fair when deciding cases. 69 percent agree. (8) How well does the word *impartial* describe judges? 63 percent say either "well" or "very well." (9) If you were in a lawsuit in Illinois, do you think the judge would be fair and impartial? 64 percent say yes. (10) The courts in your state can usually be trusted to make rulings that are right for the state as a whole. 64 percent agree either "strongly" or "somewhat." (11) The Kentucky Supreme Court can usually be trusted to make decisions that are right for the state as a whole. 66 percent agree. (12) How well does the word *impartial* describe judges? 78 percent say either "well" or "very well." (13) The state courts can usually be trusted to make decisions that are right for the state as a whole. 42 percent agree. The political questions and responses for each of the thirteen polls (following the order listed in note 25) are as follows. (1) Court decisions are influenced by political considerations. 71 percent agree. (2) Judges are too influenced by politics. 80 percent agree. (3) Politics play a major role in Connecticut court decisions. 75 percent agree. (4) Judges' decisions are influenced by political considerations. 81 percent agree. (5) Judges' decisions are influenced by political considerations. 76 percent agree. (6) Judges' decisions are influenced by political considerations. 81 percent agree. (7) Judges' decisions are influenced by the political parties in power. 62 percent agree. (8) How well does the word *political* describe judges? 76 percent say either "well" or "very well." (9) How well does the word *political* describe judges? 66 percent say either "quite well" or "very well." (10) The courts in your state are sometimes politically motivated in their rulings. 64 percent agree. (11) The Kentucky Supreme Court gets too mixed up in politics. 48 percent agree. (12) Judges' decisions are influenced by the political party currently in power. 77 percent agree either "strongly" or "somewhat." (13) The decisions of the state courts are too often mixed up in politics. 59 percent agree.

27. There is a developing empirical debate about precisely which aspects of state judicial behavior appear political to the public. See James L. Gibson, "Challenges to the Impartiality of State Supreme Courts: Legitimacy Theory and 'New-Style' Judicial Campaigns," *American Political Science Review* 102 (2008): 59–75; "Campaigning for the Bench: The Corrosive Effects of Campaign Speech?" *Law and Society Review* 42(2008): 899–928; and "New-Style' Judicial Campaigns and the Legitimacy of State High Courts," *The Journal of Politics* 71 (2009): 1285–1304. Some evidence suggests that campaign contributions and negative campaign advertisements detract from popular beliefs in judicial impartiality, while policy statements by judicial candidates do not have a similar effect (at least in those states that rely on elections to select or retain their judges). As this empirical debate refines our understanding of how different kinds of judicial action trigger different public responses, it also underscores the point I am making: we live in a time of contradictory judicial appearances, with large majorities of

the public seeing state judges as impartial arbiters and as political actors. Indeed, as one of the studies in this area found, people tend to hold contradictory expectations of the courts, believing at once that judicial decisionmaking will be political and that judges will strictly follow the law. See Footnote 9 of James L. Gibson, "Judging the Politics of Judging."

28. Briffault, *Judicial Campaign Codes*, at 200. For evidence that elected judges and unelected judges actually decide cases differently, see Paul Brace and Brent D. Boyea, "Judicial Selection Methods and Capital Punishment in the American States," in Matthew J. Streb, ed., *Running for Judge: The Rising Political, Financial, and Legal Stakes of Judicial Elections* (New York: New York University Press, 2007), 168–203. For evidence that elections undermine the legitimacy of state courts and state legislatures in some of the same ways, see Gibson, "Challenges to the Impartiality." For specific evidence indicating that the mere offer of a campaign contribution to a judicial candidate may undercut the public's perceived legitimacy and impartiality of that candidate, see James L. Gibson and Gregory A. Caldeira, "Campaign Support, Conflicts of Interest, and Judicial Impartiality: Can the Legitimacy of Courts Be Rescued by Recusals?" October 19, 2009, http://ssrn.com/abstract=1491289 (last accessed December 1, 2009). See also *Caperton*. The claim that the practice of judging and popular elections are incompatible is an old one. See Renee Lettow Lerner, "The New York Bar and Reform of the Elected Judiciary After the Civil War," George Washington University Law School Public Law and Legal Theory Working Paper No. 139, April 4, 2005, http://ssrn.com/abstract=697902 (last accessed August 30, 2009). See also Cheek and Champagne, *Partisan Judicial Elections*, at 1375–60. The debate over the propriety of judicial elections continues today. For arguments against judicial elections, see Geyh, *Why Judicial Elections Stink*; Steven Zeidman, *To Elect or Not to Elect: A Case Study of Judicial Selection in New York City, 1977–2002*, 37 U. MICH. J. L. REFORM 791, 791–836 (2004); and Penny J. White, *Relinquished Responsibilities*, 123 HARV. L. REV. 120 (2009). For pro-elections arguments, see Judicial Elections White Paper Task Force, *Judicial Selection White Papers*; Peter Paul Olszewski Sr. *Who's Judging Whom? Why Popular Elections are Preferable to Merit Selection Systems*, 109 PENN ST. L. REV 1, 1–16 (2004); and Harold See, "An Essay on Judicial Selection," in Keith J. Bybee, ed., *Bench Press: The Collision of Courts, Politics, and the Media* (Stanford, CA: Stanford University Press, 2007), 77–113. For an argument in favor of the legislative (as opposed to popular) election of judges, see Joanne F. Alper, "Selecting the Judiciary: Who Should Be the Judge?," in Keith J. Bybee, ed., *Bench Press: The Collision of Courts, Politics, and the Media* (Stanford, CA: Stanford University Press, 2007), 131–50.

29. Cheek and Champagne, *Partisan Judicial Elections*, at 1359–60.

30. Sample, Jones, and Weiss, "New Politics of Judicial Elections," at 25.

31. Larry T. Aspin and William K. Hall, *Retention Elections and Judicial Behavior*, 77 JUDICATURE 307 (1994). Of course, not all retention elections are uncontroversial.

See Traciel V. Reid, *The Politicization of Retention Elections: Lessons from the Defeat of Justices Lanphier and White*, 83 JUDICATURE 68, 68–77 (1999).

32. Larry T. Aspin, *Trends in Judicial Retention Elections, 1964–1998*, 83 JUDICATURE 79, 79–81 (1999); Aspin and Hall, *Retention Elections*, at 307.

33. Robert F. Bauer, *Thoughts on the Democratic Basis for Restrictions on Judicial Campaign Speech*, 35 IND. L. REV. 747, 750 (2002).

34. Randall T. Shepard, *Telephone Justice, Pandering, and Judges Who Speak Out of School*, 29 FORDHAM URB. L.J. 811, 811–25 (2002); and *What Judges Can Do About Legal Professionalism*, 32 WAKE FOREST L. REV. 621, 621–33 (1997). For the argument that electorally insulated state judges issue more deliberative decisions than directly elected judges, see Michael J. Woodruff, "Deliberative Expectations and Electoral Incentives for State Supreme Court Justices," March 30, 2009, http://ssrn.com/abstract=1440868 (last accessed December 1, 2009).

35. The line of scholarship reaching this conclusion stretches back more than three decades. See Malia Reddick, *Merit Selection: A Review of the Social Scientific Literature*, 106 DICK. L. REV. 729, 729–45 (2002).

36. For a personal account of appointment politics, see James E. Graves Jr., "Judicial Independence: The Courts and the Media," in Keith J. Bybee, ed., *Bench Press: The Collision of Courts, Politics, and the Media* (Stanford, CA: Stanford University Press, 2007), 114–122.

37. Aspin and Hall, *Retention Elections*, at 312–15.

38. Gregory A. Huber and Sanford C. Gordon, "Accountability and Coercion: Is Justice Blind When It Runs for Office?" *American Journal of Political Science* 48 (2004): 247–63; and Brandice Canes-Wrone, Tom S. Clark, and Jee-Kwang Park, "Judicial Independence and Retention Elections," September 19, 2009, http://ssrn.com/abstract=1475657 (last accessed December 1, 2009).

39. The National Center for State Courts, "How the Public Views the State Courts." In this vein, it is also worth noting that two of the surveys I discuss in notes 25 and 26 are from states that do not have judicial elections (Connecticut and Rhode Island). In both instances, a strong majority of respondents say that state judicial decisions are influenced by politics. Of course, as one might expect given the conflicting nature of the public's views, the flipside is that the public also tends to see appointed and elected judges as equally impartial. When asked whether judges appointed to office are more likely, less likely, or just as likely to be as fair and impartial as judges who are elected, 42 percent said "just as likely." See Princeton Survey Research Associates International, "2006 Annenberg Judicial Independence Survey." It is also the case that the public credibility of the courts varies little between states that elect their supreme courts and those that do not. See Princeton Survey Research Associates International, "Separate Branches, Shared Responsibilities." Moreover, as the other eleven polls in notes 25 and 26 show, the residents in states with judicial elections have as much or

more faith in the fairness of their state courts as the residents of Rhode Island and Connecticut.

40. Tarr, *Rethinking the Selection*, at 1459, and "Politicizing the Process." See also William D. Popkin, *Evolution of Judicial Opinion: Institutional and Individual Styles* (New York: New York University Press, 2007), 127–41; Michael R. Dimino, *Judicial Elections Versus Merit Selection: The Futile Quest for a System of Judicial "Merit" Selection*, 67 ALB. L. REV. 803, 803–19 (2004); and Bonneau and Hall, *In Defense of Judicial Elections*, 14–15.

41. The caseload in state courts has ballooned in recent decades: from 1987 to 2004 non-traffic state court case filings grew by almost 45 percent (Langton and Cohen, *State Court Organization*, 1). As the caseload has increased, the number of fragmented judicial opinions issued by state supreme courts has grown (Popkin, *Evolution*, 128, 135–41). The role of ideology in judicial decisionmaking is perhaps most evident in politically charged constitutional disputes, but this is not the only place such influence can be found. For the argument that ideology shapes judicial decisionmaking even in highly technical fields of law, see Banks Miller and Brett Curry, "Expertise, Experience, and Ideology on Specialized Courts: The Case of the Court of Appeals for the Federal Circuit," *Law and Society Review* 43 (2009): 839–64.

42. Tarr, Rethinking the Selection, at 1460. For empirical evidence of such cynicism, see Gibson, "Challenges to the Impartiality," 66–67, in which survey respondents, when asked to recall a hypothetical vignette that they had been read, reported that judges had received campaign contributions and made policy promises even though the hypothetical vignette in fact made no mention of either contributions or promises.

43. *Constitution of the United States*, Art. III, sec. 1.

44. Alexander Hamilton, "Federalist Paper No. 78," in Alexander Hamilton, James Madison, and John Jay, *The Federalist Papers*, Clinton Rossiter, ed. (New York: Mentor, 1961), 465, 469. On the Federalists in general, see Gordon S. Wood, *The Creation of the American Republic, 1776–1787* (New York: Norton, 1972).

45. "Essays of Brutus" in Herbert Storing, ed., *The Anti-Federalist* (Chicago: University of Chicago Press, 1985), 183. On the Anti-Federalists in general, see Cecelia Kenyon, "Introduction," in Cecelia Kenyon, ed., *The Anti-Federalists* (Indianapolis: Bobbs-Merrill, 1966); and Herbert J. Storing (with the editorial assistance of Murray Dry), *What the Anti-Federalists Were For: The Political Thought of the Opponents of the Constitution* (Chicago: University of Chicago Press, 1981). In noting the objections made by the Anti-Federalists, I am not suggesting that there was a deep and bitter divide over life tenure for federal judges at the founding. In fact, the Anti-Federalists, for the most part, did not strongly oppose life tenure during the ratification process. See Charles Gardner Geyh, *When Courts and Congress Collide: The Struggle for Control of America's Judicial System* (Ann Arbor: University of Michigan Press, 2006), 24–44.

46. Sanford Levinson, *Bush v. Gore and the French Revolution: A Tentative List of Some Early Lessons*, 65 LAW & CONTEMP. PROBS. 7, 11 (2002); see also John Ferejohn, *Judicializing Politics, Politicizing Law*, 65 LAW & CONTEMP. PROBS. 41, 64 (2002); and Brian Z. Tamanaha, "The Perils of Pervasive Instrumentalism," Montesquieu Lecture Series, Tilburg University, 1 (2005): 49–56, http://ssrn.com/abstract=725582 (last accessed August 30, 2009). As I noted earlier, there is also evidence that ideology shapes judicial decisionmaking even in highly technical fields of law. See Miller and Curry, "Expertise, Experience, and Ideology."

47. Laurence H. Tribe, *American Constitutional Law*, 3rd ed., Vol. I (New York: Foundation Press, 2000).

48. Laurence H. Tribe, "An Open Letter to Readers of *American Constitutional Law*," April 29, 2005, 9, http://www.scotusblog.com/movabletype/archives/Tribe-Treatise-Green%20Bag%202005%20low%20res.pdf (last accessed August 30, 2009).

49. Popkin, *Evolution*, 118.

50. Partisanship plays a prominent role from the very start of the appointments process. Studies show that roughly 90 percent of both lower federal court and Supreme Court nominations have gone to candidates with the same party affiliations as the nominating president. Indeed, the majority of judicial nominees are more than fellow party members: they are party activists with established records of organizing, campaigning, or fundraising on their party's behalf. See Lee Epstein and Jeffrey A. Segal, *Advice and Consent: The Politics of Judicial Appointments* (New York: Oxford University Press, 2005), 26–27, 60–61. For a demonstration that the Supreme Court nomination process (and, in particular, the political spots run by interest groups during the process) lead public opinion to a political view of the Court, see James L. Gibson and Gregory A. Caldeira, "Supreme Court Nominations, Legitimacy Theory and the American Public: A Dynamic Test of the Theory of Positivity Bias," July 4, 2007, http://ssrn.com/abstract=998283 (last accessed August 30, 2009).

51. Mark Silverstein, *Judicious Choices: The New Politics of Supreme Court Confirmations* (New York: W.W. Norton, 1994).

52. Sarah Binder and Forrest Maltzman, "Senatorial Delay in Confirming Federal Judges," *American Journal of Political Science* 46 (2002): 190–99; and Tajuana D. Massie, Thomas G. Hansford, and Donald Songer, "The Timing of Presidential Nominations to the Lower Federal Courts," *Political Research Quarterly* 57 (2004): 145–54. This general point was spectacularly illustrated in the 2005 battles over the Senate's use of the filibuster in judicial confirmations. For histories of the growing contentiousness of federal court nominations, see Nancy Scherer, *Scoring Points: Politicians, Activists, and the Lower Federal Court Appointments Process* (Stanford, CA: Stanford University Press, 2005); and Roger E. Hartley and Lisa M. Holmes, "The Increasing Senate Scrutiny of Lower Federal Court Nominees," *Political Science Quarterly* 117 (2002): 259–78.

53. Rorie L. Spill and Zoe M. Oxley, *Philosopher Kings or Political Actors? How the Media Portray the Supreme Court*, 87 JUDICATURE 23, 23–39 (2003). For critiques of media practice, see Ruth Bader Ginsburg, *Speaking in a Judicial Voice*, 67 N.Y.U. L. REV. 1185, 1191–92 (1992); Mark Obbie, "Winners and Losers," in Keith J. Bybee, ed., *Bench Press: The Collision of Courts, Politics, and the Media* (Stanford, CA: Stanford University Press, 2007), 153–76; Dahlia Lithwick, "The Internet and the Judiciary: We Are All Experts Now," in Keith J. Bybee, ed., *Bench Press: The Collision of Courts, Politics, and the Media* (Stanford, CA: Stanford University Press, 2007), 177–84; and Tom Goldstein, "The Distance Between Judges and Journalists," in Keith J. Bybee, ed., *Bench Press: The Collision of Courts, Politics, and the Media* (Stanford, CA: Stanford University Press, 2007), 185–96.

54. The scholarly literature documenting the decline of consensus on the Supreme Court is large. See, for example, Thomas G. Walker, Lee Epstein, and William Dixon, "On the Mysterious Demise of Consensual Norms in the United States Supreme Court," *The Journal of Politics* 50 (1988): 361–89; Scott D. Gerber and Keeok Park, "The Quixotic Search for Consensus on the U.S. Supreme Court: A Cross-Judicial Empirical Analysis of the Rehnquist Court Justices," *American Political Science Review* 91 (1997): 390–408; Gregory A. Caldeira and Christopher Zorn, "Of Time and Consensual Norms on the Supreme Court," *American Journal of Political Science* 42 (1998): 874–902; Sandra L. Wood, Linda Camp Keith, Drew Noble Lanier, and Ayo Ogundele, "The Supreme Court, 1888–1940: An Empirical Analysis," *Social Science History* 22 (1998): 201–24; Robert Post, *The Supreme Court Opinion as an Institutional Practice: Dissent, Legal Scholarship, and Decisionmaking in the Taft Court*, 85 MINN. L. REV. 1267, 1267–1390 (2001); Lee Epstein, Jeffrey A. Segal, and Harold J. Spaeth, "The Norm of Consensus on the Supreme Court," *American Journal of Political Science* 45 (2001): 362–77; and *Nine Justices, Ten Years: A Statistical Retrospective*, 118 HARV. L. REV. 510, 510–23 (2004).

55. The quoted phrase comes from Gerber and Park, "Quixotic Search," 391.

56. It is for this reason that Chief Justice Roberts has called for greater unanimity on the Court. See Jeffery Rosen, "Roberts's Rules," *The Atlantic Monthly* (January/February 2007), http://www.theatlantic.com/doc/200701/john-roberts (last accessed August 30, 2009).

57. See Walker, Epstein, and Dixon, "Mysterious Demise," 362. For the argument that the rise in dissents serves the Court's political purposes, see M. Todd Henderson, *From Seriatim to Consensus and Back Again: A Theory of Dissent*, 2007 SUPREME COURT REVIEW 283, 283–344 (2007). The sense of a "politicized" Court also extends to the decision of which law clerks to hire. Scholars have found that over the course of the twentieth century Supreme Court justices have increasingly drawn clerks from courts of appeals judges who are ideologically similar to themselves. See Lawrence Baum, *Judges and Their Audiences: A Perspective on Judicial Behavior* (Princeton, NJ: Princeton University Press, 2006), 129–31. In turn, Supreme Court clerks end up pursuing politically

divergent career paths. See William E. Nelson, Harvey Rishikof, I. Scott Messinger, and Michael Jo, *The Supreme Court Clerkship and the Polarization of the Court: Can the Polarization Be Fixed?*, 13 GREEN BAG 2D 59 (Autumn 2009).

58. John Russonello, "Speak to Values: How to Promote the Courts and Blunt Attacks on the Judiciary," *Court Review* (Summer 2004): 10–12; John M. Scheb II and William Lyons, "Judicial Behavior and Public Opinion: Popular Expectations Regarding Factors That Influence Supreme Court Decisions," *Political Behavior* 23 (2001): 181–94; and Gibson and Caldeira, "Supreme Court Nominations." For the argument that important subsets of the general public, such as lawyers and legal scholars, constitute especially important judicial audiences that place a strong emphasis on legal reasoning and skilled legal interpretation, see Baum, *Judges and Their Audiences*, chapter 4. Such elites appear to have a particularly strong belief in the Court's legal nature. When surveyed, 80 percent of lawyers admitted to practice in either the U.S. Supreme Court or a U.S. court of appeals agreed with the statement "Most of the time the Supreme Court Justices closely follow the Constitution, the law, and the precedents in deciding cases." Kevin T. McGuire, "The Judicial Branch: Judging America's Judges," in Kathleen Hall Jamieson, ed., *A Republic Divided: The Annenberg Democracy Project* (New York: Oxford University Press, 2007), 202.

59. Gregory A. Caldeira and James L. Gibson, "The Etiology of Public Support for the Supreme Court," *American Political Science Review* 36 (1992): 635–64; James L. Gibson, Gregory A. Caldeira, and Lester Kenyatta Spence, "Measuring Attitudes Toward the United States Supreme Court," *American Journal of Political Science* 47 (2003): 354–76; James L. Gibson, "The Legitimacy of the U.S. Supreme Court in a Polarized Polity," *Journal of Empirical Legal Studies* 4 (2007): 507–38; and Gibson and Caldeira, "Supreme Court Nominations."

60. "Judicial Independence, Final Report September 2006," prepared for Annenberg Public Policy Center, September 2006, http://www.annenbergpublicpolicycenter. org/ (last accessed August 30, 2009). See also McGuire, "Judicial Branch."

61. "Poll: Americans Don't Want Politicians Constraining Judges," CNN.com, October 28, 2006, http://www.cnn.com/2006/POLITICS/10/27/activist.judges/ (last accessed August 30, 2009).

62. Richard W. Stevenson and Neil A. Lewis, "Alito Says Judges Shouldn't Bring Agenda to Cases," *New York Times*, January 9, 2006, A1, A16. See also John M. Walker Jr., "Politics and the Confirmation Process: Thoughts on the Roberts and Alito Hearings," in Keith J. Bybee, ed., *Bench Press: The Collision of Courts, Politics, and the Media* (Stanford, CA: Stanford University Press, 2007), 123–30; and American Bar Association, "Justice in Jeopardy."

63. Belden Russonello and Stewart Communications, "Americans Consider Judicial Independence: Findings of a National Survey Regarding Attitudes Toward the Federal Courts," April 1998. As is the case with surveys of opinions about state judges (including

the polls discussed in notes 25 and 26), the very same polls that indicate strong political skepticism of the federal judges also indicate a strong belief in the impartiality of federal judges. Thus the Belden et. al. poll finds that 67 percent of those surveyed believe the terms *fair* and *impartial* describe the federal courts either very or somewhat well. For the argument that the forms of public support for federal and state courts are nonetheless different because citizens are more likely to have had personal experience in state courts, see Susan M. Olson and David A. Huth, "Explaining Public Attitudes Toward Local Courts," *The Justice System Journal* 20 (1998): 41–61.

64. Gibson and Caldeira, "Supreme Court Nominations," 51, table 1. See also Gibson et. al., "Measuring Attitudes," 358; Scheb and Lyons, "Judicial Behavior," 184–90; Gibson, "Legitimacy of the U.S. Supreme Court," 519; and James L. Gibson, Gregory A. Caldeira, and Lester Kenyatta Spence, "Why Do People Accept Public Policies They Oppose? Testing Legitimacy Theory with a Survey-Based Experiment," *Political Research Quarterly* 58 (2005): 187–201. According to some polls, up to 70 percent of Americans agree that the Court favors some groups more than others (McGuire, "The Judicial Branch," 203).

65. Thirteen polls conducted by the Gallup Poll News Service from 2000 through 2007 show that Americans' overall ratings of the Court are clearly related to their party affiliation. See Gallup Poll News Service, "Slim Majority of Americans Approve of the Supreme Court," September 26, 2007, http://www.gallup.com/poll/28798/Slim-Majority-Americans-Approve-Supreme-Court.aspx (last accessed August 30, 2009).

66. The Pew Research Center for the People & the Press, "Court Critics Now on Both Left and Right: Supreme Court's Image Declines as Nomination Battles Loom, National Survey Conducted June 8–12, 2005," http://people-press.org/report/247/supreme-courts-image-declines-as-nomination-battle-looms (last accessed August 30, 2009). There is also some evidence indicating that conservatives react to judicial decisions they dislike differently than liberals do, with conservatives considering the Court to be less legitimate when it issues a disfavored decision while liberals' rating of Court legitimacy remains largely unaffected by their evaluation of an individual decision. See Patrick J. Egan and Jack Citrin, "Opinion Leadership, Backlash, and Delegitimation: Supreme Court Rulings and Public Opinion," August 4, 2009, http://ssrn.com/abstract=1443631 (last accessed December 1, 2009). For extended discussions of how opinion elites and African Americans evaluate the Supreme Court in political terms, see Caldeira and Gibson, "Etiology of Public Support," 655–58; Gibson, "Legitimacy of the U.S. Supreme Court," 531; and James L. Gibson and Gregory A. Caldeira, "Blacks and the United States Supreme Court: Models of Diffuse Support," *The Journal of Politics* 54 (1992): 1120–45.

67. Susan Page, "What Americans Want in O'Connor Court Vacancy," *USA Today*, July 13, 2005, http://www.usatoday.com/news/nation/2005-07-13-court-cover_x.htm (last accessed August 30, 2009).

68. As I indicated in note 58, specific subsets in the population may come down a bit differently on this issue. The less educated are somewhat more likely to see the Supreme Court in political terms, while lawyers admitted to practice in federal appellate courts and the Supreme Court are somewhat more likely to see the high bench in legal terms (See McGuire, "The Judicial Branch").

69. The survey was of both state and federal judges in the 6th, 7th, and 8th Circuits. The responses of the two classes of judges were not tabulated separately, although there was some indication that state judges were slightly more likely to agree that courts were under increasing pressure to be directly accountable to public opinion. See Kevin M. Esterling, *Judicial Independence, Public Confidence in Courts, and State-Federal Cooperation in the Midwest: A Research Report on the Midwest Regional Conference on State-Federal Judicial Relationships with Survey Findings and Recommendations* (Chicago: American Judicature Society, 1998).

70. For the argument that judges compulsively reassert their legal standing whenever confronted with political perceptions of their decisions in the same way that individuals coming out of the closet compulsively reassert their heterosexuality when confronted with evidence of being gay or lesbian, see Susan Burgess, *The Founding Fathers, Pop Culture, and Constitutional Law* (Burlington, VT: Ashgate Publishing, 2008), 93–94. For an exception to the general rule of judges asserting their apolitical approach, see Theodore A. McKee, *Judges as Umpires*, 35 Hofstra. L. Rev. 1709, 1709–24 (2007).

71. Alex Kozinski, *What I Ate for Breakfast and Other Mysteries of Judicial Decision Making*, 26 Loy. L.A. L. Rev. 993, 993–94, 997 (1993). For a similar message delivered in different language, see John M. Walker Jr., *Current Threats to Judicial Independence and Appropriate Responses: A Presentation to the American Bar Association*, 12 St. John's J. Legal Comment. 45, 45–58 (1996). Like sitting federal judges, nominees to the federal bench also routinely distance themselves from any hint of political judging. For instance, during his confirmation hearings, William G. Myers III, a nominee for the Ninth Circuit Court of Appeals, faced criticism that his past work as a lobbyist for the mining and timber industries compromised his ability to judge environmental disputes impartially. As Senator Charles Schumer told Myers, "Your record screams 'passionate advocate' and it doesn't even whisper 'impartial judge.'" In response, Myers insisted that his record of anti-environmentalist remarks would not follow him onto the bench; he had been "a forceful advocate for my clients" and, if confirmed, he would be "a forceful advocate for the law." See Neil A. Lewis, "Democrats on Senate Panel Pummel Judicial Nominee," *New York Times*, March 2, 2005, A16. Similarly, John G. Roberts Jr. criticized the idea of political judging in his confirmation hearings for the D.C. Circuit (Roberts joined the Supreme Court two years later). See Jeffrey Toobin, "Sex and the Supremes," *The New Yorker*, August 1, 2005, 32–7.

72. Alex Kozinski, "The Appearance of Propriety," *Legal Affairs* (January/February 2005), http://www.legalaffairs.org/issues/January-February-2005/argument_kozinski_janfeb05.msp (last accessed August 30, 2009).

73. *Bush v. Gore*, 531 U.S. 98 (2000). Linda Greenhouse, "The 43rd President: Another Kind of Bitter Split," *New York Times*, December 14, 2000, A1.

74. Greenhouse, "The 43rd President," A1.

75. Although I have treated the state judiciary and federal judiciary as units for purposes of discussion, there are different kinds of courts within each judiciary, including trial courts, appellate courts, and specialty courts devoted to particular subjects. One could argue that each type of court, like the state and federal judiciaries overall, also generates conflicting political and legal appearances. For example, as arbiters of first instance, trial judges may appear to be governed by principle because they are more likely than appellate judges to find themselves handling those conflicts that can be addressed with straightforward applications of existing precedent. On the other hand, trial judges may use their own preferences and political commitments to shape legal proceedings in a number of ways (see Frank, *Law and the Modern Mind* and my discussion in note 100). Similarly, one could argue that decisionmaking in substantively specialized courts is more likely to be driven by technical knowledge than by partisan preference, leading the public to see the judges serving on specialized courts as neutral experts rather than as political actors. At the same time, the specialized courts have also been shown to be arenas where the political beliefs of judges are influential (see Miller and Curry, "Expertise, Experience, and Ideology").

76. Lynn Mather, "Courts in Popular Culture," in Kermit L. Hall and Kevin T. McGuire, eds., *The Judicial Branch* (New York: Oxford University Press, 2005), 233–61. See also Susan Bandes, *We Lost It at the Movies: The Rule of Law Goes from Washington to Hollywood and Back Again*, 40 Loy. L.A. L. Rev. 539 (2007). There are also other images of judges in popular culture. For assessments, see Steven A. Kohm, "The People's Law Versus Judge Judy Justice: Two Models of Law in American Reality-Based Courtroom TV," *Law and Society Review* 40 (2006): 693–727; and David Ray Papke, "From Flat to Round: Changing Portrayals of the Judge in American Popular Culture," Marquette Law School Legal Studies Paper No. 06-24, May 2006, http://ssrn.com/abstract=902125 (last accessed August 30, 2009).

77. Syracuse University's Campbell Public Affairs Institute, "The Maxwell Poll on Civic Engagement and Inequality," October 2005, <http://www.maxwell.syr.edu/campbell/programs/maxwellpoll/data.htm> (last accessed August 30, 2009). The sample size was 609 and the margin of error was plus or minus 5 percent. I should note that the minor discrepancies between the results listed on the Web and the results listed above are due to the fact that that the Web link reports unweighted scores while the text above reports data weighted so that the presence of age, sex, and race groups within the overall results are equivalent to that of the population in the continental United States.

For analysis of this poll in addition to the analysis supplied in the text, see Keith J. By-bee, "The Two Faces of Judicial Power," in Keith J. Bybee, ed., *Bench Press: The Collision of Courts, Politics, and the Media* (Stanford, CA: Stanford University Press, 2007), 1–17.

78. As other surveys have shown, when given a choice between electing and appointing federal judges, large majorities of Americans, across all race, age, income, and education-level groups, prefer election. Belden et. al., "Americans Consider Judicial Independence."

79. Liberals (77 percent), moderates (82 percent), conservatives, (77 percent), frequent church goers (78 percent), non-church goers (83 percent), and "distrusting" respondents (73 percent).

80. People demand judicial involvement (47 percent), elected officials fail to deal with the controversies themselves (21 percent), judges are activist (11 percent). The political ideology of respondents does play a role here. Conservatives (19 percent) are more likely than liberals (8 percent) to say that many conflicts end up in court because judges actively involve themselves in controversies. Given the amount of conservative rhetoric about the errant ways of "activist judges," it is not surprising to find a difference of opinion between conservatives and liberals on this question. Even so, it is worth noting that the most common response of both conservatives (46 percent) and liberals (52 percent) was to say that many conflicts end up in court because most people want to get the courts involved. Thus, in spite of the steady stream of conservative criticism targeting judicial activism, a large plurality of conservatives nonetheless believe that crowded, controversial court dockets are the result of popular demand. In a related vein, it is worth noting that nearly three-quarters of Americans believe that state courts should maintain their ability to decide controversial issues. This strong majority generally holds across party lines. See Princeton Survey Research Associates International, "Separate Branches, Shared Responsibilities."

81. Princeton Survey Research Associates International, "2006 Annenberg Judicial Independence Survey."

82. In other words, the public seems cynical about the courts, but not entirely so. If the public was wholly cynical, then a new kind of legal system would be in order. For a development of this point in slightly different terms, see note 12. For a more thoroughly cynical view of the American courts, as well as an indication of the changes to the legal system such cynicism would entail, see J. Mark Ramseyer, "Not So Ordinary Judges in Ordinary Courts: Teaching *Jordan v. Duff & Phelps*," Harvard Law and Economics Discussion Paper No. 557, August 2006, http://ssrn.com/abstract=927862 (last accessed August 30, 2009). Suppose, Ramseyer writes, that judges "are only modestly intelligent, frequently wrong, badly harried, and in the pockets of the lawyers who funded their reelection campaigns; or that juries only randomly determine the facts correctly. Suppose, in short, that we live in the world that we do. If so, then the right legal rule may not be the one that places the loss on the least cost-avoider. In a second-best world, the

right legal rule is not one that tries to get the 'right result' every time. . . . [In this world], the easiest rule to implement is . . . : tell the plaintiff to get lost" (7–8).

83. In saying that the judicial process is appearing more evidently political, I am not arguing that politicization of the judiciary process is merely a modern phenomenon. Consider judicial appointments. It is true, as Epstein and Segal write, that "the appointments process is and always has been mired in politics" (*Advice and Consent*, 119; although, as Scherer demonstrates, the form that appointment politics has taken—at least for the lower federal courts—has changed markedly over American history; see *Scoring Points*). For my purposes, the important point is that the politics of judicial appointments has become more publicly apparent. As Epstein and Segal note, even though the confirmation of Supreme Court nominees has always been political, Court confirmations now unfold in the glare of unprecedented media coverage (*Advice and Consent*, 94). This increased publicity, coupled with the other factors I have discussed, has raised the public profile of judicial politics.

84. Geyh, *When Courts and Congress Collide*, 263.

85. Anthony Lewis, "Afterword: The State of Judicial Independence. A similar concern is voiced by virtually all of the authors in the Bybee volume.

86. The *Oxford English Dictionary*, 2nd ed. (Oxford: Oxford University Press, 1989) defines *hypocrisy* as "the assuming of a false appearance of virtue or goodness, with dissimulation of real character or inclinations, especially in respect to religious life or beliefs." According to *OED*, the earliest mention of the word *hypocrite* (from the year 1225) is in a religious context. See also William Ian Miller, *Faking It* (New York: Cambridge University Press, 2003).

87. For discussions of different kinds of insincerity, see Christine McKinnon, "Varieties of Insincerity," *International Journal of Applied Philosophy* 20 (2006): 23–40; and Harry G. Frankfurt, *On Bullshit* (Princeton, NJ: Princeton University Press, 2005).

88. Both definitions in this paragraph are from the *OED*. It is also worth noting that hypocrisy, unlike insincerity, is connected with the act of judgment. At its etymological root, hypocrisy is a composite of the Greek *hypo* (under or lower) and *krinein* (to decide, determine, judge). See the *OED*.

89. James L. Gibson and Gregory A. Caldeira, "Have Segal and Spaeth Damaged the Legitimacy of the U.S. Supreme Court?," July 17, 2009, http://ssrn.com/abstract=1436426 (last accessed August 30, 2009).

90. *Ibid.*, 13.

91. *Ibid.*

92. Ultimately, Gibson and Caldeira do not interpret this finding as a sign that Supreme Court legitimacy is in crisis, and neither do I. Yet we reach our shared conclusion by different means. Gibson and Caldeira argue that the political view of the Court does not undermine Court legitimacy because people understand Court politics to be a matter of principled ideological decisionmaking. I take a different approach (as indicated in Part

III). Let me say two things here. First, Gibson and Caldeira concede that they are only discussing a relatively small portion of the public when they talk about Americans who believe the Court has a high level of discretion that is exercised in a principled, political way (around 75 percent of the public does not hold this view). Second, as I note in my discussion of Peretti's work further on, the claim of principled and consistent ideological decisionmaking is contrary to how participants in the judicial process actually describe their own actions. Clearly, one can coherently talk about consistent ideological decision-making—but that talk simply is not the stuff of legal argument. Instead, the judicial process is filled with claims of impartiality, and these claims are at odds with the political perceptions of the courts. The task, as I see it, is to explore the significance of this tension.

93. Martin Shapiro, *Courts: A Comparative and Political Analysis* (Chicago: University of Chicago Press, 1981).

94. Dennis F. Thompson, "Hypocrisy and Democracy," in Bernard Yack, ed., *Liberalism Without Illusions: Essays on Liberal Theory and the Political Vision of Judith Shklar* (Chicago: University of Chicago Press, 1996), 173–90.

95. The quotations in this paragraph are from Brian Z. Tamanaha, *Law as a Means to an End: Threat to the Rule of Law* (New York: Cambridge University Press, 2006), 225.

96. I thank Brian Tamanaha for suggesting this example.

97. Lawrence Baum, *The Puzzle of Judicial Behavior* (Ann Arbor: University of Michigan Press, 1997), 127; Baum, *Judges and Their Audiences*, 173. See also Andreas Schedler, "Arguing and Observing: Internal and External Critiques of Judicial Impartiality," *The Journal of Political Philosophy* 12 (2004): 245–65.

98. On the link between popular perceptions of judicial legitimacy and the courts' capacity to pin decisions on "the law," see James L. Gibson, Gregory A. Caldeira, and Vanessa Baird, "On the Legitimacy of National High Courts," *American Political Science Review* 92 (1998): 343–58; Trevor L. Brown and Charles R. Wise, "Constitutional Courts and Legislative-Executive Relations: The Case of Ukraine," *Political Science Quarterly* 119 (2004): 143–69; and Gibson and Caldeira, "Segal and Spaeth." For a discussion of how the Court's "mantle of legality" increases public acquiescence of unpopular decisions, see Gibson et. al. "Why Do People Accept." For a discussion of the importance of perceptions of fairness at the level of local and state courts, see Olson and Huth, "Explaining Public Attitudes," and Kevin Buckler, Francis T. Cullen, and James D. Unnever, "Citizen Assessment of Local Criminal Courts: Does Fairness Matter?" *Journal of Criminal Justice* 35 (2007): 524–36.

99. For evidence that the appearance of judicial bias reflects the presence of actual bias, see Chris W. Bonneau and Damon M. Cann, "The Effect of Campaign Contributions on Judicial Decisionmaking," February 4, 2009, http://ssrn.com/abstract=1337668 (last accessed August 30, 2009).

100. See Peter David Blanck, Robert Rosenthal, and LaDoris Hazzard Cordell, *Note: The Appearance of Justice: Judges' Verbal and Nonverbal Behavior in Criminal Jury*

Trials, 38 Stan. L. Rev. 89, 89–90 (1985); and Peter David Blanck, *Calibrating the Scales of Justice: Studying Judges' Behavior in Bench Trials*, 68 Ind. L.J. 1119, 1119–98 (1993). See also *Caperton*. Blanck and his coauthors argue that in spite of efforts to appear impartial, information about judicial preferences often "leaks out" in a wide range of nonverbal cues.

101. In this paragraph and the next, I draw on Geyh, "Preserving Public Confidence."

102. *Ibid.*, 29.

103. The Code of Conduct for United States Judges, adopted in 2009, contains the first-ever definition of "appearance of impropriety" to appear in the federal code— a move that advances the trend toward regulating judicial appearances. See Code of Conduct for United States Judges, Canon 2, http://www.uscourts.gov/library/code OfConduct/Revised_Code_Effective_July-01-09.pdf (last accessed August 30, 2009). For instances in which judges have been disciplined for failing to appear impartial, see James J. Alfini, Steven Lubet, Jeffrey M. Shaman, and Charles Gardner Geyh (eds.), *Judicial Conduct and Ethics* 4th ed. (Newark, NJ: LexisNexis Matthew Bender, 2007), Appendix A, A-1, A-4, Tables 1 and 2. Of course, with a political view of judges held by much of the public, one should expect that some will object to the Code's special emphasis on regulating the appearance of judicial behavior and argue instead that judges should be more or less free to behave like other elected officials so long as individual judges may be recused if they cannot actually be impartial in a given case. Geyh details this alternative view in "Preserving Public Confidence." See also Deborah Goldberg, James Sample, and David Pozen, *The Best Defense: Why Elected Courts Should Lead Recusal Reform*, 46 Washburn L.J. 504, 504–34 (2007). In fact, in its reevaluation of the Code in 2007, the American Bar Association's special commission charged with updating the Code initially stated that it would change the instruction to "avoid impropriety and the appearance of impropriety" from an enforceable, mandatory rule to nonbinding advice. See Adam Liptak, "A.B.A. Panel Would Weaken Code Governing Judges' Conduct," *New York Times*, February 6, 2007, http://www.nytimes.com/2007/02/06/ us/06aba.html?ex=1171688400&en=a94f7b90a925703c&ei=5070&emc=eta1 (last accessed August 30, 2009). The announcement was greeted with controversy and led one of the commission's advisors to resign in protest. The commission then reversed itself and reinstated the Code's original formulation. See James Podgers, "Judging Judicial Behavior," *ABA Journal eReport*, February 16, 2007, http://www.abanet.org/journal/ereport/f16code .html (last accessed August 30, 2009).

104. The quotations are from Ferejohn, *Judicializing Politics*, at 65. For an empirical study of how litigant beliefs about judicial politics actually affect litigation filings, see Ahmed E. Taha, "'Judges' Political Orientations and the Selection of Disputes for Litigation," Wake Forest University Legal Studies Research Paper Series No. 963468, January 2007, http://ssrn.com/abstract=963468 (August 30, 2009). See also Geyh, *When Courts and Congress Collide*.

105. McGuire, "The Judicial Branch," 199.

106. Belden et. al., "Americans Consider Judicial Independence."

107. Zogby International, "Nationwide Poll, 7/21/06-7/27/06," http://www.zogby. com/wf-AOL%20National.pdf (last accessed August 30, 2009). The record of public ignorance about the courts is well-established and can be found in surveys dating from the late 1970s. See National Center for State Courts, "State Courts: A Blueprint for the Future," prepared for the Proceedings of the Second National Conference on the Judiciary," Williamsburg, Virginia, March 19–22, 1978. Yet, as I will argue, the public's ignorance about some kinds of detailed knowledge by no means demonstrates that the public knows nothing of importance about the courts.

108. Institute for the Advancement of the American Legal System and the League of Women Voters of Colorado Education Fund, "2007 Colorado Voter Opinions on the Judiciary," July 2007, http://www.du.edu/legalinstitute/publications2007.html (last accessed August 30, 2009).

109. Ronald A. Cass, *The Rule of Law in America* (Baltimore: The Johns Hopkins University Press, 2001).

110. *Ibid.*, 19.

111. According to Cass, *Bush v. Gore* has been unfairly denounced as being driven by the political preferences of the justices (*Rule of Law*, 91–7).

112. Peretti, *In Defense of a Political Court*, 3.

113. The quotations in this sentence and the previous one are drawn from the discussion of Peretti's work in Howard Gillman, *The Votes That Counted: How the Court Decided the 2000 Presidential Election* (Chicago: University of Chicago Press, 2001), 7. See also Sanford Levinson, "Return of Legal Realism," *The Nation,* January 8, 2001, http://www.thenation.com/doc/20010108/levinson (last accessed August 30, 2009) and Gibson and Caldeira, "Segal and Spaeth."

114. See, for example, Michael Bailey and Forrest Maltzman, "Does Legal Doctrine Matter? Unpacking Law and Policy Preferences on the Supreme Court," *American Political Science Review* 102 (2008): 369–84; and Joshua B. Fischman and David S. Law, "What Is Judicial Ideology, and How Should We Measure It?," October 19, 2008, http://ssrn.com/abstract=1121228 (last accessed August 30, 2009). For a recent study emphasizing the political nature of state supreme courts, see Bonneau and Hall, In Defense of *Judicial Elections.*

115. Cass and Peretti could also both be right if they are read as simply providing alternative methodologies for studying the courts (see Schedler, "Arguing and Observing"). I understand Cass and Peretti to be providing accounts of how the courts do and should work; thus I do not understand them to be offering mere methodologies. I think they are both right because they each accurately describe basic (albeit contradictory) elements of the judicial process. For a thoughtful analysis of how these contradictory elements cross-pressure members of the Supreme Court, see Thomas M. Keck, "Party, Policy, or Duty:

Why Does the Supreme Court Invalidate Federal Statutes?," *American Political Science Review* 101 (2007): 321–38.

116. In saying this, the judge is, as Hart put it, expressing an "attitude of shared acceptance" of the same set of normative rules. That is, the judge is using the "language of one assessing a situation by reference to rules which he in common with others acknowledges as appropriate for this purpose." See Hart, *Concept of Law*, 102. See also Rogers M. Smith, "If Politics Matters: Implications for a 'New Institutional'," *Studies in a American Political Development* 6 (1992), 1–36; Lief H. Carter and Thomas F. Burke, *Reason in Law*, Updated 7th ed., (New York: Pearson Education, Inc., 2007), 184–86 and *passim*. The claims of impartiality and principle are general features of adjudication, but this is not to say that all judges speak from the bench in such terms all the time. As I note in Part III, judges will occasionally drop legal language and speak as ordinary citizens addressing the mundane reality apart from law's formalisms.

117. For a discussion of the "schizophrenia" between political understandings of the courts and the way in which judges talk about their work, see Cornell W. Clayton, "The Supreme Court and Political Jurisprudence: New and Old Institutionalisms," in Cornell W. Clayton and Howard Gillman, eds., *Supreme Court Decisionmaking: New Institutionalist Approaches* (Chicago: University of Chicago Press, 1999), 15–41. For the argument that judicial ways of reasoning may themselves promote such schizophrenic views, see John Dewey, "Logical Method and the Law," *Cornell Law Quarterly* 10 (1924): 17–27.

118. The quotations here and in the previous sentence are from Paul W. Kahn, *The Cultural Study of Law: Reconstructing Legal Scholarship* (Chicago: University of Chicago Press, 1999), 73. It is worth noting, as I indicated in note 12, that leading legal realists did not share Peretti's belief that judicial decisionmaking could openly present itself as being exclusively anchored in something other than the law and, at the same time, easily remain a legitimate "legal" process.

119. Geyh, *When Courts and Congress Collide*, 280. I discuss the more general relationship between habit and the rule of law in Part III.

120. The quotations in this paragraph are from Shapiro, *Courts*, 19–20. For a recent validation of Shapiro's work, see Ran Hirschl, *Towards Juristocracy: The Origins and Consequences of the New Constitutionalism* (Cambridge: Harvard University Press, 2004).

121. *Ibid.*, 18. Thus one could say that Shapiro argues—contrary to Hart—that judges may not have an "internal perspective" that normatively attaches the judge to legal rules and leads her to use the rules as the basis for her judgments. Hart does entertain the idea that judges might make up their minds on non-legal bases and then "merely choose from a catalogue of legal rules one which, they pretended, resembled the case at hand. . . . " But Hart rejects this as an improbable view: "it is surely evident that for the most part decisions, like the chess-player's moves, are reached either by

genuine effort to conform to rules consciously taken as guiding standards of decision or, if intuitively reached, are justified by rules which the judge was antecedently disposed to observe and whose relevance to the case in hand would generally be acknowledged." See Hart, *Concept of Law*, 140–1. Shapiro's study, coupled with my arguments here, suggest that Hart's view is not evident to many ordinary people (of course, Hart might agree that the suspicion that judges are not following legal rules is warranted "at the fringe" where judges are free to fill in the law's open texture—*ibid.*, 153–4; my argument is that the suspicion judges are not following the law is far more common). I take up this issue again in Part III.

122. Patricia Ewick and Susan Silbey, *The Common Place of Law: Stories from Everyday Life* (Chicago: University of Chicago Press, 1998). Ewick and Silbey examine popular understandings of law and the legal process as a whole. For studies that look specifically at the popular understanding of lawyers and reach conclusions similar to those of Ewick and Silbey, see Marc Galanter, *Lowering the Bar: Lawyer Jokes and Legal Culture* (Madison: University of Wisconsin Press, 2005) and Marvin W. Mindes with Alan C. Acock, "Trickster, Hero, Helper: A Report on the Lawyer Image," *American Bar Foundation Research Journal* 7 (1982): 177–233.

123. Ewick and Silbey, *Common Place*, 28.

124. *Ibid.*, 223. Ewick and Silbey argue that the maintenance of contradictory views lends law hegemonic power: it is because law can at any given time be seen as a "reified transcendent realm" and as "a game" that the law as a whole deflects critique. "Challenges to legality for being only a game, or a gimmick, can be repulsed by invoking legality's transcendent reified character. Similarly, dismissals of law for being irrelevant to daily life can be answered by invoking its gamelike purposes" (231). Ewick and Silbey also argue that the recognition of law's contradictions may lead some individuals to resistance—to being "against the law." "Because legality is an ongoing production that is created anew daily, rather than a fixed and external reality, personal engagements, in the fact and in the retelling, have the capacity to reproduce as well as challenge legal hegemony" (244). As will become clear in Part III, I agree with Ewick and Silbey that contradictory perceptions actually help sustain the rule of law. Our approaches are nonetheless distinct because I identify somewhat different mechanisms through which perceived contradictions become enabling, and I do so without framing my argument in terms of hegemony.

125. For a recent effort along such lines, see Stephen M. Feldman, "The Rule of Law or the Rule of Politics? Harmonizing the Internal and External Views of Supreme Court Decisionmaking," *Law and Social Inquiry* 30 (2005): 89–135.

126. *Ibid.*, 93.

127. *Ibid.*, 109.

128. As John Brigham has observed, the public is thus in a kind of "bind" when it comes to evaluating bodies like the Supreme Court. On the one hand, the public knows

"the Court is political" and pays "a great deal of attention to [its] policy formation and outcomes." On the other hand, "the uniquely 'judicial' is still significant." See John Brigham, *The Cult of the Court* (Philadelphia: Temple University Press, 1987), 219.

129. Samuel L. Popkin, *The Reasoning Voter: Communication and Persuasion in Presidential Campaigns*, 2nd ed. (Chicago: University of Chicago Press, 1994); and Samuel L. Popkin, John W. Gorman, Charles Phillips and Jeffrey A. Smith, "Comment: What Have You Done for Me Lately? Toward an Investment Theory of Voting," *American Political Science Review* 70 (1976): 779–805.

130. Indeed, when pollsters specifically change question wording so as to not presuppose that the public's knowledge of the courts is highly detailed, respondents demonstrate that they do know a number of things about the judiciary. See James L. Gibson and Gregory A. Caldeira, "Knowing About Courts," June 20, 2007, http://ssrn.com/abstract=956562 (last accessed August 30, 2009); and Sara C. Benesh, Nancy Scherer, and Amy Steigerwalt, "Public Perceptions of the Lower Federal Courts," August 3, 2009, http://ssrn.com/abstract=1443434 (last accessed December 1, 2009).

131. According to the Maxwell Poll, 68 percent of Americans agree that media coverage of the courts pays more attention to partisan affiliation than to the reasoning that judges use to justify their decisions. For further discussion, see Bybee, "Two Faces." See also the discussion of media coverage in Spill and Oxley, "Philosopher Kings," and Obbie, "Winners and Losers." This is not to say that all cases are covered in political terms or that all judges receive equal press coverage. See William Haltom, *Reporting on the Courts: How the Mass Media Cover Judicial Actions* (Chicago: Nelson-Hall Publishers, 1998) and Brian F. Schaffner and Jennifer Segal Diascro, "Judicial Elections in the News," in Matthew J. Streb, ed., *Running for Judge: The Rising Political, Financial, and Legal Stakes of Judicial Elections* (New York: New York University Press, 2007), 115–39. Nor is it to say that the idea of partisanship affecting judicial decisionmaking is the only view of the law generally propagated by the media. See William Haltom and Michael McCann, *Distorting the Law: Politics, Media, and the Litigation Crisis* (Chicago: University of Chicago Press, 2004). For a review of the various ways in the which one court has attempted to manage its own media image, see Richard Davis, *Decisions and Images: The Supreme Court and the Press* (Englewood Cliffs, NJ: Prentice Hall, 1994).

132. Ninety-three percent of those who said they "follow news about court decisions a lot" believe that the partisan background of judges influences court decisions either some or a lot, while only 74 percent of those who said they do not follow court news believed that judges were driven by partisan influence. At the same time, 79 percent of those who follow news about court decisions a lot thought that judges should be shielded from outside pressure and allowed to make their decisions on the basis of an independent reading of the law, while only 70 percent of those who do not follow court news shared the same view (although this difference falls within the poll's margin of error, it is suggestive). Given their sharper sense of the judiciary's half-politics-half-law

status, Americans who attend to court news the most are also more likely to suspect judges of not meaning what they say: 66 percent of them agree that judges in many cases really base their decisions on personal views (even though judges always cite the law and the Constitution), while only 59 percent of those who do not follow court news hold this view (this difference is suggestive, though it falls within the margin of error).

133. Princeton Survey Research Associates International, "Separate Branches, Shared Responsibilities: A National Survey of Public Expectations on Solving Justice Issues.

134. Neither the Maxwell Poll nor the Princeton Survey poll contains questions that break down levels of popular support for the courts in terms of "diffuse support" (i.e., do individuals support the judiciary as an institution) and "specific support" (i.e., do individuals support a court's resolution of a particular controversy). Yet even though these polls do not disaggregate precise elements of opinion, their Janus-faced findings (that those who follow court-related news most carefully are more likely to believe that judges are influenced by politics *and* to believe that judges should be treated as impartial arbiters) may speak indirectly to a set of contradictory findings about public support of the judiciary. Early opinion studies showed that those individuals best informed about the courts were the most dissatisfied by the courts (e.g., National Center for State Courts, "State Courts") For a critique of the early study, see Herbert M. Kritzer and John Voelker, *How Wisconsin Citizens View Their Courts*, 82 JUDICATURE 64 (1998–1999). More recent studies have found that the more individuals know about the courts, the more satisfied with the courts they are (e.g., Gibson et. al., "On the Legitimacy of National High Courts" and Gibson, "Legitimacy of the U.S. Supreme Court"). If we understand a political view of the courts to be a negative view of the courts, then the Maxwell and Princeton Survey findings show that both early and more recent findings about the relationship between information and support capture something important: the more one knows about the courts, the stronger one's negative *and* positive assessments of the courts become. For an extended argument along these lines, see Gibson and Caldeira, "Supreme Court Nominations" and "Segal and Spaeth."

135. As I indicated earlier, the information individuals have about the courts does not just come from the news conveyed by television and newspapers. See note 76.

136. See Popkin, *Evolution* and H. Jefferson Powell, *Constitutional Conscience: The Moral Dimension of Judicial Decision* (Chicago: The University of Chicago Press, 2008).

137. Popkin, *Evolution*, 126.

138. As I indicated in note 12, several legal realists argued that judicial decisionmaking could not openly purport to be anchored in something other than the law and, at the same time, easily remain a legitimate "legal" process. Absent a radical transformation in citizen expectations and beliefs, new judicial behavior is likely to create a new crisis in judicial legitimacy.

139. See Judith N. Shklar, *Ordinary Vices* (Cambridge, MA: The Belknap Press of Harvard University, 1984); Ruth W. Grant, *Hypocrisy and Integrity: Machiavelli,*

Rousseau, and the Ethics of Politics (Chicago: University of Chicago Press, 1997); David Runciman, *Political Hypocrisy: The Mask of Power, From Hobbes to Orwell and Beyond* (Princeton, NJ: Princeton University Press, 2008); Jenny Davidson, *Hypocrisy and the Politics of Politeness: Manners and Morals from Locke to Austen* (New York: Cambridge University Press, 2004); Ewick and Silbey, *Common Place;* Charles P. Curtis, *The Ethics of Advocacy*, 4 STAN. L. REV. 3, 3–32 (1951); Robert C. Post, *On the Popular Image of Lawyers: Reflections in a Dark Glass*, 75 CAL. L. REV. 379, 379–89 (1987); John M. Kang, "The Case for Insincerity," *Studies in Law, Politics, and Society* 29 (2003): 143–64; John M. Kang, "The Uses of Insincerity: Thomas Hobbes's Theory of Law and Society," *Law and Literature* 15 (2003): 371–93; John M. Kang, *The Irrelevance of Sincerity: Deliberative Democracy in the Supreme Court*, 48 ST. LOUIS U. L.J. 305, 305–26 (2004); Stephen D. Krasner, *Sovereignty: Organized Hypocrisy* (Princeton, NJ: Princeton University Press, 1999); and Keith J. Bybee, "Legal Realism, Common Courtesy, and Hypocrisy," *Law, Culture and the Humanities*, 1 (2005): 75–102.

Part II

1. Jenny Davidson, *Hypocrisy and the Politics of Politeness: Manners and Morals from Locke to Austen* (Cambridge: Cambridge University Press, 2004), 1. For a philosophical discussion of hypocrisy, see Christine McKinnon, "Hypocrisy, Cheating, and Character Possession," *The Journal of Value Inquiry*, 39 no. 3–4 (December 2005): 1–16.

2. The *Oxford English Dictionary*, 2nd ed. (Oxford: Oxford University Press, 1989) defines *pharmacon* as "drug, medicine, poison."

3. The term *false friends* comes from Ruth W. Grant, *Hypocrisy and Integrity: Machiavelli, Rousseau, and the Ethics of Politics* (Chicago: University of Chicago Press, 1997), 20–21.

4. Although I will make my case by relying on a variety of literatures, I do not draw directly on the large body of work in sociolinguistics on "politeness theory." Politeness theories are highly technical efforts to produce scientific descriptions of specific communicative acts—as such, politeness theories are generally outside the scope of my argument. Even so, it is worth noting that politeness theory as a whole reaches some of the same conclusions that I do. Politeness theorists understand politeness to be a basic strategy of conflict avoidance. They also take politeness to be involved with "social indexing" in the sense that politeness is "directly dependent on the social characteristics of the interactants, and thus is a reflection of their respective social positions." See Gino Eelen, *A Critique of Politeness Theories* (Manchester, U.K.: St. Jerome, 2001), 21–22.

5. I draw my definitions of these terms from *Merriam-Webster's Collegiate Dictionary*, 10th ed. (Springfield, MA: Merriam-Webster, Incorporated: 1995) and *Oxford English Dictionary*, 2nd ed. (Oxford: Oxford University Press, 1989). Some discussions of civility stray from the dictionary definitions I use here and impute far more substance to civility, treating it as a positive and critically important moral virtue that good citizens

ought to cultivate. There is an element of truth to this moral understanding of civility. But, as I discuss further on, this moral understanding is ultimately at odds with the conception of human nature on which manners rely.

6. In considering courtesy to be the most ordinary form of good manners, I have occasionally adopted formulations that other authors have assigned to different forms of good manners. For example, the subtitle of this book features an adaptation of the definition Ambrose Bierce gave to *politeness* (see *The Devil's Dictionary,* available at http://www.alcyone.com/max/lit/devils/) (last accessed August 30, 2009). I thank Bruce Bybee for suggesting the adaptation of Bierce's definition.

7. Elizabeth L. Post, *Emily Post on Etiquette* (New York: Harper & Row, 1987), 18, 73. See also the long list of publications offered by the Emily Post Institute, http://www.emilypost.com/ (last accessed August 30, 2009).

8. See, for example, George Washington, *Rules of Civility & Decent Behaviour in Company and Conversation,* available at http://www.earlyamerica.us/Almanack/life/manners/rules2.cfm (last accessed August 30, 2009). See also Eric Sloane, *Don't: A Little Book of Early American Gentility* (New York: Funk & Wagnalls, 1968).

9. Judith Martin, "The World's Oldest Virtue," *First Things* 33 (1993): 24.

10. Judith Martin, *Miss Manners Rescues Civilization from Sexual Harassment, Frivolous Lawsuits, Dissing and Other Lapses in Civility* (New York: Crown Publishers, 1996), 134–5.

11. Committee on Civility of the Seventh Federal Judicial Circuit, "Interim Report," April 1991, reprinted in 143 F.R.D. 371, 448 (7th Cir. 1992).

12. My tally is drawn primarily from the list of professional codes for lawyers and judges maintained by the American Bar Association (ABA Website), http://www.abanet.org/cpr/professionalism/profcodes.html (last accessed August 30, 2009). The ABA list identifies a number of courtesy codes, but it is incomplete. It does not include, for example, the code adopted by a federal district court in *Dondi Properties Corp. v. Commerce Savings & Loan Ass'n,* 121 F.R.D. 284 (N.D.Tex. 1988)—see Committee on Civility, "Interim Report" at 414–5. It is also likely that many bar associations and courts with courtesy codes have appended these codes to existing standards of professional conduct that do not themselves mention "civility" or "courtesy" in their titles—and therefore such "embedded" courtesy codes would not be evident on the ABA list. The end result is that my tally probably under-represents the number of courtesy codes in the United States. It is worth noting that courtesy codes are endorsed by the American Bar Association and several national organizations, including the American Inns of Courts, a national legal association with 325 chapters and over 75,000 active and alumni members. See http://www.innsofcourt.org/ (last accessed August 30, 2009). The importance of professional legal courtesy has also been publicly endorsed by at least two of the justices currently sitting on the United States Supreme Court. See Paul L. Friedman, *Taking the High Road: Civility, Judicial Independence, and the Rule of Law,* 58 N.Y.U. ANN. SURV.

Am. L. 187, 187–202 (2001); and Ruth Bader Ginsburg, *Speaking in a Judicial Voice*, 67 N.Y.U. L. Rev. 1185, 1185–1209 (1992). Finally, as one might expect from my discussion of *Republican Party of Minnesota v. White*, 536 U.S. 765 (2002) in Part I (a decision in which the Supreme Court overturned part of the Minnesota state judicial conduct code on First Amendment grounds), there has been some resistance to courtesy and civility codes from lawyers and judges who believe such codes infringe their constitutional rights. In fact, critics of the courtesy provisions in Michigan succeeded in having the provisions invalidated as violations of free speech and due process rights. See *Fieger v. Mich. Supreme Court*, 2007 U.S. Dist. LEXIS 64973 (E.D. Mich. Sept. 4, 2007), available at http://www.northcountrygazette.org/documents/fiegermemo00904407.pdf (last accessed August 30, 2009).

13. Martin, *Miss Manners Rescues Civilization*, 241. For other reactions to the effort to inject courtesy (or at least civility) into the legal process, see Joseph N. Hosteny, "Civility or Honesty? Which Should You Choose?," *Intellectual Property Today* (January 2002):18–19; Raymond M. Ripple, *Learning Outside the Fire: The Need for Civility Instruction in Law School*, 15 Notre Dame J.L. Ethics & Pub. Pol'y 359 (2001); Austin Sarat, *Enactments of Professionalism: A Study of Judges' and Lawyers' Accounts of Ethics and Civility in Litigation*, 67 Fordham L. Rev. 809 (1998); and Randall T. Shepard, *The Special Professional Challenges of Appellate Judging*, 35 Ind. L. Rev. 381 (2002). And for the argument that lawyers ought to adhere to a much older code of honor, see Douglas H. Yarn, *The Attorney as Duelist's Friend: Lessons from the Code Duello*, 51 Case W. L. Rev. 69 (2000).

14. The long historical process during which the inculcation of manners gradually became part of the internal governance in the family is documented in Norbert Elias, *The History of Manners*, Vol. I of *The Civilizing Process*, trans. Edmund Jephcott (New York: Urizen, 1978, originally published 1939) and *Power and Civility*, Vol. II of *The Civilizing Process*, trans. Edmund Jephcott (New York: Pantheon, 1982, originally published 1939). I will have more to say about courtesy and childhood further on.

15. Martin, *Miss Manners Rescues Civilization*, 32. For influential treatments of the effort to incorporate shaming into legal punishment, see Dan M. Kahan, *What Do Alternative Sanctions Mean?*, 63 U. Chi. L. Rev. 591 (1996); and Dan M. Kahan, *What's Really Wrong with Shaming Sanctions?* (Yale Law School Public Law and Legal Theory Working Paper No. 125, July 1, 2006, http://ssrn.com/abstract=914503 (last accessed August 30, 2009). For a philosophical argument that some forms of shaming are more politically beneficial than others, see Christina Tarnopolsky, "Prudes, Perverts, and Tyrants: Plato and the Contemporary Politics of Shame," *Political Theory* 32 (2004): 468–94. For an empirical discussion of how shaming penalties might be made more effective, see Tom R. Tyler, Lawrence Sherman, Heather Strang, Geoffrey C. Barnes, and Daniel Woods, "Reintegrative Shaming, Procedural Justice, and Recidivism: The

Engagement of Offenders' Psychological Mechanisms in the Canberra RISE Drinking-and-Driving Experiment," *Law and Society Review* 41(2007): 553–86.

16. H.L.A. Hart, *The Concept of Law*, 2nd ed. (New York: Oxford University Press, 1994).

17. Mark Caldwell, *A Short History of Rudeness* (New York: Picador USA, 1999), 240.

18. According to Hart, the introduction of legal rules that manage and order other legal rules is "a step forward as important to society as the invention of the wheel" (Hart, *Concept of Law*, 42).

19. For an overview of the ways in which good manners and law may pull in different directions, see George W. Jarecke and Nancy K. Plant, *Seeking Civility: Common Courtesy and the Common Law* (Boston: Northeastern University Press, 2003). In this vein, some have argued that it is advantageous to maintain a tension between law and courtesy, and that society would be improved by encouraging a certain level of rudeness. See Richard C. Sinopoli, "Thick-Skinned Liberalism: Redefining Civility," *American Political Science Review* 89 (1995): 612–20.

20. K. N. Llewellyn, *The Bramble Bush: Some Lectures on Law and Its Study* (New York: Tentative Printing for Use of Students at Columbia University School of Law), 114.

21. Thomas Hobbes, *Leviathan* (New York: Penguin English Library, 1981), 160. Hobbes did, however, appreciate the importance of "compleasance" or mutual accommodation in society. See Anna Bryson, *From Courtesy to Civility: Changing Codes of Conduct in Early Modern England* (Oxford: Clarendon Press, 1998), 223. As I argue further on, courtesy is centrally concerned with the achievement of such accommodation. See also Jacob T. Levy, "Multicultural Manners," May 12, 2009, http://ssrn.com/abstract=1403687 (last accessed August 30, 2009).

22. For a recent argument in this vein, see Lynne Truss, *Talk to the Hand: The Utter Bloody Rudeness of the World Today, or Six Good Reasons to Stay Home and Bolt the Door* (New York: Gotham Books, 2005).

23. Fanny Trollope, *The Domestic Manners of Americans*, ed. Richard Mullen (New York: Oxford University Press, 1984).

24. John F. Kasson, *Rudeness and Civility: Manners in Nineteenth-Century Urban America* (New York: Hill and Wang, 1990).

25. Trollope, *Domestic Manners*, 101.

26. Kasson, *Rudeness and Civility*, 258

27. Emrys Westacott, "The Rights and Wrongs of Rudeness," *International Journal of Applied Philosophy* 20 (2006): 1–20. As I shall argue, courtesy also depends on habit and pleasure, and these dependencies increase the difficulty of adapting manners to changed circumstances.

28. The ongoing reconstruction of courtesy does not mean that manners adopt an entirely new form each time. As I argue further on, codes of courtesy are closely tied to

patterns of dominance, and across the changes in etiquette one can find an unvarying support for whatever hierarchies happen to prevail.

29. Kasson, *Rudeness and Civility*, 62.

30. Laura Claridge, *Emily Post: Daughter of the Gilded Age, Mistress of American Manners* (New York: Random House, 2008), 245, 367, 251, 261.

31. *Ibid.*, 435.

32. Deborah Robertson Hodges, *Etiquette: An Annotated Bibliography of Literature Published in the English in the United States, 1900 Through 1987* (Jefferson, NC: McFarland and Company, 1989).

33. "The Great *Reader's Digest* Global Courtesy Test: How Polite Are We?" July 2006, available at http://www.readersdigest.ca/mag/2006/07/polite.php (last accessed August 30, 2009); and Diana C. Muntz, "Effects of 'In-Your-Face' Television Discourse on Perceptions of a Legitimate Opposition," *American Political Science Review* 101 (2007): 621–35.

34. Jennifer Lee, *Civility in the City: Blacks, Jews, and Koreans in Urban America* (Cambridge: Harvard University Press, 2002). Indeed, some commentators have argued that levels of courtesy are highest in the cities: "Can any number of small-town grocery clerks smiling while saying 'have a nice day' rival the politeness of a single overstuffed metro car moving from place to place without incident?" (Levy, "Multicultural Manners," 10).

35. For an extended elaboration of this point, see Caldwell, *History of Rudeness*.

36. Elias, *History of Manners*, 68.

37. *Ibid.*, 106.

38. *Ibid.*, 129.

39. Of course, manners are more significant where there is broad agreement about them, as there is in traditional rank-ordered societies defined by clear hierarchies and well-established roles.

40. Erving Goffman, *Behavior in Public Places: Notes on the Social Organization of Gatherings* (New York: The Free Press, 1963), 5, emphasis original.

41. *Ibid.*, 234. Goffman considered the effects of such rules to be quite serious: those who consistently violate the rules of social interaction are typically viewed as being mentally ill.

42. *Ibid.*, 247.

43. Desiderius Erasmus, "On Good Manners for Boys/*De civilitate morum puerilium*," trans. Brian McGregor, in J. K. Sowards, ed., *Literary and Educational Writings 3*, 273–89, Volume 25 of J. K. Sowards, ed., *Collected Works of Erasmus* (Toronto: University of Toronto Press, 1978–1993).

44. Kevin A. Clarke and David M. Primo, "Modernizing Political Science: A Model-Based Approach," *Perspectives on Politics* 5 (December 2007): 742.

45. "Civility in the House of Representatives: Statement of Donald R. Wolfensberger," Subcommittee on the Rules and Organization of the House, House Committee on Rules, Thursday, April 17, 1997, available at http://www.rules.house.gov/archives/tran01.htm (last accessed August 30, 2009). Although my goal in this book is to use courtesy to help explain the rule of law, the congressional reliance on comity and the frequency of hypocrisy in public life suggest that one could extend my analysis of courtesy to politics more generally.

46. "Civility in the House of Representatives: Executive Summary," prepared by Kathleen Hall Jamieson for the Subcommittee on the Rules and Organization of the House, House Committee on Rules, Thursday, April 17, 1997, available at http://www.annenberg publicpolicycenter.org/NewsDetails.aspx?myId=195 (last accessed August 30, 2009).

47. *Ibid.*

48. There are cases in which governmental institutions have tried to impose codes of courtesy even more broadly. In the run-up to the 2008 Olympic games in Beijing, for example, the Chinese government attempted to instill new forms of elegant behavior en masse. In addition to printing manuals, passing ordinances, and deploying agents to enforce good manners, the government attempted to habituate Beijing residents to queuing by encouraging them to practice forming lines on the 11th of each month beginning in February 2007. See Reshma Patil, "Two Claps, Arms Stretched, Two Claps, Arms Up . . . ," July, 27, 2008, http://www.livemint.com/2008/07/26000951/Two-claps-arms-stretched-two.html (last accessed August 30, 2009). See also Loretta Chao, "For Beijing, Etiquette Isn't a Game," August 1, 2008, http://online.wsj.com/public/article/SB121752752638401551-1iYic5O4z5mFSQ3EQAhS8_aS1NU_20080830.html?mod=tff_main_tff_top (last accessed August 30, 2009).

49. "Civility: Executive Summary," and Kathleen Hall Jamieson and Erika Falk, "Civility in the House of Representatives: An Update," March 1998; "Civility in the House of Representatives: The 105th Congress," March 1999; and "Civility in the House of Representatives: The 106th Congress," March 2001. Available, respectively, at http://www.annenbergpublicpolicycenter.org/Downloads/Political_Communication/105th CongressCivil/REP20.PDF, http://www.annenbergpublicpolicycenter.org/Downloads/Political_Communication/105thCongressCivil/REP26.PDF, and http://www.annenberg publicpolicycenter.org/Downloads/Political_Communication/106thCongressCivil/20 01_civility106th.pdf (last accessed August 30, 2009). See also the essays collected in Burdett A. Loomis, ed., *Esteemed Colleagues: Civility and Deliberation in the U.S. Senate* (Washington, DC: Brookings Institution Press, 2000).

50. "Civility in the House of Representatives: Statement of Stephen Frantzich," Subcommittee on the Rules and Organization of the House, House Committee on Rules, Thursday, May 1, 1997, available at http://www.house.gov/rules/tran01b.htm (last accessed August 30, 2009).

51. Kasson, *Rudeness and Civility*; Caldwell, *History of Rudeness*.

52. The Miss Manners quotations in this paragraph are taken from Judith Martin, "In What Respect Do You Mean 'Respect'?," *Washington Post*, July 2, 2008, C7.

53. Kasson, *Rudeness and Civility*, 93.

54. Martin, *Miss Manners Rescues Civilization*, 15.

55. Grant, *Hypocrisy and Integrity*, 20–34.

56. *Ibid.*, 20.

57. *Ibid.*, 30–31.

58. Here I am paraphrasing the advice that House Speaker Sam Rayburn famously gave new members of Congress: "If you want to get along, go along." Arguing along the same lines as Grant, Jenny Davidson makes a similar point about the double meaning of hypocrisy: "Forms of deception that seem unforgiveable when they are considered from the viewpoint of a victim of an individual hypocrite bent on self-advancement may be sanctioned by the need to build consensus or community." Davidson, *Hypocrisy and Politics*, 147.

59. Grant, *Hypocrisy and Integrity*, 49.

60. *Ibid.*, 50.

61. *Ibid.*, 52.

62. La Rochefoucauld, *Maxims*, trans. Leonard Tancock (London: Penguin, 1959), 65, 48; Edmund Burke, *Reflections on the Revolution in France*, ed. J.G.A. Pocock, (Indianapolis: Hackett,), 67. Similar understandings can also be found in Hume, Swift, Mandeville, and Hobbes. See Davidson, *Hypocrisy and Politics*; David Runciman, *Political Hypocrisy: The Mask of Power, From Hobbes to Orwell and Beyond* (Princeton, NJ: Princeton University Press, 2008); and L. E. Klein, "The Political Significance of Politeness in Early Eighteenth-Century Britain," in Gordon J. Schochet, ed., with Patricia E. Tatspaugh and Carol Brobeck, *Politics, Politeness, and Patriotism*, Proceedings of the Folger Institute, Center for the History of British Political Thought, Volume 5 (Washington, DC: The Folger Institute, 1993): 73–108.

63. The classic discussion of the links between Machiavellian and American political thought is J.G.A. Pocock, *The Machiavellian Moment: Florentine Political Thought and the Atlantic Republican Tradition* (Princeton, NJ: Princeton University Press, 1975). As David Runciman notes, the connection usually drawn between Machiavelli and American political thought is in terms of republican virtue (one of Machiavelli's central concerns in *The Discourses*), and not in terms of the vanities embedded in human nature (one of Machiavelli's central concerns in *The Prince*). But the emphasis on virtue and innate human sociability was not shared equally by all Americans, as evidenced by Madison's view, among others. See Runciman, *Political Hypocrisy*, 79.

64. James Madison, "Federalist Paper No. 55" and "Federalist Paper No. 10" in Alexander Hamilton, James Madison, and John Jay, *The Federalist Papers*, Clinton Rossiter, ed. (New York: Mentor, 1961), 346 and 78–9. For a more detailed account of Madi-

son's view of human nature and its connection to his understanding of constitutional design, see Jack N. Rakove, *Original Meanings: Politics and Ideas in the Making of the Constitution* (New York: Vintage Books, 1997), especially 35–56.

65. Runciman, *Political Hypocrisy*, 10. Runciman is writing about hypocrisy in general, but I would argue that his formulation also applies to courtesy in particular.

66. Lord Chesterfield, *Letters*, ed. David Roberts (New York: Cambridge University Press, 1992), 18, 89, 57, 144.

67. Judith Martin, *Common Courtesy: In Which Miss Manners Solves the Problem That Baffled Mr. Jefferson* (New York: Athenaeum, 1985), 12.

68. Martin, "World's Oldest Virtue," 22.

69. Martin, *Miss Manners Rescues Civilization*, 22–3.

70. Chesterfield, *Letters*, 262.

71. *Ibid.*, 106.

72. Bryson, *Courtesy to Civility*, 198–99. Erasmus's understanding of good manners as a kind of "private virtue made public" is still with us. As Peggy Post writes, civility and courtesy are "in essence, the outward expressions of human decency." *Emily Post's Etiquette*, 17th ed. (New York: HarperCollins, 2004), 6.

73. See Lionel Trilling, *Sincerity and Authenticity* (Cambridge, MA: Harvard University Press, 1972).

74. In saying this, I should emphasize that I do not mean to deny that performance and pretense are embedded elements of modern society. My point here is that the ubiquity of such phenomena does not, in itself, make the possibility of hypocritical behavior any less reviled.

75. Runciman, *Political Hypocrisy*, 18.

76. Kasson, *Rudeness and Civility*, 116.

77. P. M. Forni, *Choosing Civility: The Twenty-Five Rules of Considerate Conduct* (New York: St. Martin's Press, 2002), 9; and Stephen L. Carter, *Civility: Manners, Morals, and the Etiquette of Democracy* (New York: Basic Books, 1998), xii. See also Edward Shils, *The Virtue of Civility: Selected Essays on Liberalism, Tradition, and Civil Society*, ed. Steven Grosby (Indianapolis: Liberty Fund, 1997); and Os Guinness, *The Case for Civility: And Why Our Future Depends on It* (New York: HarperCollins, 2008).

78. Forni, *Choosing Civility*, 11.

79. Shils, *Virtue of Civility*, 345.

80. *Ibid.*, 4.

81. As I indicated in my earlier discussion of congressional comity, courtesy does provide a way of conveying genuine respect. See also Sarah Buss, "Appearing Respectful: The Moral Significance of Manners," *Ethics* 109 (July 1999): 795–826. Buss argues that the essential point of manners is moral even though "our code of manners may have originated as a way of encouraging peaceful coexistence among people, or as a way for the powerful to retain control over the resentful weak, or as a way for the resentful

weak to claim power for themselves" (805). Buss admits that manners may indeed still serve these original purposes. But she also insists the persistence of original purposes does not mean that manners are not also, here and now, essentially moral. I disagree. As I argue further on, the original purposes Buss assigns to manners are more consistent with the understanding of human nature on which courtesy relies (as well as the way in which courtesy actually works) than the moral functions Buss advocates. As for the connection Buss draws between courtesy and power, I will have more to say about that later on in my discussion of hierarchy.

82. Cheshire Calhoun, "The Virtue of Civility," *Philosophy and Public Affairs* 29 (2000): 251–76.

83. Judith N. Shklar, *Ordinary Vices* (Cambridge, MA: The Belknap Press of Harvard University, 1984), 78, 77. For recent extensions of Shklar's argument, see John M. Kang, "The Case for Insincerity," *Studies in Law, Politics, and Society* 29 (2003): 143–64; John M. Kang, "The Uses of Insincerity: Thomas Hobbes's Theory of Law and Society," *Law and Literature* 15 (2003): 371–93; and John M. Kang, *The Irrelevance of Sincerity: Deliberative Democracy in the Supreme Court*," 48 St. Louis U. L.J. 305, 305–26 (2004). For a critical response to Shklar's argument that nonetheless accepts the notion that democratic civility is based on hypocrisy, see Dennis F. Thompson, "Hypocrisy and Democracy," in Bernard Yack, ed., *Liberalism Without Illusions: Essays on Liberal Theory and the Political Vision of Judith Shklar* (Chicago: University of Chicago Press, 1996), 173–90.

84. The tension between the disapproval of hypocritical behavior and this behavior's usefulness is often resolved by strategies that allow those engaging in hypocrisy to deny that they are being hypocritical. See Michael Lipson, "Peacekeeping: Organized Hypocrisy?" *European Journal of International Relations* 13 (2007): 5–34. For a broader discussion of organized hypocrisy in the context of international relations, see Stephen D. Krasner, *Sovereignty: Organized Hypocrisy* (Princeton, NJ: Princeton University Press, 1999).

85. As Shklar recognized, the discomfort with hypocrisy not only may result in denial, but also may lead to active crusades against hypocrisy. In her view, such anti-hypocrisy campaigns inevitably end up inflicting far higher costs than the vice they seek to eliminate. See Shklar, *Ordinary Vices*, 45–86. See also Elizabeth Markovitz, *The Politics of Sincerity: Plato, Frank Speech, and Democratic Government* (University Park: The Pennsylvania State University Press, 2008) and Hannah Arendt, *On Revolution* (New York: Pelican Books, 1977), 96–106.

86. Martin, *Common Courtesy*, 11–12.

87. Goffman, *Behavior*, 35.

88. *Ibid.*

89. This is not to say that habit, pleasure, and utility will work together perfectly in every respect. For example, as I argue further on, the practice of mutual accommodation

that makes courtesy useful contains some modest guarantees of equal treatment that may be at odds with the habits and pleasures that draw individuals to good manners.

90. As I indicated in note 14, the teaching of manners has not always been considered to be part of family life. For historical discussions of British and American etiquette manuals concerned with raising children, see Davidson, *Hypocrisy and Politics*, and Kasson, *Rudeness and Civility*. For a recent sampling of children's etiquette books, see Peggy Post and Cindy Post Senning, *Emily's Everyday Manners*, illus. Steve Bjorkman (New York: Collins, 2006); Whoopi Goldberg, *Whoopi's Big Book of Manners*, illus. Olo (New York: Hyperion Books for Children, 2006); David Greenberg, *Don't Forget Your Etiquette!*, illus. Nadine Bernard Westcott (New York: Melanie Kroupa Books/Farrar, Straus & Giroux, 2006); and Alan Katz, *Are You Quite Polite? Silly Dilly Manners Songs*, illus. David Catrow (New York: Margaret K. McElderry Books/Simon & Schuster, 2006).

91. Erasmus, "Good Manners," 277.

92. Martin, *Miss Manners Rescues Civilization*, 318.

93. Judith Martin, *Miss Manners' Guide to Rearing Perfect Children*, illus. Gloria Kaman (New York: Athenaeum, 1984), 3.

94. Martin, *Common Courtesy*, 10–11. William Miller suggests that authorities of all stripes have depended on the capacity of action to generate a version of true belief: "The church forcing people to say the credo, totalitarian regimes making people swear allegiance, even liberal regimes demanding loyalty oaths, might do so as a sign of their power to constrain people's wills but, mostly they do it because they know it works. You say it, we got you. You say you believe long enough and you will believe, if only after a fashion." See William Ian Miller, *Faking It* (New York: Cambridge University Press, 2003), 74–75.

95. Emphasis original. The quote here, as well as the quotes in the preceding two sentences, come from Alan Houston, *Benjamin Franklin and the Politics of Improvement* (New Haven, CT: Yale University Press, 2008), 40.

96. *Ibid.*

97. Caldwell, *History of Rudeness*, 9.

98. Burke, *Reflections*, 67.

99. Oscar Wilde, "The Decay of Lying," in Oscar Wilde, *Intentions* (New York: Brentano, 1905), 14–15.

100. Those who see no place for hypocrisies in political life understandably reject Burke's defense of taste and elegance. For example, Thomas Paine, who has been described "as pure an anti-hypocrite as it is possible to meet in the history of modern political thought" (Runciman, *Political Hypocrisy*, 80), excoriated Burke because he ignored the "reality of distress" that motivated the French Revolution. "[Burke] pities the plumage," Paine wrote, "but forgets the dying bird." See Thomas Paine, *Rights of Man* (New York: Viking Penguin, 1984), 51. See also Davidson, *Hypocrisy and Politics*.

101. Burke, *Reflections*, 70.

102. Chesterfield, *Letters*, 90, 61, 185, 88.

103. As I indicate in note 89 and as I argue further on, this is not to say that the considerations of habit, pleasure, and utility will always work together perfectly in every respect.

104. Elias, *History of Manners* and *Power and Civility*; Bryson, *Courtesy to Civility*.

105. Virginia Sapiro, "Considering Political Civility Historically: A Case Study of the United States," prepared for the annual meeting of the International Society for Political Psychology, Amsterdam, The Netherlands, July 1999), 11.

106. Michel Foucault, *Power/Knowledge: Selected Interviews and Other Writings, 1972–1977*, ed. Colin Gordon, trans. Colin Gordon, Leo Marshall, John Mepham, and Kate Soper (New York: Pantheon Books, 1980); and *Discipline and Punish: The Birth of the Prison*, trans. Alan Sheridan (Middlesex, U.K.: Penguin Books, 1979).

107. Kasson, *Rudeness and Civility*, 116 and passim.

108. *Ibid.*, 161. See also Sapiro, "Considering Political Civility."

109. It is worth remembering that the subordination of women during this period occurred in a social context that Fanny Trollope considered to be overrun with egalitarianism (see text associated with notes 23–25). As a believer in the older rank-ordered society that Americans had destabilized, Trollope argued that nineteenth century American women were being given far too much equality—even though they were by no means being treated as equal to men.

110. Martin Luther King Jr., "Letter from a Birmingham Jail," in Robert A. Godwin, ed., *On Civil Disobedience: Essays Old and New* (Chicago: Rand McNally, 1968), 65.

111. Deborah B. Gould, "Life During Wartime: Emotions and the Development of ACT UP," *Mobilization* 7 (2002): 177–200. See also Keith J. Bybee, "The Polite Thing to Do," in H. N. Hirsch, ed., *The Future of Gay Rights in America* (New York: Routledge, 2005), 297–302.

112. Gould, "Life During Wartime," 188, quoting the activist Ferd Eggan.

113. The phrase comes from Davidson, *Hypocrisy and Politics*, 11.

114. For an extended discussion of this point, see Kasson, *Rudeness and Civility*.

115. Davidson, *Hypocrisy and Politics*, 163. This was not a situation restricted to the nineteenth century. Well into the twentieth century women were advised to accept the benefits that came from working within a system that treated women as subordinates. As the 1953 etiquette manual "The Woman You Want To Be" put it: "You must participate in a conversation in order to influence it." Quoted in Caldwell, *History of Rudeness*, 185.

116. For a general discussion of how efforts to act "as if" there are no deep inequalities actually serve to perpetuate inequality, see Nancy Fraser, "Rethinking the Public Sphere: A Contribution to the Critique of Actually Existing Democracy," in Craig Calhoun, ed., *Habermas and the Public Sphere* (Cambridge, MA: MIT Press, 1990), 109–42.

117. Martin, *Common Courtesy*, 65.

118. Caldwell, *History of Rudeness*, 185.

119. Claridge, *Emily Post*, 114.

120. Randall Kennedy, "The Case Against Civility," *The American Prospect* 9 (November 1, 1998–December 1, 1998), available at http://www.prospect.org/cs/articles?article=the _case_against_civility (last accessed August 30, 2009).

Part III

1. Blaise Pascal, *Pascal's Pensées* (New York: E.P. Dutton, 1958), 90.

2. *Ibid.*

3. *Ibid.*

4. As I indicated in Part I, note 13, by "rule of law" I mean the general cluster of political beliefs, habits of mind, and cultural practices that inform and sustain judicial decisionmaking. My discussion of the rule of law, so understood, does not assess legal doctrine in detail and does not examine the experiences that individuals may have in specific legal circumstances. For an account of how law is experienced in the highly particular context of trials, see Robert P. Burns, *A Theory of the Trial* (Princeton, NJ: Princeton University Press, 1999).

5. I draw the term *false friends* from Ruth W. Grant, *Hypocrisy and Integrity: Machiavelli, Rousseau, and the Ethics of Politics* (Chicago: University of Chicago Press, 1997), 20–21.

6. David Runciman, *Political Hypocrisy: The Mask of Power, From Hobbes to Orwell and Beyond* (Princeton, NJ: Princeton University Press, 2008), 10.

7. Ruth Bader Ginsburg, *Speaking in a Judicial Voice*, 67 N.Y.U. L. Rev. 1185 (1992).

8. Lief H. Carter and Thomas F. Burke, *Reason in Law*, Updated 7th ed. (New York: Pearson Education, 2007). For other accounts of legal reasoning that emphasize its facilitative role, see Edward Levi, *An Introduction to Legal Reasoning* (Chicago: University of Chicago Press, 1949) and Cass R. Sunstein, *Once Case at a Time: Judicial Minimalism on the Supreme Court* (Cambridge, MA: Harvard University Press, 1999).

9. Carter and Burke, *Reason*, 147. The authors take the injunction to "look outside [one's] own will for criteria of judgment" from Robert Cover.

10. *Ibid.*, 3, emphasis original.

11. *Ibid.*, 184.

12. *Ibid.*

13. *Ibid.*

14. *Ibid.*, 164.

15. *Ibid.*, 186.

16. For the argument that proceduralism is the basic mode for the rule of law in liberal societies, see Brian Z. Tamanaha, *On the Rule of Law: History, Politics, and Theory* (New York: Cambridge University Press, 2004), 41 and passim.

17. I discuss these differences at greater length in Part II.

18. Marc Galanter has identified a broad continuum of dispute-resolving mechanisms, ranging from the informal mediation provided by ethnic clubs and associations to the formal, full-scale litigation offered in the state's official courts. See Marc Galanter, "Why the 'Haves' Come Out Ahead: Speculations on the Limits of Legal Change," *Law and Society Review* 9 (1974): 95–160.

19. I discuss these regulations and their history in Part I.

20. Tamanaha, *Rule of Law*, 141, emphasis original.

21. As I shall argue further on, public acceptance of law is also bolstered by considerations of habit, pleasure, and hierarchy.

22. Charles P. Curtis, *The Ethics of Advocacy*, 4 STAN. L. REV. 3, 3–32 (1951).

23. Carter and Burke, *Reason*, 10.

24. *Ibid.*, 143, 144.

25. *Ibid.*, 3.

26. *Ibid.*, 187.

27. *Ibid.*, 7.

28. I discuss this point of view at length in Part I.

29. Sanford Levinson, "Foreword," in Carter and Burke, *Reason*, vi, emphasis original.

30. I discuss the public's lack of detailed knowledge about the courts in Part I. For Carter and Burke's response to the criticism that most of the public is "almost totally ignorant" of judicial opinions, see Carter and Burke, *Reason*, 147.

31. Stuart Hampshire, *Justice Is Conflict* (Princeton, NJ: Princeton University Press, 2000), 94.

32. *Ibid.*, 25.

33. Albert O. Hirschman, *The Passions and the Interests: Political Arguments for Capitalism Before Its Triumph*, Twentieth Anniversary ed. (Princeton, NJ: Princeton University Press, 1997).

34. *Ibid.*, 20.

35. *Ibid.*, 43–44.

36. Hirschman focuses his attention on the passion for acquiring wealth and does not specifically discuss courtesy. He argues that the love of money is particularly well-suited to serve as a countervailing passion because of its "constancy, doggedness, and sameness from one day to the next and from person to person" (Hirschman, *Passions*, 54). But love of money is not the only countervailing passion and, as originally understood, "interests" (as countervailing passions came to be called) were not restricted to money or the pursuit of material goods. On the contrary, Hirschman writes, interests "comprised the totality of human aspirations, but denoted an element of reflection and calculation with respect to the manner in which these aspirations were to be pursued" (*ibid.*, 32). What matters, then, is not the particular passion that is placed in the coun-

tervailing role but the considered way in which the countervailing passion is deployed. Thus courtesy and the passions on which it depends comfortably fit within the tradition that Hirschman describes.

37. Alan Houston, *Benjamin Franklin and the Politics of Improvement* (New Haven, CT: Yale University Press, 2008), 69. Although Houston's subject is the way in which Franklin managed conflict in his own public life, his words also apply to the courtesy-based view of law I am setting forth here. For a more general discussion that touches on the same themes as Houston does, see John M. Kang, "The Case for Insincerity," *Studies in Law, Politics, and Society* 29 (2003): 143–64.

38. I discuss Holmes's view in the opening section of Part I.

39. Curtis, *Ethics of Advocacy*, at 12.

40. *Ibid.*, at 13, 12. See also Robert A. Kagan, *Adversarial Legalism: The American Way of Law* (Cambridge, MA: Harvard University Press, 2001), 55–56, 244.

41. Richard A. Posner, *What Do Judges Maximize? (The Same Thing Everybody Else Does)*, 3 SUP. CT. ECON. REV. 1, 1–41 (1993).

42. *Ibid.*, at 26. In spite of the importance that legal academics assign to judicial reasoning, Posner claims that most judges assign little weight to the work of written justification and have consequently left the task of opinion writing almost entirely in the hands of "eager law clerks" (*Ibid.*, at 19).

43. In this paragraph and the next I draw on Keith J. Bybee, "The Rule of Law Is Dead! Long Live the Rule of Law!," March 2009, http://ssrn.com/abstract=1404600 (last accessed August 30, 2009).

44. I discuss further on the specific propensity dominant groups have for turning law to their purposes.

45. Judith N. Shklar, *Legalism: Law, Morals, and Political Trials* (Cambridge, MA: Harvard University Press, 1964).

46. *Ibid.*, x.

47. *Ibid.*

48. I am using a threshold definition of gaming that I draw from H.L.A. Hart, *The Concept of Law*, 2nd ed. (New York: Oxford University Press, 1994). The definition of a game might be elaborated so that one has a more detailed understanding of what constitutes a "good game." Such an understanding could then be used as a normative ideal around which legal reform could be organized. For a thoughtful development of a normative account of a "good game" applied to law, see Lief H. Carter, *Law and Politics as Play*, 83 CHI.-KENT L. REV. 1333 (2008).

49. See Hart, *Concept of Law*, 257.

50. Scott J. Shapiro, "What Is the Internal Point of View?," October 14, 2006, http://ssrn.com/abstract=937337 (last accessed August 30, 2009). See also Eric J. Miller, "Judging in Bad Faith," August 25, 2009, http://ssrn.com/abstract=1461496 (December

1, 2009); and Mathilde Cohen, "Sincerity and Reason Giving: When May Legal De-cision-Makers Lie?" May 8, 2009, http://ssrn.com/abstract=1401705 (last accessed De-cember 1, 2009).

51. Hart, *Concept of Law*, 140. As I indicated in note 121 in Part I, Hart recognized the possibility of judicial "window dressing" raised by the game analogy, but dismissed it as an exceptional occurrence. "Some judicial decisions may be like this," Hart wrote, "but it is surely evident that for the most part decisions, like the chess-player's moves, are reached either by genuine effort to conform to rules consciously taken as guiding standards of decision or, if intuitively reached, are justified by rules which the judge was antecedently disposed to observe and whose relevance to the case in hand would generally be acknowledged." See *Ibid.*, 141. Posner adopts a position similar to Hart's (see Posner, *What Do Judges Maximize?*, 28). The arguments and evidence I presented in Part I suggest that Hart's and Posner's estimations are too optimistic. See also Andreas Schedler, "Arguing and Observing: Internal and External Critiques of Judicial Impar-tiality," *The Journal of Political Philosophy* 12 (2004): 245–65, 261–2.

52. As Posner writes, "in our system the line between law and policy, the judging game and the legislating game, is blurred. Many cases cannot be decided by reasoning from conventional legal materials. . . . [T]he rules of the judicial game [may] require the judge to act the part of the legislator and therefore vote his values, although the rules do not require and may even forbid him to acknowledge that this is what he is doing." See Posner, *What Do Judges Maximize?*, 28, 40.

53. Tamanaha, *Rule of Law*, 126.

54. Stanley Fish, "The Law Wishes to Have a Formal Existence," in Austin Sarat and Thomas R. Kearns, eds., *The Fate of the Law* (Ann Arbor: University of Michigan Press, 1991), 172, emphasis original. For empirical evidence that the public lends greater support to courts that take a most legalistic path to their conclusions, see Dion Far-ganis, "Does Reasoning Matter? The Impact of Opinion Content on Supreme Court Legitimacy," July 15, 2009, http://ssrn.com/abstract=1434726 (last accessed December 1, 2009).

55. Fish, "The Law Wishes," 172. Oscar Wilde expressed a similar idea when he com-pared the "true liar" to the lawyer. According to Wilde, members of the bar do not have a direct relationship to the truth. They deploy "feigned ardours and unreal rhetoric" and can "make the worse appear the better cause." Yet Wilde argued that lawyers should not be seen as true liars. Lawyers are "briefed by the prosaic" and feel obligated to "appeal to precedent," while the true liar has a "healthy, natural disdain for proof of any kind." Wilde considered this to be a critical difference. See Oscar Wilde, "The Decay of Ly-ing," in Oscar Wilde, *Intentions* (New York: Brentano, 1905), 6.

56. See Ronald Dworkin, "Justice Sotomayor: The Unjust Hearings," *The New York Review of Books* 56 (September 24, 2009), p. 14, available at http://www.nybooks.com/articles/23052 (last accessed December 1, 2009).

57. For a noted example, see *Zell v. American Seating Co.*, 138 F.2d 641 (2d Cir. 1943).

58. See, respectively, Justice Blackmun, dissenting, *DeShaney v. Winnebago County Department of Social Services*, 489 U.S. 189, 212 (1989) and Justice Scalia, dissenting, *Lawrence v. Texas*, 539 U.S. 558, 591 (2003).

59. Hart, *Concept of Law*, 24. Hart took this term from John Austin.

60. *Ibid.*, 52.

61. *Ibid.*

62. *Ibid.*

63. *Ibid.*, 114.

64. *Ibid.*, 115. In this section, I am addressing legal habits in a broad sense. There are also more specific kinds of legal habit. For example, as I indicated in my discussion of Peretti in Part I, judges are, by virtue of their specialized education and professional experience, habituated to reason in legal terms.

65. Tamanaha, *Rule of Law*, 15.

66. *Ibid.*, 23.

67. *Ibid.*, 22.

68. *Ibid.*, 116.

69. Kagan, *Adversarial Legalism*, 42.

70. Alexis de Tocqueville, *Democracy in America*, ed. J. P. Mayer, trans. George Lawrence (New York: Harper & Row, 1966), 270.

71. Kagan, *Adversarial Legalism*, 5.

72. Ravit Reichman, "Making a Mess of Things: The Trifles of Legal Pleasure," *Law, Culture and the Humanities* 1 (2005): 14–34, 19.

73. *Ibid.*, 26, 19.

74. Patricia Ewick and Susan Silbey, *The Common Place of Law: Stories from Everyday Life* (Chicago: University of Chicago Press, 1998), 219.

75. Hampshire, *Justice Is Conflict*, 8–9.

76. Ewick and Silbey, *Common Place*, 134.

77. Posner, *What Do Judges Maximize?*, 30.

78. *Ibid.*

79. Ewick and Silbey, *Common Place*, 134.

80. See Tom R. Tyler, *Why People Obey the Law* (New Haven, CT: Yale University Press, 1990) and Tom R. Tyler and Yuen J. Hou, *Trust in the Law: Encouraging Public Cooperation with the Police and the Courts* (New York: Russell Sage Foundation, 2002).

81. Tyler and Hou, *Trust*, 12. This finding also suggests that there is a symbiotic relationship between courtesy and law. I discuss this symbiosis at some length in Part II.

82. See, for example, *Plessy v. Ferguson*, 163 U.S. 537 (1896); *Bradwell v. Illinois*, 83 U.S. 130 (1872); and *Bowers v. Hardwick*, 478 U.S. 186 (1986). The substantive biases of law can be more subtle than the enforcement of cramped notions of specific concepts may suggest. Law may be used, as I indicate in the text, to uphold hierarchy by defining

"equality" in such a way that manifest inequalities are rendered as unproblematic. But law may also be used to shield existing inequalities from change by defining action in terms of individualized agency and individualized conflict that conceal the structural forces actually producing hierarchy. See William Haltom and Michael McCann, *Distorting the Law: Politics, Media, and the Litigation Crisis* (Chicago: University of Chicago Press, 2004).

83. Hart, *Concept of Law*, 117.

84. Galanter, "Why the 'Haves' Come Out Ahead," 97. The terms *one shotters* and *repeat players* are Galanter's. For elaborations and development of Galanter's argument, see Catherine Albiston, "The Rule of Law and the Litigation Process: The Paradox of Losing by Winning," *Law and Society Review* 33(1999): 869–910 and the essays collected in Herbert Kritzer and Susan Silbey, eds., *In Litigation: Do the "Haves" Still Come Out Ahead?* (Stanford, CA: Stanford University Press, 2003).

85. Galanter, "Why the 'Haves' Come Out Ahead," 135.

86. In this way litigation helps produce substantively biased concepts and doctrines that support hierarchy. See note 82.

87. Albiston thus describes the predicament of the individual one shotter as the "paradox of losing by winning." See Albiston, "Rule of Law," 901.

88. For a discussion of the advantages of law over violence, framed in the context of the African American struggle for voting rights, see Keith J. Bybee, *Mistaken Identity: The Supreme Court and the Politics of Minority Representation* (Princeton, NJ: Princeton University Press, 1998), 14–16.

89. As I argue in Part I, there is good reason to believe that public perceptions of the courts, in addition to being important, manage to express truths about how the judiciary actually functions.

90. For an extended discussion of "against the law" relationships with law, see Ewick and Silbey, *Common Place*.

91. As I suggested in note 48, the unfairness of the current system is not a necessary consequence of understanding law as a game. Nor, more broadly, is the unfairness a necessary consequence of analogizing from courtesy. It is possible to develop a normative account of a "good game" that may be then be used to model a more just judicial process. And, as indicated in Part II, it is also possible to develop an account of an ideal society in which manners serve as guardians of a just status quo. I do not develop such accounts myself because, as I indicate in the conclusion to Part III, my project has been to explain how the current system works, not to outline how it should be reformed.

Bibliography

Albiston, Catherine. "The Rule of Law and the Litigation Process: The Paradox of Losing by Winning." *Law and Society Review* 33 (1999): 869–910.

Alfini, James J., Steven Lubet, Jeffrey M. Shaman, and Charles Gardner Geyh, eds. *Judicial Conduct and Ethics* 4th ed. Newark, NJ: LexisNexis Matthew Bender, 2007.

Alper, Joanne F. "Selecting the Judiciary: Who Should Be the Judge?" In *Bench Press: The Collision of Courts, Politics, and the Media*, edited by Keith J. Bybee, 131–50. Stanford, CA: Stanford University Press, 2007.

American Bar Association Commission on the 21st Century Judiciary. "Justice in Jeopardy." July 2003, http://www.abanet.org/judind/jeopardy/pdf/report.pdf (last accessed August 30, 2009).

Anderson, Niebuhr and Associates, Inc., "1999–2000 Minnesota Supreme Court Public Opinion of the Courts Study," 2000.

Arendt, Hannah. *On Revolution*. New York: Pelican Books, 1977.

Arnold, Thurman W. *The Symbols of Government*. New Haven, CT: Yale University Press, 1935.

Aspin, Larry T., *Trends in Judicial Retention Elections, 1964–1998*, 83 JUDICATURE 79 (1999).

Aspin, Larry T., and William K. Hall, *Retention Elections and Judicial Behavior*, 77 JUDICATURE 307 (1994).

Bailey, Michael, and Forrest Maltzman. "Does Legal Doctrine Matter? Unpacking Law and Policy Preferences on the Supreme Court." *American Political Science Review* 102 (2008): 369–84.

Bandes, Susan, *We Lost It at the Movies: The Rule of Law Goes from Washington to Hollywood and Back Again*, 40 LOY. L.A. L. REV. 539 (2007).

Bauer, Robert F. *Thoughts on the Democratic Basis for Restrictions on Judicial Campaign Speech*, 35 IND. L. REV. 747 (2002).

Baum, Lawrence. *Judges and Their Audiences: A Perspective on Judicial Behavior*. Princeton, NJ: Princeton University Press, 2006.

Baum, Lawrence. *The Puzzle of Judicial Behavior*. Ann Arbor: University of Michigan Press, 1997.

Belden Russonello and Stewart Communications. "Americans Consider Judicial Independence: Findings of a National Survey Regarding Attitudes Toward the Federal Courts." Washington, DC, April 1998.

Benesh, Sara C., Nancy Scherer, and Amy Steigerwalt. "Public Perceptions of the Lower Federal Courts." August 3, 2009, http://ssrn.com/abstract=1443434 (last accessed December 1, 2009).

Bierce, Ambrose. *The Devil's Dictionary*. http://www.alcyone.com/max/lit/devils/ (last accessed August 30, 2009).

Binder, Sarah, and Forrest Maltzman. "Senatorial Delay in Confirming Federal Judges." *American Journal of Political Science* 46 (2002): 190–99.

Blanck, Peter David, *Calibrating the Scales of Justice: Studying Judges' Behavior in Bench Trials*, 68 IND. L.J. 1119 (1993).

Blanck, Peter David, Robert Rosenthal, and LaDoris Hazzard Cordell, *Note: The Appearance of Justice: Judges' Verbal and Nonverbal Behavior in Criminal Jury Trials*, 38 STAN. L. REV. 89 (1985).

Bonneau, Chris W., and Damon M. Cann. "The Effect of Campaign Contributions on Judicial Decision-Making." February 4, 2009, http://ssrn.com/abstract=1337668 (last accessed August 30, 2009).

Bonneau, Chris W., and Melinda Gann Hall. *In Defense of Judicial Elections*. New York: Routledge, 2009.

Brace, Paul, and Brent D. Boyea. "Judicial Selection Methods and Capital Punishment in the American States." In *Running for Judge: The Rising Political, Financial, and Legal Stakes of Judicial Elections*, edited by Matthew J. Streb, 186–203. New York: New York University Press, 2007.

Briffault, Richard, *Judicial Campaign Codes After Republican Party of Minnesota v. White*, 153 U. PA. L. REV. 181 (2004).

Brigham, John. *The Cult of the Court*. Philadelphia: Temple University Press, 1987.

Brown, Trevor L., and Charles R. Wise. "Constitutional Courts and Legislative-Executive Relations: The Case of Ukraine." *Political Science Quarterly* 119 (2004): 143–69.

Bryson, Anna. *From Courtesy to Civility: Changing Codes of Conduct in Early Modern England*. Oxford: Clarendon Press, 1998.

Buckler, Kevin, Francis T. Cullen, and James D. Unnever. "Citizen Assessment of Local Criminal Courts: Does Fairness Matter?" *Journal of Criminal Justice* 35 (2007): 524–36.

Burgess, Susan. *The Founding Fathers, Pop Culture, and Constitutional Law*. Burlington, VT: Ashgate Publishing, 2008.

Burke, Edmund. *Reflections on the Revolution in France*, edited by J.G.A. Pocock. Indianapolis: Hackett, 1987.

Burns, Robert P. *A Theory of the Trial*. Princeton, NJ: Princeton University Press, 1999.

Buss, Sarah. "Appearing Respectful: The Moral Significance of Manners." *Ethics* 109 (July 1999): 795–826.

Bybee, Keith J. "Legal Realism, Common Courtesy, and Hypocrisy." *Law, Culture and the Humanities* 1 (2005): 75–102.

Bybee, Keith J. *Mistaken Identity: The Supreme Court and the Politics of Minority Representation*. Princeton, NJ: Princeton University Press, 1998.

Bybee, Keith J. "The Polite Thing to Do." In *The Future of Gay Rights in America*, edited by H. N. Hirsch, 297–302. New York: Routledge, 2005.

Bybee, Keith J. "The Rule of Law Is Dead! Long Live the Rule of Law!" March 2009, http://ssrn.com/abstract=1404600 (last accessed August 30, 2009).

Bybee, Keith J. "The Two Faces of Judicial Power." In *Bench Press: The Collision of Courts, Politics, and the Media*, edited by Keith J. Bybee, 1–17. Stanford, CA: Stanford University Press, 2007.

Caldeira, Gregory A., and James L. Gibson. "The Etiology of Public Support for the Supreme Court." *American Political Science Review* 36 (1992): 635–64.

Caldeira, Gregory A., and Christopher Zorn. "Of Time and Consensual Norms on the Supreme Court." *American Journal of Political Science* 42 (1998): 874–902.

Caldwell, Mark. *A Short History of Rudeness*. New York: Picador USA, 1999.

Calhoun, Cheshire. "The Virtue of Civility." *Philosophy and Public Affairs* 29 (2000): 251–76.

Canes-Wrone, Brandice, Tom S. Clark, and Jee-Kwang Park. "Judicial Independence and Retention Elections." September 19, 2009, http://ssrn.com/abstract=1475657 (last accessed December 1, 2009).

Carter, Lief H., *Law and Politics as Play*, 83 Chi.-Kent L. Rev. 1333 (2008).

Carter, Lief H., and Thomas F. Burke. *Reason in Law*. Updated 7th ed. New York: Pearson Education, 2007.

Carter, Stephen L. *Civility: Manners, Morals, and the Etiquette of Democracy*. New York: Basic Books, 1998.

Cass, Ronald A. *The Rule of Law in America*. Baltimore: The Johns Hopkins University Press, 2001.

Caufield, Rachel P. "The Changing Tone of Judicial Election Campaigns as a Result of White." In *Running for Judge: The Rising Political, Financial, and Legal Stakes of Judicial Elections*, edited by Matthew J. Streb, 34–58. New York: New York University Press, 2007.

Center for Research and Public Policy, "Statewide Public Trust and Confidence Study." Prepared for the Connecticut Judicial Branch and the Connecticut Commission on Public Trust and Confidence, August 1998.

Chao, Loretta. "For Beijing, Etiquette Isn't a Game." August 1, 2008, http://online.wsj.com/public/article/SB121752752638401551-1iY1c5O4z5mFSQ3EQAhS8_aS1NU_20080830.html?mod=tff_main_tff_top (last accessed August 30, 2009).

Cheek, Kyle D., and Anthony Champagne, *Partisan Judicial Elections: Lessons from a Bellwether State*, 39 Willamette L. Rev. 1357 (2003).

"Civility in the House of Representatives: Executive Summary." Prepared by Kathleen Hall Jamieson for the Subcommittee on the Rules and Organization of the House, House Committee on Rules, Thursday, April 17, 1997, http://www.annenbergpublicpolicycenter.org/NewsDetails.aspx?myId=195 (last accessed August 30, 2009).

"Civility in the House of Representatives: Statement of Donald R. Wolfensberger." Subcommittee on the Rules and Organization of the House, House Committee on Rules, Thursday, April 17, 1997, http://www.rules.house.gov/archives/tran01.htm (last accessed August 30, 2009).

"Civility in the House of Representatives: Statement of Stephen Frantzich." Subcommittee on the Rules and Organization of the House, House Committee on Rules, Thursday, May 1, 1997, http://www.house.gov/rules/tran01b.htm (last accessed August 30, 2009).

Claridge, Laura. *Emily Post: Daughter of the Gilded Age, Mistress of American Manners.* New York: Random House, 2008.

Clarke, Kevin A., and David M. Primo. "Modernizing Political Science: A Model-Based Approach." *Perspectives on Politics* 5 (December 2007): 741–53.

Clayton, Cornell W. "The Supreme Court and Political Jurisprudence: New and Old Institutionalisms." In *Supreme Court Decisionmaking: New Institutionalist Approaches,* edited by Cornell W. Clayton and Howard Gillman, 15–41. Chicago: University of Chicago Press, 1999.

Code of Conduct for United States Judges, Canon 2. http://www.uscourts.gov/library/codeOfConduct/Revised_Code_Effective_July-01-09.pdf (last accessed August 30, 2009).

Cohen, Mathilde. "Sincerity and Reason Giving: When May Legal Decision-Makers Lie?" May 8, 2009, http://ssrn.com/abstract=1401705 (last accessed December 1, 2009).

Committee on Civility of the Seventh Federal Judicial Circuit, "Interim Report," April 1991, reprinted in 143 F.R.D. 371 (7th Cir. 1992).

Curtis, Charles P., *The Ethics of Advocacy,* 4 STAN. L. REV. 3 (1951).

Davidson, Jenny. *Hypocrisy and the Politics of Politeness: Manners and Morals from Locke to Austen.* New York: Cambridge University Press, 2004.

Davis, Richard. *Decisions and Images: The Supreme Court and the Press.* Englewood Cliffs, NJ: Prentice Hall, 1994.

De Tocqueville, Alexis. *Democracy in America,* edited by J. P. Mayer and translated by George Lawrence. New York: Harper & Row, 1966.

Dewey, John. "Logical Method and the Law." *Cornell Law Quarterly* 10 (1924): 17–27.

Dimino, Michael R., *Judicial Elections Versus Merit Selection: The Futile Quest for a System of Judicial "Merit" Selection,* 67 ALB. L. REV. 803 (2004).

Duxbury, Neil. *Patterns of American Jurisprudence.* New York: Oxford University Press, 1995.

Dworkin, Ronald. "Justice Sotomayor: The Unjust Hearings." *The New York Review of Books* 56 (September 24, 2009), p. 14, http://www.nybooks.com/articles/23052 (last accessed December 1, 2009).

Eelen, Gino. *A Critique of Politeness Theories.* Manchester, U.K.: St. Jerome, 2001.

Egan, Patrick J., and Jack Citrin. "Opinion Leadership, Backlash, and Delegitimation: Supreme Court Rulings and Public Opinion." August 4, 2009, http://ssrn.com/abstract=1443631 (last accessed December 1, 2009).

Elias, Norbert. "The History of Manners." Vol. I of *The Civilizing Process*, translated by Edmund Jephcott. New York: Urizen, 1978, originally published 1939.

Elias, Norbert. "Power and Civility." Vol. II of *The Civilizing Process*, translated by Edmund Jephcott. New York: Pantheon, 1982, originally published 1939.

Epstein, Lee, and Jeffrey A. Segal, *Advice and Consent: The Politics of Judicial Appointments*. New York: Oxford University Press, 2005.

Epstein, Lee, Jeffrey A. Segal, and Harold J. Spaeth. "The Norm of Consensus on the Supreme Court." *American Journal of Political Science* 45 (2001): 362–77.

Erasmus, Desiderius. "On Good Manners for Boys/*De civilitate morum puerilium*," translated by Brian McGregor. In *Literary and Educational Writings 3*, 273–89, Volume 25 of J. K. Sowards, ed., *Collected Works of Erasmus*. Toronto: University of Toronto Press, 1985.

"Essays of Brutus." In *The Anti-Federalist: An Abridgment of the Complete Anti-Federalist*, edited by Herbert Storing, 103–197. Chicago: University of Chicago Press, 1985.

Esterling, Kevin M. *Judicial Independence, Public Confidence in Courts, and State-Federal Cooperation in the Midwest: A Research Report on the Midwest Regional Conference on State-Federal Judicial Relationships with Survey Findings and Recommendations*. Chicago: American Judicature Society, 1998.

Ewick, Patricia, and Susan Silbey. *The Common Place of Law: Stories from Everyday Life*. Chicago: University of Chicago Press, 1998.

Farganis, Dion. "Does Reasoning Matter? The Impact of Opinion Content on Supreme Court Legitimacy." July 15, 2009, http://ssrn.com/abstract=1434726 (last accessed December 1, 2009).

Feldman, Stephen M. *American Legal Thought from Premodernism to Postmodernism: An Intellectual Voyage*. New York: Oxford University Press, 2000.

Feldman, Stephen M. "The Rule of Law or the Rule of Politics? Harmonizing the Internal and External Views of Supreme Court Decision-Making." *Law and Social Inquiry* 30 (2005): 89–135.

Ferejohn, John, *Judicializing Politics, Politicizing Law*, 65 LAW & CONTEMP. PROBS. 41 (2002).

Fischman, Joshua B., and David S. Law. "What Is Judicial Ideology, and How Should We Measure It?" October 19, 2008, http://ssrn.com/abstract=1121228 (last accessed August 30, 2009).

Fish, Stanley. "The Law Wishes to Have a Formal Existence." In *The Fate of the Law*, edited by Austin Sarat and Thomas R. Kearns, 159–208. Ann Arbor: University of Michigan Press, 1991.

Fleming and Associates, "An Analysis of Attitudes and Perspectives in the State of Rhode Island Towards the Rhode Island Court System for the Rhode Island Judicial Branch," April 1989.

Forni, P. M. *Choosing Civility: The Twenty-Five Rules of Considerate Conduct*. New York: St. Martin's Press, 2002.

Foucault, Michel. *Discipline and Punish: The Birth of the Prison*, translated by Alan Sheridan. Middlesex, U.K.: Penguin Books, 1979.

Foucault, Michel. *Power/Knowledge: Selected Interviews and Other Writings, 1972–1977*, edited by Colin Gordon, and translated by Colin Gordon, Leo Marshall, John Mepham, and Kate Soper. New York: Pantheon Books, 1980.

Frank, Jerome. *Law and the Modern Mind*. Gloucester, MA: Peter Smith, 1970.

Frankfurt, Harry G. *On Bullshit*. Princeton, NJ: Princeton University Press, 2005.

Fraser, Nancy. "Rethinking the Public Sphere: A Contribution to the Critique of Actually Existing Democracy." In *Habermas and the Public Sphere*, edited by Craig Calhoun, 109–42. Cambridge, MA: MIT Press, 1990.

Friedman, Paul L., *Taking the High Road: Civility, Judicial Independence, and the Rule of Law*, 58 N.Y.U. ANN. SURV. AM. L. 187 (2001).

Galanter, Marc. *Lowering the Bar: Lawyer Jokes and Legal Culture*. Madison: University of Wisconsin Press, 2005.

Galanter, Marc. "Why the 'Haves' Come Out Ahead: Speculations on the Limits of Legal Change." *Law and Society Review* 9 (1974): 95–160.

Gallup Poll News Service. "Slim Majority of Americans Approve of the Supreme Court," September 26, 2007, http://www.gallup.com/poll/28798/Slim-Majority-Americans-Approve-Supreme-Court.aspx (last accessed August 30, 2009).

Gerber, Scott D., and Keeok Park. "The Quixotic Search for Consensus on the U.S. Supreme Court: A Cross-Judicial Empirical Analysis of the Rehnquist Court Justices." *American Political Science Review* 91 (1997): 390–408.

Geyh, Charles Gardner. "Preserving Public Confidence in the Courts in an Age of Individual Rights and Public Skepticism." In *Bench Press: The Collision of Courts, Politics, and the Media*, edited by Keith J. Bybee, 21–51. Stanford, CA: Stanford University Press, 2007.

Geyh, Charles Gardner. *When Courts and Congress Collide: The Struggle for Control of America's Judicial System*. Ann Arbor: University of Michigan Press, 2006.

Geyh, Charles Gardner, *Why Judicial Elections Stink*, 64 OHIO ST. L.J. 43 (2003).

Gibson, James L. "Campaigning for the Bench: The Corrosive Effects of Campaign Speech?" *Law and Society Review* 42 (2008): 899–928.

Gibson, James L. "Challenges to the Impartiality of State Supreme Courts: Legitimacy Theory and 'New-Style' Judicial Campaigns." *American Political Science Review* 102 (2008): 59–75.

Gibson, James L. "Judging the Politics of Judging: Are Politicians in Robes Inevitably Illegitimate?" Paper prepared for the "What's Law Got to Do with It?" Conference, Indiana University School of Law, March 27–28, 2009.

Gibson, James L. "The Legitimacy of the U.S. Supreme Court in a Polarized Polity." *Journal of Empirical Legal Studies* 4 (2007): 507–38.

Gibson, James L. "New-Style' Judicial Campaigns and the Legitimacy of State High Courts." *The Journal of Politics* 71 (2009): 1285–1305.

Gibson, James L., and Gregory A. Caldeira. "Blacks and the United States Supreme Court: Models of Diffuse Support." *The Journal of Politics* 54 (1992): 1120–45.

Gibson, James L., and Gregory A. Caldeira. "Campaign Support, Conflicts of Interest, and Judicial Impartiality: Can the Legitimacy of Courts Be Rescued by Recusals?" October 19, 2009, http://ssrn.com/abstract=1491289 (last accessed December 1, 2009).

Gibson, James L., and Gregory A. Caldeira. "Have Segal and Spaeth Damaged the Legitimacy of the U.S. Supreme Court?" July 17, 2009, http://ssrn.com/abstract=1436426 (last accessed August 30, 2009).

Gibson, James L., and Gregory A. Caldeira. "Knowing About Courts." June 20, 2007, http://ssrn.com/abstract=956562 (last accessed August 30, 2009).

Gibson, James L., and Gregory A. Caldeira. "Supreme Court Nominations, Legitimacy Theory and the American Public: A Dynamic Test of the Theory of Positivity Bias." July 4, 2007, http://ssrn.com/abstract=998283 (last accessed August 30, 2009).

Gibson, James L., Gregory A. Caldeira, and Vanessa Baird. "On the Legitimacy of National High Courts." *American Political Science Review* 92 (1998): 343–58.

Gibson, James L., Gregory A. Caldeira, and Lester Kenyatta Spence. "Measuring Attitudes Toward the United States Supreme Court." *American Journal of Political Science* 47 (2003): 354–76.

Gibson, James L., Gregory A. Caldeira, and Lester Kenyatta Spence. "Why Do People Accept Public Policies They Oppose? Testing Legitimacy Theory with a Survey-Based Experiment." *Political Research Quarterly* 58 (2005): 187–201.

Gillman, Howard. *The Votes That Counted: How the Court Decided the 2000 Presidential Election.* Chicago: University of Chicago Press, 2001.

Ginsburg, Ruth Bader, *Speaking in a Judicial Voice,* 67 N.Y.U. L. Rev. 1185 (1992).

GMA Research Corporation, "How the Public Views the Courts: A 1999 Washington Statewide Survey Compared to a 1999 National Survey." Prepared for the Office of the Administrator of the Courts, State of Washington, 1999.

Goffman, Erving. *Behavior in Public Places: Notes on the Social Organization of Gatherings.* New York: The Free Press, 1963.

Goldberg, Deborah, James Sample, and David Pozen, *The Best Defense: Why Elected Courts Should Lead Recusal Reform,* 46 Washburn L.J. 504 (2007).

Goldberg, Whoopi. *Whoopi's Big Book of Manners,* illustrated by Olo. New York: Hyperion Books for Children, 2006.

Goldstein, Tom. "The Distance Between Judges and Journalists." In *Bench Press: The Collision of Courts, Politics, and the Media,* edited by Keith J. Bybee, 185–96. Stanford, CA: Stanford University Press, 2007.

Gould, Deborah B. "Life During Wartime: Emotions and the Development of ACT UP." *Mobilization* 7 (2002): 177–200.

Grant, Ruth W. *Hypocrisy and Integrity: Machiavelli, Rousseau, and the Ethics of Politics.* Chicago: University of Chicago Press, 1997.

Graves, James E. Jr. "Judicial Independence: The Courts and the Media." In *Bench Press: The Collision of Courts, Politics, and the Media,* edited by Keith J. Bybee, 114–22. Stanford, CA: Stanford University Press, 2007.

"The Great *Reader's Digest* Global Courtesy Test: How Polite Are We?" July 2006, http://www.readersdigest.ca/mag/2006/07/polite.php (last accessed August 30, 2009).

Greenberg, David. *Don't Forget Your Etiquette!*, illustrated by Nadine Bernard Westcott. New York: Melanie Kroupa Books/Farrar, Straus & Giroux, 2006.

Greenberg, Quinlan, Rosner Research Inc. "Justice at Stake National Survey of American Voters, October 30–November 7, 2001," http://faircourts.org/files/JASNational SurveyResults.pdf (last accessed August 30, 2009).

Greenberg, Quinlan, Rosner Research Inc. "Justice at Stake National Survey of State Judges, November 5, 2001–January 2, 2002," http://faircourts.org/files/JASJudges SurveyResults.pdf (last accessed August 30, 2009).

Guinness, Os. *The Case for Civility: And Why Our Future Depends on It*. New York: HarperCollins, 2008.

Haltom, William. *Reporting on the Courts: How the Mass Media Cover Judicial Actions* Chicago: Nelson-Hall, 1998.

Haltom, William, and Michael McCann. *Distorting the Law: Politics, Media, and the Litigation Crisis*. Chicago: University of Chicago Press, 2004.

Hamilton, Alexander. "Federalist Paper No. 78." In Alexander Hamilton, James Madison, and John Jay, *The Federalist Papers*, edited by Clinton Rossiter, 463–78. New York: Mentor, 1961.

Hampshire, Stuart. *Justice Is Conflict*. Princeton, NJ: Princeton University Press, 2000.

Hart, H.L.A. *The Concept of Law*. 2nd ed. New York: Oxford University Press, 1994.

Hartley, Roger E., and Lisa M. Holmes. "The Increasing Senate Scrutiny of Lower Federal Court Nominees." *Political Science Quarterly* 117 (2002): 259–78.

Henderson, M. Todd, *From Seriatim to Consensus and Back Again: A Theory of Dissent*, 2007 SUPREME COURT REVIEW 283 (2007).

Hensler, Deborah L., *Do We Need an Empirical Research Agenda on Judicial Independence?*, 72 S. CAL. L. REV. 707 (1999).

Hirschl, Ran. *Towards Juristocracy: The Origins and Consequences of the New Constitutionalism*. Cambridge, MA: Harvard University Press, 2004.

Hirschman, Albert O. *The Passions and the Interests: Political Arguments for Capitalism Before Its Triumph*, Twentieth Anniversary ed. Princeton, NJ: Princeton University Press, 1997.

Hobbes, Thomas. *Leviathan*. New York: Penguin English Library, 1981.

Hodges, Deborah Robertson. *Etiquette: An Annotated Bibliography of Literature Published in the English in the United States, 1900 Through 1987*. Jefferson, NC: McFarland and Company, 1989.

Holmes, Oliver Wendell, *The Path of the Law*, 10 HARV. L. REV. 457 (1897).

Horwitz, Morton J. *The Transformation of American Law, 1870–1960: The Crisis of Legal Orthodoxy*. New York: Oxford University Press, 1992.

Hosteny, Joseph N. "Civility or Honesty? Which Should You Choose?" *Intellectual Property Today* (January 2002): 18–19.

Houston, Alan. *Benjamin Franklin and the Politics of Improvement*. New Haven, CT: Yale University Press, 2008.

Huber, Gregory A., and Sanford C. Gordon, "Accountability and Coercion: Is Justice Blind When It Runs for Office?" *American Journal of Political Science* 48 (2004): 247–63.

Institute for the Advancement of the American Legal System and the League of Women Voters of Colorado Education Fund. "2007 Colorado Voter Opinions on the Judiciary." July 2007, http://www.du.edu/legalinstitute/publications2007.html (last accessed August 30, 2009).

Institute for Public Affairs, University of Illinois at Springfield, "2002 Illinois Statewide Survey on Judicial Selection Issues." Prepared for Illinois Campaign for Political Reform, August 2002.

Jamieson, Kathleen Hall, and Erika Falk. "Civility in the House of Representatives: An Update." March 1998, http://www.annenbergpublicpolicycenter.org/Downloads/Political_Communication/105thCongressCivil/REP20.PDF (last accessed August 30, 2009).

Jamieson, Kathleen Hall, and Erika Falk. "Civility in the House of Representatives: The 105th Congress." March 1999, http://www.annenbergpublicpolicycenter.org/Downloads/Political_Communication/105thCongressCivil/REP26.PDF (last accessed August 30, 2009).

Jamieson, Kathleen Hall, and Erika Falk. "Civility in the House of Representatives: The 106th Congress." March 2001, http://www.annenbergpublicpolicycenter.org/Downloads/Political_Communication/106thCongressCivil/2001_civility106th.pdf (last accessed August 30, 2009).

Jarecke, George W., and Nancy K. Plant. *Seeking Civility: Common Courtesy and the Common Law*. Boston: Northeastern University Press, 2003.

Judicial Elections White Paper Task Force, *Judicial Selection White Papers: The Case for Partisan Judicial Elections*, 22 TOL. L. REV 393 (2002).

"Judicial Independence, Final Report September 2006." Prepared for Annenberg Public Policy Center, September 2006, http://www.annenbergpublicpolicycenter.org/ (last accessed August 30, 2009).

Justice at Stake, Minnesota Statewide Poll, conducted by Decision Resources, Ltd., January 2008.

Kagan, Robert A. *Adversarial Legalism: The American Way of Law*. Cambridge, MA: Harvard University Press, 2001.

Kahan, Dan M., *What Do Alternative Sanctions Mean?*, 63 U. CHI. L. REV. 591 (1996).

Kahan, Dan M. "What's Really Wrong with Shaming Sanctions?" Yale Law School Public Law and Legal Theory Working Paper No. 125, July 1, 2006, http://ssrn.com/abstract=914503 (last accessed August 30, 2009).

Kahn, Paul W. *The Cultural Study of Law: Reconstructing Legal Scholarship*. Chicago: University of Chicago Press, 1999.

Kalman, Laura. *Legal Realism at Yale, 1927–1960*. Chapel Hill: University of North Carolina Press, 1986.

Kang, John M. "The Case for Insincerity." *Studies in Law, Politics, and Society* 29 (2003): 143–64.

Kang, John M., *The Irrelevance of Sincerity: Deliberative Democracy in the Supreme Court*, 48 ST. LOUIS U. L.J. 305 (2004).

Kang, John M. "The Uses of Insincerity: Thomas Hobbes's Theory of Law and Society." *Law and Literature* 15 (2003): 371–93.

Karlan, Pamela S., *Electing Judges, Judging Elections, and the Lessons of Caperton*, 123 HARV. L. REV. 80 (2009).

Kasson, John F. *Rudeness and Civility: Manners in Nineteenth-Century Urban America*. New York: Hill and Wang, 1990.

Katz, Alan. *Are You Quite Polite? Silly Dilly Manners Songs*, illustrated by David Catrow. New York: Margaret K. McElderry Books/Simon & Schuster, 2006.

Keck, Thomas M. "Party, Policy, or Duty: Why Does the Supreme Court Invalidate Federal Statutes?" *American Political Science Review* 101 (2007): 321–38.

Kennedy, Randall. "The Case Against Civility." *The American Prospect*. November 1, 1998–December 1, 1998, http://www.prospect.org/cs/articles?article=the_case_against_civility (last accessed August 30, 2009).

Kenyon, Cecelia. "Introduction." In *The Anti-Federalists*, edited by Cecelia Kenyon, xxi–xxxii. Indianapolis, IN: Bobbs-Merrill, 1966.

King, Martin Luther Jr. "Letter from a Birmingham Jail." In *On Civil Disobedience: Essays Old and New*, edited by Robert A. Godwin, 65. Chicago: Rand McNally, 1968.

Klein, L. E. "The Political Significance of Politeness in Early Eighteenth-Century Britain." In *Politics, Politeness, and Patriotism*, edited by Gordon J. Schochet, with Patricia E. Tatspaugh and Carol Brobeck, 73–108. Proceedings of the Folger Institute, Center for the History of British Political Thought, Volume 5. Washington, DC: The Folger Institute, 1993.

Kohm, Steven A. "The People's Law Versus Judge Judy Justice: Two Models of Law in American Reality-Based Courtroom TV." *Law and Society Review* 40 (2006): 693–727.

Kozinski, Alex. "The Appearance of Propriety." *Legal Affairs*. January-February 2005, http://www.legalaffairs.org/issues/January-February-2005/argument_kozinski_janfeb05.msp (last accessed August 30, 2009).

Kozinski, Alex, *What I Ate for Breakfast and Other Mysteries of Judicial Decision Making*, 26 LOY. L.A. L. REV. 993 (1993).

Krasner, Stephen D. *Sovereignty: Organized Hypocrisy*. Princeton, NJ: Princeton University Press, 1999.

Kritzer, Herbert, and Susan Silbey, eds. *In Litigation: Do the "Haves" Still Come Out Ahead?* Stanford, CA: Stanford University Press, 2003.

Kritzer, Herbert M., and John Voelker, *How Wisconsin Citizens View Their Courts*, 82 JUDICATURE 64 (1998–1999).

La Rochefoucauld. *Maxims*, translated by Leonard Tancock. London: Penguin, 1959.

Langton, Lynn, and Thomas H. Cohen. *State Court Organization, 1987–2004*. Bureau of Justice Statistics, Office of Justice Programs, United States Department of Justice, 2007.

Lee, Jennifer. *Civility in the City: Blacks, Jews, and Koreans in Urban America*. Cambridge, MA: Harvard University Press, 2002.

Lerner, Renee Lettow. "The New York Bar and Reform of the Elected Judiciary After the Civil War." George Washington University Law School Public Law and Legal Theory Working Paper No. 139, April 4, 2005, http://ssrn.com/abstract=697902 (last accessed August 30, 2009).

Levi, Edward. *An Introduction to Legal Reasoning*. Chicago: University of Chicago Press, 1949.

Levinson, Sanford, *Bush v. Gore and the French Revolution: A Tentative List of Some Early Lessons*, 65 LAW & CONTEMP. PROBS. 7 (2002).

Levinson, Sanford. "Foreword." In *Reason in Law*, updated 7th ed., edited by Lief H. Carter and Thomas F. Burke. New York: Pearson Education, 2007.

Levinson, Sanford. "Return of Legal Realism." *The Nation*. January 8, 2001, http://www.thenation.com/doc/20010108/levinson (last accessed August 30, 2009).

Levy, Jacob T. "Multicultural Manners." May 12, 2009, http://ssrn.com/abstract=1403687 (last accessed August 30, 2009).

Lewis, Anthony. "Afterword: The State of Judicial Independence." In *Bench Press: The Collision of Courts, Politics, and the Media*, edited by Keith J. Bybee, 197–201. Stanford, CA: Stanford University Press, 2007.

Lipson, Michael. "Peacekeeping: Organized Hypocrisy?" *European Journal of International Relations* 13 (2007): 5–34.

Lithwick, Dahlia. "The Internet and the Judiciary: We Are All Experts Now." In *Bench Press: The Collision of Courts, Politics, and the Media*, edited by Keith J. Bybee, 177–84. Stanford, CA: Stanford University Press, 2007.

Llewellyn, K. N. *The Bramble Bush: Some Lectures on Law and Its Study*. New York: Tentative Printing for Use of Students at Columbia University School of Law.

Loomis, Burdett A., ed. *Esteemed Colleagues: Civility and Deliberation in the U.S. Senate*. Washington, DC: Brookings Institution Press, 2000.

Lord Chesterfield. *Letters*, edited by David Roberts. New York: Cambridge University Press, 1992.

Madison, James. "Federalist Paper No. 10." In Alexander Hamilton, James Madison, and John Jay, *The Federalist Papers*, edited by Clinton Rossiter, 78–9. New York: Mentor, 1961.

Madison, James. "Federalist Paper No. 78." In Alexander Hamilton, James Madison, and John Jay, *The Federalist Papers*, edited by Clinton Rossiter, 346. New York: Mentor, 1961.

Markovitz, Elizabeth. *The Politics of Sincerity: Plato, Frank Speech, and Democratic Government*. University Park: The Pennsylvania State University Press, 2008.

Martin, Judith. *Common Courtesy: In Which Miss Manners Solves the Problem That Baffled Mr. Jefferson.* New York: Athenaeum, 1985.

Martin, Judith. *Miss Manners' Guide to Rearing Perfect Children,* illustrated by Gloria Kaman. New York: Athenaeum, 1984.

Martin, Judith. *Miss Manners Rescues Civilization from Sexual Harassment, Frivolous Lawsuits, Dissing and Other Lapses in Civility.* New York: Crown Publishers, 1996.

Martin, Judith. "The World's Oldest Virtue." *First Things* 33 (1993): 22–25.

Massie, Tajuana D., Thomas G. Hansford, and Donald Songer. "The Timing of Presidential Nominations to the Lower Federal Courts." *Political Research Quarterly* 57 (2004): 145–54.

Mather, Lynn. "Courts in Popular Culture." In *The Judicial Branch,* edited by Kermit L. Hall and Kevin T. McGuire, 233–61. New York: Oxford University Press, 2005.

McGuire, Kevin T. "The Judicial Branch: Judging America's Judges." In *A Republic Divided: The Annenberg Democracy Project,* edited by Kathleen Hall Jamieson, 194–213. New York: Oxford University Press, 2007.

McKee, Theodore A., *Judges as Umpires,* 35 Hofstra. L. Rev. 1709 (2007).

McKinnon, Christine. "Hypocrisy, Cheating, and Character Possession." *The Journal of Value Inquiry* 39 no. 3–4 (December 2005): 1–16.

McKinnon, Christine. "Varieties of Insincerity." *International Journal of Applied Philosophy* 20 (2006): 23–40.

Merriam-Webster's Collegiate Dictionary 10th ed. Springfield, MA: Merriam-Webster, 1995.

Miller, Banks, and Brett Curry. "Expertise, Experience, and Ideology on Specialized Courts: The Case of the Court of Appeals for the Federal Circuit." *Law and Society Review* 43 (2009): 839–64.

Miller, Eric J. "Judging in Bad Faith." August 25, 2009, http://ssrn.com/abstract=1461496 (last accessed December 1, 2009).

Miller, William Ian. *Faking It.* New York: Cambridge University Press, 2003.

Mindes, Marvin W., with Alan C. Acock. "Trickster, Hero, Helper: A Report on the Lawyer Image." *American Bar Foundation Research Journal* 7 (1982): 177–233.

Muntz, Diana C. "Effects of 'In-Your-Face' Television Discourse on Perceptions of a Legitimate Opposition." *American Political Science Review* 101 (2007): 621–35.

National Center for State Courts. "State Courts: A Blueprint for the Future." Prepared for the Proceedings of the Second National Conference on the Judiciary, Williamsburg, Virginia, March 19–22, 1978.

National Center for State Courts, "How the Public Views the State Courts: A 1999 National Survey." Presented at the Conference on Public Trust and Confidence in the Justice System, Washington, DC, May 14, 1999.

Nelson, William E., Harvey Rishikof, I. Scott Messinger, and Michael Jo, *The Supreme Court Clerkship and the Polarization of the Court: Can the Polarization Be Fixed?,* 13 Green Bag 2d 59 (Autumn 2009).

Nine Justices, Ten Years: A Statistical Retrospective, 118 Harv. L. Rev. 510 (2004).

Obbie, Mark. "Winners and Losers." In *Bench Press: The Collision of Courts, Politics, and the Media*, edited by Keith J. Bybee, 153–76. Stanford, CA: Stanford University Press, 2007.

Olson, Susan M., and David A. Huth. "Explaining Public Attitudes Toward Local Courts." *The Justice System Journal* 20 (1998): 41–61.

Olszewski, Peter Paul Sr., *Who's Judging Whom? Why Popular Elections Are Preferable to Merit Selection Systems*, 109 PENN ST. L. REV 1 (2004).

Oxford English Dictionary, 2nd ed. Oxford: Oxford University Press, 1989.

Paine, Thomas. *Rights of Man*. New York: Viking Penguin, 1984.

Papke, David Ray. "From Flat to Round: Changing Portrayals of the Judge in American Popular Culture." Marquette Law School Legal Studies Paper No. 06-24, May 2006, http://ssrn.com/abstract=902125 (last accessed August 30, 2009).

Pascal, Blaise. *Pascal's Pensées*. New York: E.P. Dutton, 1958.

Patil, Reshma. "Two Claps, Arms Stretched, Two Claps, Arms Up . . ." July, 27, 2008, http://www.livemint.com/2008/07/26000951/Two-claps-arms-stretched-two.html (last accessed August 30, 2009).

Peretti, Terri Jennings. *In Defense of a Political Court*. Princeton, NJ: Princeton University Press, 1999.

Pew Research Center for the People & the Press. "Court Critics Now on Both Left and Right: Supreme Court's Image Declines as Nomination Battles Loom, National Survey Conducted June 8–12, 2005." http://people-press.org/report/247/supreme-courts-image-declines-as-nomination-battle-looms (accessed August 30, 2009).

Pocock, J.G.A. *The Machiavellian Moment: Florentine Political Thought and the Atlantic Republican Tradition*. Princeton, NJ: Princeton University Press, 1975.

Podgers, James. "Judging Judicial Behavior," *ABA Journal eReport*, February 16, 2007, http://www.abanet.org/journal/ereport/f16code.html (last accessed August 30, 2009).

Popkin, Samuel L. *The Reasoning Voter: Communication and Persuasion in Presidential Campaigns*, 2nd ed. Chicago: University of Chicago Press, 1994.

Popkin, Samuel L., John W. Gorman, Charles Phillips, and Jeffrey A. Smith. "Comment: What Have You Done for Me Lately? Toward an Investment Theory of Voting." *American Political Science Review* 70 (1976): 779–805.

Popkin, William D. *Evolution of Judicial Opinion: Institutional and Individual Styles*. New York: New York University Press, 2007.

Posner, Richard A., *What Do Judges Maximize? (The Same Thing Everybody Else Does)*, 3 SUP. CT. ECON. REV. 1 (1993).

Post, Elizabeth L. *Emily Post on Etiquette*. New York: Harper & Row, 1987.

Post, Peggy. *Emily Post's Etiquette*, 17th ed. New York: HarperCollins, 2004.

Post, Peggy, and Cindy Post Senning. *Emily's Everyday Manners*, illustrated by Steve Bjorkman. New York: Collins, 2006.

Post, Robert C., *On the Popular Image of Lawyers: Reflections in a Dark Glass*, 75 CAL. L. REV. 379 (1987).

Post, Robert, *The Supreme Court Opinion as an Institutional Practice: Dissent, Legal Scholarship, and Decisionmaking in the Taft Court*, 85 Minn. L. Rev. 1267 (2001).

Powell, H. Jefferson. *Constitutional Conscience: The Moral Dimension of Judicial Decision*. Chicago: University of Chicago Press, 2008.

Princeton Survey Research Associates International. "Separate Branches, Shared Responsibilities: A National Survey of Public Expectations on Solving Justice Issues." Conducted on Behalf of the National Center for State Courts, April 2009.

Princeton Survey Research Associates International. "2006 Annenberg Judicial Independence Survey." Prepared for the Annenberg Foundation Trust at Sunnylands, August 2006.

Purcell, Edward A. Jr. *The Crisis of Democratic Theory: Scientific Naturalism and the Problem of Value*. Lexington: University Press of Kentucky, 1973.

Rakove, Jack N. *Original Meanings: Politics and Ideas in the Making of the Constitution*. New York: Vintage Books, 1997.

Ramseyer, J. Mark. "Not So Ordinary Judges in Ordinary Courts: Teaching *Jordan v. Duff & Phelps*." Harvard Law and Economics Discussion Paper No. 557, August 2006, http://ssrn.com/abstract=927862 (last accessed August 30, 2009).

Reddick, Malia, *Merit Selection: A Review of the Social Scientific Literature*, 106 Dick. L. Rev. 729 (2002).

Reichman, Ravit. "Making a Mess of Things: The Trifles of Legal Pleasure." *Law, Culture and the Humanities* 1 (2005): 14–34.

Reid, Traciel V., *The Politicization of Retention Elections: Lessons from the Defeat of Justices Lanphier and White*, 83 Judicature 68 (1999).

Ripple, Raymond M., *Learning Outside the Fire: The Need for Civility Instruction in Law School*, 15 Notre Dame J.L. Ethics & Pub. Pol'y 359 (2001).

Rosen, Jeffery. "Roberts's Rules." *The Atlantic Monthly*, January-February 2007, http://www.theatlantic.com/doc/200701/john-roberts (last accessed August 30, 2009).

Rottman, David B. "Public Perceptions of the State Courts: A Primer." Paper prepared for presentation at the Third National Symposium on Court Management, Atlanta, GA, August 13–19, 2000.

Runciman, David. *Political Hypocrisy: The Mask of Power, From Hobbes to Orwell and Beyond*. Princeton, NJ: Princeton University Press, 2008.

Russonello, John. "Speak to Values: How to Promote the Courts and Blunt Attacks on the Judiciary." *Court Review* (Summer 2004): 10–12.

Sample, James, Lauren Jones, and Rachel Weiss. "The New Politics of Judicial Elections, 2006." Justice at Stake Campaign and The Brennan Center of Justice at NYU Law School, 2007, http://www.justiceatstake.org/contentViewer.asp?breadcrumb=3,570,979 (last accessed August 30, 2009).

Sapiro, Virginia. "Considering Political Civility Historically: A Case Study of the United States." Prepared for the annual meeting of the International Society for Political Psychology, Amsterdam, The Netherlands, July 1999.

Sarat, Austin, *Enactments of Professionalism: A Study of Judges' and Lawyers' Accounts of Ethics and Civility in Litigation*, 67 FORDHAM L. REV. 809 (1998).

Schaffner, Brian F., and Jennifer Segal Diascro. "Judicial Elections in the News." In *Running for Judge: The Rising Political, Financial, and Legal Stakes of Judicial Elections*, edited by Matthew J. Streb, 115–39. New York: New York University Press, 2007.

Scheb, John M. II, and William Lyons. "Judicial Behavior and Public Opinion: Popular Expectations Regarding Factors That Influence Supreme Court Decisions." *Political Behavior* 23 (2001): 181–94.

Schedler, Andreas. "Arguing and Observing: Internal and External Critiques of Judicial Impartiality." *The Journal of Political Philosophy* 12 (2004): 245–65.

Schelegel, John Henry. *American Legal Realism and Empirical Social Science*. Chapel Hill: University of North Carolina Press, 1995.

Scherer, Nancy. *Scoring Points: Politicians, Activists, and the Lower Federal Court Appointments Process*. Stanford, CA: Stanford University Press, 2005.

Schotland, Roy A. "Should Judges Be More Like Politicians?" *Court Review* 39 (2002): 8–11.

Schultz, David, *Republican Party of Minnesota v. White and the Future of Judicial Selection*, 69 ALB. L. REV. 985 (2004).

See, Harold. "An Essay on Judicial Selection." In *Bench Press: The Collision of Courts, Politics, and the Media*, edited by Keith J. Bybee, 77–113. Stanford, CA: Stanford University Press, 2007.

Shaening and Associates, Inc., "How New Mexicans View the State Courts: How Do We Compare to the National Picture and How Perceptions Have Changed Since 1997." Prepared for the Administrative Office of the Courts, February 2000.

Shane, Peter M., *Interbranch Accountability in State Government and the Constitutional Requirement of Judicial Independence*, 61 LAW & CONTEMP. PROBS. 21 (1998).

Shapiro, Martin. *Courts: A Comparative and Political Analysis*. Chicago: University of Chicago Press, 1981.

Shapiro, Scott J. "What Is the Internal Point of View?" October 14, 2006, http://ssrn.com/abstract=937337 (last accessed August 30, 2009).

Shepard, Randall T., *The Special Professional Challenges of Appellate Judging*, 35 IND. L. REV. 381 (2002).

Shepard, Randall T., *Telephone Justice, Pandering, and Judges Who Speak Out of School*, 29 FORDHAM URB. L.J. 811 (2002).

Shepard, Randall T., *What Judges Can Do About Legal Professionalism*, 32 WAKE FOREST L. REV. 621 (1997).

Shils, Edward. *The Virtue of Civility: Selected Essays on Liberalism, Tradition, and Civil Society*, edited by Steven Grosby. Indianapolis: Liberty Fund, 1997.

Shklar, Judith N. *Legalism: Law, Morals, and Political Trials*. Cambridge, MA: Harvard University Press, 1964.

Shklar, Judith N. *Ordinary Vices*. Cambridge, MA: The Belknap Press of Harvard University, 1984.

Silverstein, Mark. *Judicious Choices: The New Politics of Supreme Court Confirmations*. New York: W.W. Norton, 1994.

Sinopoli, Richard C. "Thick-Skinned Liberalism: Redefining Civility." *American Political Science Review* 89 (1995): 612–20.

Sloane, Eric. *Don't: A Little Book of Early American Gentility*. New York: Funk & Wagnalls, 1968.

Smith, Rogers M. "If Politics Matters: Implications for a 'New Institutional'." *Studies in American Political Development* 6 (1992): 1–36.

Spargo, Thomas J., *A Peripatetic View of Judicial Free Speech*, 68 ALB. L. REV. 629 (2005).

Spill, Rorie L., and Zoe M. Oxley, *Philosopher Kings or Political Actors? How the Media Portray the Supreme Court*, 87 JUDICATURE 23 (2003).

Storing, Herbert J. *What the Anti-Federalists Were For: The Political Thought of the Opponents of the Constitution*. Chicago: University of Chicago Press, 1981.

Streb, Matthew J., ed. *Running for Judge: The Rising Political, Financial, and Legal Stakes of Judicial Elections*. New York: New York University Press, 2007.

Sunstein, Cass R. *Once Case at a Time: Judicial Minimalism on the Supreme Court*. Cambridge, MA: Harvard University Press, 1999.

Survey Research Center, University of New Orleans, "Citizen Evaluation of the Louisiana Courts: A Report to the Louisiana Supreme Court, Volume I, The Survey," June 16, 1998.

Syracuse University's Campbell Public Affairs Institute, "The Maxwell Poll on Civic Engagement and Inequality," October 2005, http://www.maxwell.syr.edu/campbell/programs/maxwellpoll/data.htm (last accessed August 30, 2009).

Taha, Ahmed E. "Judges' Political Orientations and the Selection of Disputes for Litigation," Wake Forest University Legal Studies Research Paper Series No. 963468, January 2007, http://ssrn.com/abstract=963468 (last accessed August 30, 2009).

Tamanaha, Brian Z. *Law as a Means to an End: Threat to the Rule of Law*. New York: Cambridge University Press, 2006.

Tamanaha, Brian Z. *On the Rule of Law: History, Politics, and Theory*. New York: Cambridge University Press, 2004.

Tamanaha, Brian Z. "The Perils of Pervasive Instrumentalism," Montesquieu Lecture Series, Tilburg University, 1 (2005): 49–56, http://ssrn.com/abstract=725582 (last accessed August 30, 2009).

Tarnopolsky, Christina. "Prudes, Perverts, and Tyrants: Plato and the Contemporary Politics of Shame." *Political Theory* 32 (2004): 468–94.

Tarr, G. Alan. "Politicizing the Process: The New Politics of State Judicial Elections." In *Bench Press: The Collision of Courts, Politics, and the Media*, edited by Keith J. Bybee, 52–74. Stanford, CA: Stanford University Press, 2007.

Tarr, G. Alan, *Rethinking the Selection of State Supreme Court Justices*, 39 WILLIAMETTE L. REV. 1445 (2003).

Thompson, Dennis F. "Hypocrisy and Democracy." In *Liberalism Without Illusions: Essays on Liberal Theory and the Political Vision of Judith Shklar*, edited by Bernard Yack, 173–90. Chicago: University of Chicago Press, 1996.

Toobin, Jeffrey. "Sex and the Supremes." *The New Yorker*, August 1, 2005, 32–37.

Tribe, Laurence H. *American Constitutional Law*, 3rd ed., Vol. I. New York: Foundation Press, 2000.

Tribe, Laurence H. "An Open Letter to Readers of *American Constitutional Law*." http:// www.scotusblog.com/movabletype/archives/Tribe-Treatise-Green%20Bag%20 2005%20low%20res.pdf (last accessed August 30, 2009).

Trilling, Lionel. *Sincerity and Authenticity*. Cambridge, MA: Harvard University Press, 1972.

Trollope, Fanny. *The Domestic Manners of Americans*, edited by Richard Mullen. New York: Oxford University Press, 1984.

Truss, Lynne. *Talk to the Hand: The Utter Bloody Rudeness of the World Today, or Six Good Reasons to Stay Home and Bolt the Door*. New York: Gotham Books, 2005.

Twining, William. *Karl Llewellyn and the Realist Movement*. Norman, OK: University of Oklahoma Press, 1985.

Tyler, Tom R. *Why People Obey the Law*. New Haven, CT: Yale University Press, 1990.

Tyler, Tom R., and Yuen J. Hou. *Trust in the Law: Encouraging Public Cooperation with the Police and the Courts*. New York: Russell Sage Foundation, 2002.

Tyler, Tom R., Lawrence Sherman, Heather Strang, Geoffrey C. Barnes, and Daniel Woods. "Reintegrative Shaming, Procedural Justice, and Recidivism: The Engagement of Offenders' Psychological Mechanisms in the Canberra RISE Drinking-and-Driving Experiment." *Law and Society Review* 41 (2007): 553–86.

Walker, John M. Jr., *Current Threats to Judicial Independence and Appropriate Responses: A Presentation to the American Bar Association*, 12 St. John's J. Legal Comment. 45 (1996).

Walker, John M. Jr. "Politics and the Confirmation Process: Thoughts on the Roberts and Alito Hearings." In *Bench Press: The Collision of Courts, Politics, and the Media*, edited by Keith J. Bybee, 123–30. Stanford, CA: Stanford University Press, 2007.

Walker, Thomas G., Lee Epstein, and William Dixon. "On the Mysterious Demise of Consensual Norms in the United States Supreme Court." *The Journal of Politics* 50 (1988): 361–89.

Washington, George. *Rules of Civility & Decent Behaviour in Company and Conversation*. http://www.earlyamerica.us/Almanack/life/manners/rules2.cfm (last accessed August 30, 2009).

Wasserstrom, Richard A. *The Judicial Decision: Toward a Theory of Legal Justification*. Stanford, CA: Stanford University Press, 1961.

Westacott, Emrys. "The Rights and Wrongs of Rudeness." *International Journal of Applied Philosophy* 20 (2006): 1–20.

White, Penny J., *Relinquished Responsibilities*, 123 Harv. L. Rev. 120 (2009).

Wilde, Oscar. "The Decay of Lying." In *Intentions*, Oscar Wilde, 1–55. New York: Brentano, 1905.

Wood, Gordon S. *The Creation of the American Republic, 1776–1787*. New York: Norton, 1972.

Wood, Sandra L., Linda Camp Keith, Drew Noble Lanier, and Ayo Ogundele. "The Supreme Court, 1888–1940: An Empirical Analysis." *Social Science History* 22 (1998): 201–24.

Woodruff, Michael J. "Deliberative Expectations and Electoral Incentives for State Supreme Court Justices," March 30, 2009, http://ssrn.com/abstract=1440868 (last accessed December 1, 2009).

Yarn, Douglas H., *The Attorney as Duelist's Friend: Lessons from the Code Duello*, 51 CASE W. RES. L. REV. 69 (2000).

Zeidman, Steven, *To Elect or Not to Elect: A Case Study of Judicial Selection in New York City, 1977–2002*, 37 U. MICH. J. L. REFORM 791 (2004).

Zogby International. "Nationwide Poll, 7/21/06–7/27/06." http://www.zogby.com/wf-AOL %20National.pdf (last accessed August 30, 2009).

Table of Cases

Bradwell v. Illinois, 83 U.S. 130 (1872).

Bowers v. Hardwick, 478 U.S. 186 (1986).

Bush v. Gore, 531 U.S. 98 (2000).

Caperton v. A.T. Massey Coal Co., 129 S. Ct. 2252 (2009).

Carey v. Wolnitzek, 2006 U.S. Dist. LEXIS 73869 (E.D. Ky. Oct. 10, 2006).

DeShaney v. Winnebago County Department of Social Services, 489 U.S. 189 (1989).

Dimick v. Republican Party of Minnesota, 126 S.Ct. 1165 (2006).

Dondi Properties Corp. v. Commerce Savings & Loan Ass'n, 121 F.R.D. 284 (N.D.Tex. 1988).

Fieger v. Mich. Supreme Court, 2007 U.S. Dist. LEXIS 64973 (E.D. Mich. Sept. 4, 2007).

Lawrence v. Texas, 539 U.S. 558 (2003).

Plessy v. Ferguson, 163 U.S. 537 (1896).

Republican Party of Minnesota v. White, 416 F.3d 738 (8th Cir. 2005).

Republican Party of Minnesota v. White, 536 U.S. 765 (2002).

Spargo v. New York State Comm'n on Judicial Conduct, 244 F.Supp.2d 72 (N.D.N.Y., 2003).

Zell v. American Seating Co., 138 F.2d 641 (2d. Cir. 1943).

Acknowledgments

THIS BOOK DEVOTES EQUAL ATTENTION to the claims of law and of politics. In conceiving and crafting my argument, I have been helped along by opportunities to make new connections between the legal academy and political science.

In 2007, my university position was formally split in two and I was jointly appointed to the Syracuse University College of Law and to the Political Science Department in Syracuse University's Maxwell School of Citizenship and Public Affairs. I thank Dean Hannah Arterian of the College of Law and Dean Mitch Wallerstein of the Maxwell School for engineering the joint appointment. I am particularly grateful to Dean Arterian for making sure I felt at home in the College of Law. Her efforts have been greatly assisted and reinforced by my new colleagues on the law faculty.

The year before my joint appointment, I helped found the Institute for the Study of the Judiciary, Politics, and the Media (IJPM), a collaboration between the College of Law, the Maxwell School, and the S.I. Newhouse School of Public Communications. I have served as the director of IJPM since the institute's inception. For their shared vision and critical role in creating IJPM, I thank Dean Arterian, Dean Wallerstein, and Dean David Rubin of the Newhouse School. I also thank Syracuse University Chancellor Nancy Cantor for her strong commitment to interdisciplinary scholarship and for the seed money her Initiative Fund provided IJPM during its first years. Lisa Dolak and Mark Obbie served as IJPM associate directors during the institute's start-up phase. Lisa and Mark helped set IJPM on the right path with their good humor, wise counsel, and willingness to attend many meetings at IJPM

World Headquarters. IJPM has also benefitted from the hard work of incredibly talented graduate assistants and staff: Brandi Anderson, Shannon Johanni, Bert Kaufman, Heather McCoy, and Kyle Somers. My deep thanks also go to Paul and Joanne Alper, for their vision, energy, and unwavering support. The Alpers' generous gift established the Paul E. and Hon. Joanne F. Alper '72 Judiciary Studies Professorship at the College of Law, a position to which I was appointed in 2009. The Alpers' support, along with funds from Syracuse University's Faculty Today program, ensures that IJPM will remain actively engaged in interdisciplinary debate and scholarship for years to come.

I developed the arguments for the book in several different venues. I presented work at the Syracuse University College of Law, the Maxwell School's Campbell Public Affairs Institute, the Law and Society Association Annual Meeting, the Western Political Science Association Annual Meeting, and the New England Political Science Association Annual Meeting. I discussed sections of the book manuscript at the "What's Law Got to Do with It?" conference organized by Charlie Geyh at the Indiana University Maurer School of Law, as well as at the "Law and Media" conference jointly organized by the Federal Judicial Center and IJPM. I also taught segments of my arguments in Vernon Greene's graduate seminar on citizenship. I thank the audiences at these different venues for their constructive criticism and encouragement, and I am particularly grateful for the feedback I received from the audience of federal judges at the "Law and Media" conference. I also published preliminary formulations of some of my ideas in "The Polite Thing to Do," in *The Future of Gay Rights in America* (Routledge, 2005) and in "Legal Realism, Common Courtesy, and Hypocrisy," in *Law, Culture and the Humanities* (2005). I thank Harry Hirsch and Austin Sarat, as well as the anonymous reviewers, for their comments and suggestions on these two pieces.

I have had the good fortune to discuss my arguments with a number of very smart colleagues: Susan Burgess, Tom Burke, John Brigham, Elizabeth Cohen, Amanda DiPaolo, Cyril Ghosh, Vernon Greene, John Kang, Tom Keck, Rogan Kersh, Steven Lichtman, Shep Melnick, Glyn Morgan, Angela Narasimhan, Heather Pincock, Justin Schapp, Nancy Scherer, Susan Silbey, Heidi Swarts, Steve Teles, Keren Weinshall-Margel, and Elizabeth Wilson. As I researched and wrote the book, I was also helped by a series of highly capable research assistants: Evan Brown, Andrew Horsfall, Ellen Palminteri, Robert Siglin, Kyle Somers, and Honggang Tan. Ellen deserves special mention for the extraordinary effort she put into the notes and bibliography.

Charlie Geyh, Michael McCann, and Austin Sarat each read the book manuscript in its entirety. The range and depth of their commentary was amazing. I thank them for helping me to improve my arguments on many fronts. Lief Carter also provided detailed comments on my discussion of his classic work (coauthored with Tom Burke), *Reason in Law*. I thank Lief for being generous with his time and for giving me such insightful suggestions.

I thank Bert Brandenburg of Justice at Stake Campaign for supplying several of the state-level polls that I discuss in Part I. I also thank Judith Hibbard, Amanda Moran, Joa Suorez, and Kate Wahl at Stanford University Press, as well as David Horne and Stan Shoptaugh of Classic Typography, for helping me to make the book more accessible and for wisely managing the publication process.

Finally, I thank my family. My father, Roger Bybee, discussed the book's arguments with me, and he encouraged my writing with an inspired addition to my wardrobe: a t-shirt with the phrase "Yes, I am just being polite" emblazoned across the chest. My mother, Vee Bybee, read the whole manuscript, asked stimulating questions, and provided helpful editorial advice. She also gave the book one of the best reviews it is ever likely to receive when she said it made her "so proud to read what mi hijito has written." My siblings, Bruce, Greg, and Lisa, helped me keep my work in perspective; Bruce also suggested the phrase "acceptable hypocrisies" for the book's subtitle. My children, Evan and Ava, are beautiful and intelligent, and they have made my life better in countless ways. They also have given me many opportunities to rehearse the rules of common courtesy and to reflect on what is going on when we say people should be polite. My wife, Jennifer Champa Bybee, has been my partner through thick and thin. I constantly rely on her judgment and draw strength from her fiery determination. This book is dedicated to her and our kids.

K.J.B.
Fayetteville

Index

Advocacy, 87–88
African Americans, 67, 98
Alito, Samuel, 13
Ambivalence: and hegemonic power of law, 129*n*124; in judicial process, 89; legal power arising from, 5–6, 19, 33, 35–36, 101–2; in legal realism, 1–5, 7, 14, 19, 77; in public opinion, 4–5, 8, 18–19, 29–32, 35–36; universal appeal and usefulness grounded in, 85, 89–93, 101–3
American Bar Association, 7
Annenberg Judicial Independence Survey, 18
Anti-Federalists, 11
Appointment. *See* Judicial appointment
Arnold, Thurman, 108*n*12
Artificiality, benefits of, 37–38, 51, 56, 72, 79, 80, 83–84, 102

Baum, Lawrence, 23
Bryson, Anna, 58
Burke, Edmund, 55, 64–65, 71
Burke, Thomas, 81–86, 88–90, 95
Bush, George W., 15
Bush v. Gore, 15
Buss, Sarah, 139*n*81

Caldeira, Gregory A., 124*n*92
Caldwell, Mark, 64, 70–71
Canons of Judicial Ethics (1924), 24
Carey v. Wolnitzek, 110*n*17

Carter, Lief, 81–86, 88–90, 95
Carter, Stephen, 59, 61
Cass, Ronald, 26–28
Chesterfield, Lord, 55–59, 65
Children, inculcating manners in, 62–63
China, 137*n*48
Chivalry, 39
Civility, 39, 59–61, 132*n*5
Code of Conduct for United States Judges (2009), 126*n*103
Code of Judicial Conduct, 24
Comity, 50–51
Committee on Civility of the Seventh Judicial Circuit, 41
Community. *See* Society
Congress, 50–52
Constitution, 11
Constitutional law, 11–13
Countervailing passions, 87, 144*n*36
Courtesy, 36–74; as basis for understanding law, 43–50, 76–85; concepts related to, 39; conditions for, 36–37; congressional, 50–52; decline of, 37, 44–46; defined, 39; diversity and, 53–54, 56, 61; durability of, 37–38, 46–48, 53; enforcement of, 42–43; and equality, 68–71; habit as foundation of, 37–38, 62–66; and hierarchy, 38, 45, 66–72; hypocrisy and, 36–37, 50–59, 62; immoral character balanced by, 54–57; informal nature of, 42–44, 46; law compared to, 36, 39–50; law

in symbiosis with, 40–43, 79–80; in
legal profession, 41, 133*n*12; and morality, 38, 54–57, 59–60, 139*n*81; and
pleasure, 38, 64–66; respect granted
by means of, 37–38, 52–55, 60, 64, 65,
68, 73, 79, 85; as rule set, 36, 39–40,
42; shortcomings of, 38–39, 75–76;
significance of, 48–49; sociohistorical
specificity of, 70; in United States,
45–49, 61; usefulness of, 50–59, 68

Davidson, Jenny, 69
Dimick v. Republican Party of Minnesota,
110*n*17
Dispute management, law as means of,
81–82, 85, 87, 91, 92, 95–97, 99–100
Due Process Clause, 7
Education. *See* Legal training
Eighth Circuit Court of Appeals, 110*n*17
Elections. *See* Judicial elections
Elias, Norbert, 48, 134*n*14
Emily Post Institute, 47
Epstein, Lee, 124*n*83
Equality, 38, 45, 68–71, 142*n*109
Erasmus, Desiderius, 58, 62; "On Good
Manners for Boys," 49
Etiquette. *See* Courtesy
Etiquette manuals, 46–47
Europe, rule of law in, 94
Ewick, Patricia, 29, 129*n*124

Fairness, 8, 38, 68, 71, 73, 76, 79, 83, 84,
96, 102, 148*n*91. *See also* Impartiality
Federal courts, 10–16; appointment to,
10–12; contradictory pressures on, 14;
politics in, 11–16; public opinion on,
13–15. *See also* Supreme Court
Forni, P. M., 59–61
Foucault, Michel, 66
Frank, Jerome, 108*n*12
Franklin, Benjamin, 63

Galanter, Marc, 144*n*18
Gallantry, 39

Game analogy, 90–92, 145*n*48, 146*n*51,
148*n*91
Gender roles, 67, 69, 98
Geyh, Charles, 19, 24
Gibson, James L., 124*n*92
Ginsburg, Ruth Bader, 79
Goffman, Erving, 49, 62
Golden Rule, 59
Government legitimacy, 5, 22
Grant, Ruth, 53–54

Habit: courtesy and, 37–38, 62–66; law
and, 78, 93–95, 98
Hamilton, Alexander, 11
Hampshire, Stuart, 86
Hart, H.L.A., 90–91, 93–94, 98, 128*n*121,
145*n*48, 146*n*51
Hierarchy: courtesy and, 38, 45, 66–72;
law and, 78–79, 97–101
Hirschman, Albert, 86–87, 144*n*36
Hobbes, Thomas, 44
Hodges, Deborah Robertson, 47
Holmes, Oliver Wendell, 3–4, 87
Human nature or condition: irreducible
differences in, 36–37, 53–54, 80; mixed
quality of, 54–56, 60–61, 76, 80, 103
Hypocrisy: appearance of, 2–3, 19–25,
77; avoiding appearance of, 23–24;
congressional courtesy and, 51–52;
connotations of, 20, 35; consequences
of, 21–22; courtesy and, 36–37, 50–59,
62; difficulty of determining, 22–23;
law and, 83, 103; motivations for accepting a system that permits, 37, 53,
57, 66, 92–93; responses to, 59; social
benefits of, 53–54, 56–57, 61

Ideology: judicial appointment and,
12, 27, 117*n*50; and judicial decisionmaking, 14, 24, 27–28, 116*n*41; and
judicial policymaking, 27; and law
clerk hiring decisions, 118*n*57; public
opinion on, 13, 24–25. *See also* Partisanship; Politics

Impartiality: advocacy vs., 87–88; importance of, 7; judges' support for, 7, 13, 27; judicial appointment and, 11, 28–29; in judicial decisionmaking, 2–5, 26–28; judicial legitimacy dependent on, 83–84, 89; personal character and, 15; public opinion on, 6–8, 13, 17–18; and separation of powers, 111*n*22; training in, 3–4, 28; trust based on, 84. *See also* Fairness; Judicial independence
Independence. *See* Judicial independence
Insincerity, 20
Interpretation. *See* Legal interpretation

Jefferson, Thomas, 63
Jesus, 59
Jim Crow segregation, 67, 72
Judges: on accountability to public, 15; conflicting pressures on, 6–7, 14; on impartiality, 27–28; impartiality of, 7, 13; open-mindedness of, 111*n*21; partisan interests of, 88; political activities of, 1–2, 8–10; preconceptions of, 7; self-representation of, as impartial, 15–16, 27–28, 30, 84, 121*n*71, 128*n*121
Judicial activism, 123*n*80
Judicial appearance, 23–24, 101, 126*n*103
Judicial appointment: to federal courts, 10–12; ideology as factor in, 12, 27, 117*n*50; and impartiality, 11, 28–29; partisanship in, 117*n*50; politics of, 12, 124*n*83; to state courts, 8–9
Judicial decisionmaking: candor about, 32–33; as impartial, 2–5, 26–28; judges' characterization of their own, 15–16, 27–28, 30, 84, 121*n*71, 128*n*121; as political, 2–5, 26–28
Judicial elections: alternatives to, 8–9; costs of, 6; prevalence of, 6; retention elections, 8–10; for state courts, 6, 8–10; voting strategies in, 25
Judicial independence, 13, 17–19, 28–29. *See also* Impartiality

Judicial legitimacy, 5, 19, 22, 82–84, 89
Judicial open-mindedness, 111*n*21
Judicial tenure, 11
Judiciary, importance to American life of, 95

Kagan, Robert A., 109*n*13
Kennedy, Randall, 71
King, Martin Luther Jr., 67, 72
Kozinski, Alex, 15

La Rochefoucauld, François-Alexandre-Frédéric de, 54–55
Law: courtesy as basis for understanding, 43–50, 76–85; courtesy compared to, 36, 39–50; courtesy in symbiosis with, 40–43, 79–80; durability of, 92–93, 102–3; enforcement of, 42–43, 82; formal nature of, 42–43; as game, 90–92; "good enough" character of, 82, 99–100; habit as foundation of, 78, 93–95, 98; hierarchy and, 78–79, 97–101; hypocrisy and, 83, 103; motivations for participating in, 91; personal uses of, 88; pleasure and, 95–97; proceduralist account of, 77–78, 81–85; as rule-based system, 36, 39–40, 42, 76, 82. *See also* Rule of law
Law clerks, 118*n*57
Legal academics, 26
Legal interpretation: in constitutional law, 11–12; standards for assessment of, 10, 88
Legal realism: ambivalent status of, 1–5, 7, 14, 19, 77; history of, 3–4; judicial decisions and, 2–3; popularity of, 4; and public suspicion, 108*n*12
Legal scholarship, 26
Legal training, 3–4, 28
Legitimacy. *See* Government legitimacy; Judicial legitimacy
Levinson, Sanford, 11
LGBT community, 67–68, 98
Liars, 146*n*55
Llewellyn, Karl, 43

Machiavelli, Niccolò, 54, 86
Madison, James, 55
Manners. *See* Courtesy
Martin, Judith (Miss Manners), 40–43,
    52–53, 56–57, 62–63, 70
Maxwell Poll, 16–18, 20–21, 31
Media, 12, 31–32
Miss Manners. *See* Martin, Judith
Missouri Plan, 8–9
Morality, courtesy and, 38, 54–57, 59–60,
    139*n*81
Myers, William G., III, 121*n*71

New York State Commission on Judicial
    Conduct, 1, 107*n*6
New York Times (newspaper), 1–2

O'Connor, Sandra Day, 111*n*21
Open-mindedness. *See* Judicial open-
    mindedness
Partisanship: of judges, 88; in judicial
    appointment, 117*n*50; in public opin-
    ion, 14, 123*n*80; in Supreme Court
    decisionmaking, 12–13, 15. *See also*
    Ideology
Pascal, Blaise, 75
Peretti, Terri, 26–28
Pleasure: courtesy and, 38, 64–66; law
    and, 78, 95–97
Politeness, 39
Politeness theory, 132*n*4
Politics: constitutional law and, 11–13;
    courtesy and, 71–72; federal courts
    and, 13, 14; judges' participation in,
    1–2, 8–10; judicial appointment and,
    12, 124*n*83; judicial decisionmaking
    and, 2–5, 26–28; low vs. high, 27–28;
    of retention elections, 9–10; in struc-
    ture of judiciary, 29; Supreme Court
    and, 13–16, 26–27. *See also* Ideology;
    Judicial elections
Popkin, William, 32
Posner, Richard, 88, 146*n*52
Post, Emily, 43, 71; *Etiquette*, 46–47

Pound, Roscoe, 24
Preconceptions, legal, 7
Princeton Survey Research Associates,
    31–32
Public ignorance, 25, 30–32
Public opinion: ambivalence in, 4–5,
    8, 18–19, 29–32, 35–36; on courts in
    general, 16–18; and cynicism, 109*n*12,
    116*n*42, 123*n*82; on federal courts and
    judges, 14–15; on hypocrisy, 20–21; on
    impartiality, 6–8, 13, 17–18; impor-
    tance of, 22–25; information underly-
    ing, 25, 30–32; judicial legitimacy
    dependent on, 5, 19, 22, 82–84; on
    judicial process, 4–8, 14; partisanship
    in, 14, 120*n*66; on politics in judicial
    process, 16–18; on retention elections,
    9–10; standards for assessment of legal
    interpretation as factor in, 10; on state
    courts and judges, 7–8, 113*n*27, 115*n*39;
    on Supreme Court, 13, 14, 21, 124*n*92;
    suspicion in, 5, 10, 19–25, 85, 91

Ramseyer, J. Mark, 123*n*82
Rationality: limitations of, 56, 86; pas-
    sions linked to, 55; significance of, in
    rule of law, 3–4, 86–88
Reason. *See* Rationality
Republican Party of Minnesota v. White, 1,
    6–7, 110*n*17, 111*n*21
Respect, courtesy as means for granting,
    37–38, 52–55, 60, 64, 65, 68, 73, 79, 85
Retention elections, 8–10
Roberts, John G. Jr., 121*n*71
Rule of law: dispute management
    aided by, 81–82, 85, 87, 91, 92, 95–97,
    99–100; function of, 26; meaning of,
    109*n*13, 143*n*4; personal attachments
    transcended by, 81; process of, 81; rule
    of men vs., 91–92
Runciman, David, 59

Sapiro, Virginia, 66
Scholarship, legal, 26

Schumer, Charles, 121*n*71
Second Circuit Court of Appeals, 107*n*6
Segal, Jeffrey A., 124*n*83
Self-love, 54, 61, 65, 73, 85
Shapiro, Martin, 28–29, 128*n*121
Shils, Edward, 60, 61
Shklar, Judith, 61, 89–90
Silbey, Susan, 29, 129*n*124
Society: civility and the good of, 60;
    competing interests in, 76, 86;
    courtesy as aid to, 38, 48–49, 65, 76;
    diversity in, 61, 86; hierarchy in, 38,
    45, 66–72, 78–79, 97–99; hypocrisy as
    beneficial for, 53–54, 56–57, 61; moral
    standards in, 54; rule of law in, 26
Spargo, Thomas, 1–3, 107*n*6
*Spargo v. New York State Comm'n on
    Judicial Conduct*, 107*n*6
Specialty courts, 122*n*75
Sports officiating, 90
State courts: appointment to, 8–9, 12;
    judicial elections for, 6, 8–10; politics
    in, 6–10; public opinion on, 7–8,
    113*n*27, 115*n*39
Supreme Court: appointment to, 12;
    law clerk hiring decisions in, 118*n*57;
    partisan decisionmaking in, 12–13,
    15; politics in, 13–16, 26–27; public
    opinion on, 13, 14, 21, 124*n*92

Syracuse University, 16

Table manners, 48
Tact, 69
Tamanaha, Brian, 82–83, 125*n*96
Tarr, Alan, 10
Tenure, judicial, 11
Thomas, Clarence, 15–16
Tocqueville, Alexis de, 95
Trial judges, 122*n*75
Tribe, Laurence, 11–12
Trollope, Fanny, 45–46, 142*n*109
Trust, 84

United States: African Americans in, 67;
    courtesy in, 45–49, 61; equality in, 45;
    gender roles in, 67; habit of obedience
    to law in, 94–95; human nature and
    politics in, 55; importance of judiciary
    in, 95; LGBT community in, 67–68

Vanderbilt, Amy, *Complete Book of
    Etiquette*, 47

White, Republican Party of Minnesota v.,
    1, 6–7, 110*n*17, 111*n*21
Wilde, Oscar, 65, 146*n*55
Women: and courtesy, 67, 69, 98; and
    equality, 142*n*109

THE CULTURAL LIVES OF LAW

Austin Sarat, Editor

The Cultural Lives of Law series brings insights and approaches from cultural studies to law and tries to secure for law a place in cultural analysis. Books in the series focus on the production, interpretation, consumption, and circulation of legal meanings. They take up the challenges posed as boundaries collapse between as well as within cultures, and as the circulation of legal meanings becomes more fluid. They also attend to the ways law's power in cultural production is renewed and resisted.

Riding the Black Ram: Law, Literature, and Gender
Susan Sage Heinzelman
2010

Tort, Custom, and Karma: Globalization and Legal Consciousness in Thailand
David M. Engel and Jaruwan S. Engel
2010

Law in Crisis: The Ecstatic Subject of Natural Disaster
Ruth A. Miller
2009

The Affective Life of Law: Legal Modernism and the Literary Imagination
Ravit Reichman
2009

Fault Lines: Tort Law as Cultural Practice
Edited by David M. Engel and Michael McCann
2008

Lex Populi: The Jurisprudence of Popular Culture
William P. MacNeil
2007

The Cultural Lives of Capital Punishment: Comparative Perspectives
Edited by Austin Sarat and Christian Boulanger
2005